PENGUIN BOOKS

INTO THE WOODS

'Love storytelling? You need this inspiring book. John Yorke
dissects the structure of stories with a joyous enthusiasm allied to
precise, encyclopaedic knowledge. Guaranteed to send you back to
your writing desk with newfound excitement and drive'
Chris Chibnall, creator/writer, *Broadchurch, Gracepoint, The Great Train Robbery*

'A great book on story structure' Graham Linehan, creator/writer, *Father Ted,
The IT Crowd, Black Books, Count Arthur Strong*

'Brilliant, illuminates & explains' Susan Hill, author of *The Woman In Black*

'There is no end of books that instruct us on how to write the perfect
screenplay, but few that delve more deeply into the art of storytelling
than this erudite volume' *Financial Times*, Summer Reads

'Any consumer of books, plays, TV or films will find the experience enhanced;
and scriptwriters themselves will find useful guidance – because when you
know the why, the how is natural' *Independent on Sunday*

'Even for a convinced sceptic, John Yorke's book, with its massive field
of reference from Aristotle to *Glee*, and from Shakespeare to *Spooks*, is a
highly persuasive and hugely enjoyable read. It would be hard to beat for
information and wisdom about how and why stories are told'
Dominic Dromgoole, Artistic Director, The Globe Theatre

'Its strength is Yorke's acute perception of the wellsprings of universal narrative
structures relevant to all artistic activities' *The Times*

'A superb study of how stories work, from *Hamlet* to *Citizen Kane*' *Sunday Times*

'Part "How-to" manual, part "why-to" celebration, *Into The Woods*
is a wide-reaching and infectiously passionate exploration of
storytelling in all its guises . . . exciting and thought-provoking'
Emma Frost, writer *The White Queen, Jamaica Inn* and *Shameless*

'Every TV writer should read the first chapter alone'
Simon Ashdown, writer/series consultant, *EastEnders*

'Testing the adage that "in theory there's no difference between theory and practice but in practice there is", this is a love story to story – erudite, witty and full of practical magic. It's by far the best book of its kind I've ever read. I struggle to think of the writer who wouldn't benefit from reading it – even if they don't notice because they're too busy enjoying every page'
Neil Cross, creator/writer of *Luther*, *Crossbones* and writer of *Dr Who*, *Spooks*

'Books on story structure are ten a penny but Mistah Yorke's is the real deal' Kathryn Flett

'Terrific . . . It's a great read, wise and cogent, and a must for all screenwriters' David Eldridge, writer *Festen*, *In Basildon*

'It's a great read. It makes me smile and say "Yes!" aloud. Only this and PG Wodehouse do that.' Lucy Gannon, writer/creator *Soldier Soldier*, *Peak Practice*, *Frankie*, *The Best Of Men*

'A mind-blower . . . an incredibly dense but very readable tome about the art of storytelling . . . Really worth a read' Lenny Henry, *Independent*

'Anyone considering a career in television should read this book. Anyone with a career in television should read this book too'
Tony Grounds, writer, *Our Girl*, *Gone To The Dogs*, *Births*, *Marriages and Deaths*

ABOUT THE AUTHOR

John Yorke is the Managing Director of Company Pictures, the UK drama independent producing among others *Shameless*, *Skins*, *The White Queen* and *Wolf Hall*. As both Head of Channel Four Drama and Controller of BBC Drama Production he's worked on big popular works such as *Hustle*, *Spooks*, *Casualty* and *Holby City* alongside award-winners such as *Bodies*, *Omagh*, *Sex Traffic*, *Not Only But Always* and *The Curse of Steptoe*.

As a Commissioning Editor and Executive Producer he championed some of the defining works of British television including *Life on Mars*, *The Street*, *Shameless* and *Waterloo Road*. His television career began by story-lining *Eastenders* in its very first BAFTA-winning year – a show he went on to run and then oversee in an association of sixteen years. He's also worked as Editor of BBC Radio 4's *The Archers*.

In 2005 he created the BBC Writers Academy, the first writing course in Britain to guarantee broadcast work, and which has produced a generation of successful television writers.

John has lectured extensively on narrative structure, is Visiting Professor of English Language and Literature at the University of Newcastle-upon-Tyne, and lives and works in London. His website is at www.intothewoodsyorke.com

Into the Woods

How stories work and why we tell them

JOHN YORKE

PENGUIN BOOKS

PENGUIN BOOKS

UK | USA | Canada | Ireland | Australia
India | New Zealand | South Africa

Penguin Books is part of the Penguin Random House group of companies
whose addresses can be found at global.penguinrandomhouse.com.

First published in Penguin Books 2013
Published in this format in Penguin Books 2014

017

Copyright © John Yorke, 2013

The moral right of the author has been asserted

Typeset by Jouve (UK), Milton Keynes
Printed in Great Britain by Clays Ltd, Elcograf S.p.A.

A CIP catalogue record for this book is available from the British Library

ISBN: 978–0–141–97810–9

'Art consists of limitation. The most beautiful part of every picture is the frame.'

G. K. Chesterton

Dear Noor,

My best friend,

thank you

Noor

Contents

Contents

Introduction

A ship lands on an alien shore and a young man, desperate to prove himself, is tasked with befriending the inhabitants and extracting their secrets. Enchanted by their way of life, he falls in love with a local girl and starts to distrust his masters. Discovering their man has gone native, they in turn resolve to destroy both him and the native population once and for all.

Avatar or *Pocahontas*? As stories they're almost identical. Some have even accused James Cameron of stealing the Native American myth.[1] But it's both simpler and more complex than that, for the underlying structure is common not only to these two tales, but to all.

Take three different stories:

A dangerous monster threatens a community. One man takes it on himself to kill the beast and restore happiness to the kingdom . . .

It's the story of *Jaws*, released in 1976. But it's also the story of *Beowulf*, the Anglo-Saxon epic poem published some time between the eighth and eleventh centuries.

And it's more familiar than that: it's *The Thing*, it's *Jurassic Park*, it's *Godzilla*, it's *The Blob* – all films with real tangible monsters. If you recast the monsters in human form, it's also every James Bond film, every episode of *Spooks*, *Casualty*, *House* or *CSI*. You can see the same shape in *The Exorcist*, *The Shining*, *Fatal Attraction*, *Scream*, *Psycho* and *Saw*. The monster may change from a literal one in *Nightmare on Elm Street* to a corporation in *Erin Brockovich*, but the underlying architecture – in which a foe is vanquished and order restored to a community – stays the same. The monster can be fire in *The Towering Inferno*, an upturned boat in *The Poseidon*

Adventure, or a boy's mother in *Ordinary People*. Though superficially dissimilar, the skeletons of each are identical.

> Our hero stumbles into a brave new world. At first he is transfixed by its splendour and glamour, but slowly things become more sinister . . .

It's *Alice in Wonderland*, but it's also *The Wizard of Oz*, *Life on Mars* and *Gulliver's Travels*. And if you replace fantastical worlds with worlds that appear fantastical merely to the protagonists, then quickly you see how *Brideshead Revisited*, *Rebecca*, *The Line of Beauty* and *The Third Man* all fit the pattern too.

> When a community finds itself in peril and learns the solution lies in finding and retrieving an elixir far, far away, a member of the tribe takes it on themselves to undergo the perilous journey into the unknown . . .

It's *Raiders of the Lost Ark*, *Morte D'Arthur*, *Lord of the Rings* and *Watership Down*. And if you transplant it from fantasy into something a little more earthbound, it's *Master and Commander*, *Saving Private Ryan*, *Guns of Navarone* and *Apocalypse Now*. If you then change the object of the characters' quest, you find *Rififi*, *The Usual Suspects*, *Ocean's Eleven*, *Easy Rider* and *Thelma & Louise*.

So three different tales turn out to have multiple derivatives. Does that mean that when you boil it down there are only three different types of story? No. *Beowulf*, *Alien* and *Jaws* are 'monster' stories – but they're also about individuals plunged into a new and terrifying world. In classic 'quest' stories like *Apocalypse Now* or *Finding Nemo* the protagonists encounter both monsters *and* strange new worlds. Even 'Brave New World' stories such as *Gulliver's Travels*, *Witness* and *Legally Blonde* fit all three definitions: the characters all have some kind of quest, and all have their own monsters to vanquish too. Though they are superficially different, they all share the same framework and the same story engine: all plunge their characters into a strange new world; all involve a quest to find a way out of it; and in whatever form they choose to take, in every story 'monsters' are vanquished. All, at some level, too, have as their goal safety, security, completion and the importance of home.

But these tenets don't just appear in films, novels, or indeed TV series like *Spooks*, *Homeland* or *The Killing*. A nine-year-old child of my friend decided he wanted to tell a story. He didn't consult anyone about it, he just wrote it down:

> A family are looking forward to going on holiday. Mum has to sacrifice the holiday in order to pay the rent. Kids find map buried in garden to treasure hidden in the woods, and decide to go after it. They get in loads of trouble and are chased before they finally find it and go on even better holiday.[2]

Why would a child unconsciously echo a story form that harks back centuries? Why, when writing so spontaneously, would he display knowledge of story structure that echoes so clearly generations of tales that have gone before? Why do we all continue to draw our stories from the very same well? It could be because each successive generation copies from the last, thus allowing a series of conventions to become established. But while that may help explain the ubiquity of the pattern, its sturdy resistance to iconoclasm and the freshness and joy with which it continues to reinvent itself suggest something else is going on.

Storytelling has a shape. It dominates the way all stories are told and can be traced back not just to the Renaissance, but to the very beginnings of the recorded word. It's a structure that we absorb avidly whether in art-house or airport form and it's a shape that may be – though we must be careful – a universal archetype.

'Most writing on art is by people who are not artists: thus all the misconceptions.'

Eugène Delacroix

The quest to detect a universal story structure is not a new one. From the Prague School and the Russian Formalists of the early twentieth century, via Northrop Frye's *Anatomy of Criticism* to Christopher Booker's *The Seven Basic Plots*, many have set themselves the task of trying to understand how stories work. In my own field it's a veritable industry – there are hundreds of books about screenwriting (though almost nothing sensible about television). I've read most of them, but the more I read the more two issues nag away:

1. Most of them posit completely different systems, all of which claim to be the sole and only way to write stories. How can they all possibly claim to be right?
2. None of them ask 'Why?'[3]

Some of these tomes contain invaluable information; more than a few have worthwhile insights; all of them are keen to tell us *how* and with great fervour insist that 'there must be an inciting incident on page 12', but none of them explain *why* this should be. Which, when you think about it, is crazy: if you can't answer 'why', the 'how' is an edifice built on sand. And then, once you attempt to answer it yourself, you start to realize that much of the theory – incisive though some of it is – doesn't quite add up. Did God decree an inciting incident should occur on page 12, or that there were twelve stages to a hero's journey? Of course not: they're constructs. Unless we can find a coherent reason why these shapes exist, then there's little reason to take these people seriously. They're snake-oil salesmen, peddling their wares on the frontier.[4]

I've been telling stories for almost all my adult life, and I've had the extraordinary privilege of working on some of the most popular shows on British television. I've created storylines that have reached over 20 million viewers and I've been intimately involved with programmes that helped redefine the dramatic landscape. I've worked, almost uniquely in the industry, on both art-house and populist mainstream programmes, loved both equally, and the more I've told stories, the more I've realized that the underlying pattern of these plots – the ways in which an audience demands certain things – has an extraordinary uniformity.

Six years ago I started to read everything on storytelling. More importantly I started to interrogate all the writers I'd worked with about how they write. Some embraced the conventions of three-act structure, some refuted it – and some refuted it while not realizing they used it anyway. A few writers swore by four acts, some by five; others claimed that there were no such things as acts at all. Some had conscientiously learned from screenwriting manuals while others decried structural theory as the devil's spawn. But there was one unifying factor in every good script I read, whether authored by brand new talent or multiple BAFTA-winners, and that was that they all shared the same underlying structural traits.

By asking two simple questions – what were these traits; and why did they recur – I unlocked a cupboard crammed full of history. I soon discovered that the three-act paradigm was not an invention of the modern age but an articulation of something much more primal; that modern act structure was a reaction to dwindling audience attention spans and the invention of the curtain. Perhaps more intriguingly, the history of five-act drama took me back to the Romans, via the nineteenth-century French dramatist Eugène Scribe and German novelist Gustav Freytag to Molière, Shakespeare and Jonson. I began to understand that, if there really was an archetype, it had to apply not just to screenwriting, but to *all* narrative structures. One either tells all stories according to a pattern or none at all. If storytelling does have a universal shape, this has to be self-evident.

It was an investigation that was to produce a number of interesting offshoots. By concentrating initially on film and television, I was able to:

- explore how story structure works, not just in single-protagonist storytelling but also in multi-protagonist dramas
- explain why protagonists have to be active

- illustrate how – in more detail than ever before – the structural principles work in television
- understand how narration can destroy drama
- expound on why so many characters die in the penultimate stage of any drama
- explain why almost all cops are mavericks
- elucidate why TV drama series all have a limited lifespan, or else become parodies of themselves – normally within three years
- illustrate how characterization is not only born out of dramatic structure but is essential to it.

These were, however, discoveries that started to appear incidental to something more important. What started as a basic exploration of screenwriting morphed slowly into a historical, philosophical, scientific and psychological journey to the heart of all storytelling, and – in turn – to the realization that dramatic structure is not a construct, but a product of human psychology, biology and physics.

In *Into the Woods* I attempt to explore and unfold the extraordinary beauty of this structure; to touch on its historical development, and to understand how and why it is manifest in all aspects of fiction, from character to dialogue, but beyond that too. I may use films primarily as a reference because of their familiarity, but the scope of the book stretches beyond cinema, not just to television drama and its relationship to *The Apprentice* and *The X Factor* but further, to touch on how we narrate history, how we interpret art and advertising – even how, in a legal trial, we form our opinions on a subject's innocence or guilt. Why did *The X Factor* sweep away all before it? How does some modern art exploit its patrons' gullibility? Why were the Birmingham Six originally thought to be guilty? In the end it is all to do with story.

It's been a journey that – finally – let me articulate not only an underlying structure from which these stories are formed but, more importantly, allowed me to explain why that shape exists, and why anyone, without study, can replicate it entirely from within. How can a nine-year-old boy produce a perfect story from nowhere? It's a key question: understand that and you unlock the true shape and purpose of, indeed the true reason for, dramatic structure itself. It's a question, certainly, that no teacher of screenwriting ever appears to ask.

But do you need to know?

> You have to liberate people from [film theory], not give them a corset in which they have to fit their story, their life, their emotions, the way they feel about the world. Our curse is that the film industry is 80 per cent run by the half-informed. You have people who have read Joseph Campbell and Robert McKee, and now they're talking to you about the hero's journey, and you want to fucking cut off their dick and stuff it in their mouth.[5]

Guillermo del Toro echoes the thoughts of many writers and filmmakers; there's an ingrained belief for many that the study of structure is, implicitly, a betrayal of their genius; it's where mediocrities seek a substitute muse.[6] Such study can only end in one way. David Hare puts it well: 'The audience is bored. It can predict the exhausted UCLA film-school formulae – acts, arcs and personal journeys – from the moment that they start cranking. It's angry and insulted by being offered so much Jung-for-Beginners, courtesy of Joseph Campbell. All great work is now outside genre.'[7]

Charlie Kaufman, who has done more than most in Hollywood to push the boundaries of form, goes further: 'There's this inherent screenplay structure that everyone seems to be stuck on, this three-act thing. It doesn't really interest me. I actually think I'm probably more interested in structure than most people who write screenplays, because I think about it.'[8] But they protest too much. Hare's study of addiction *My Zinc Bed* and Kaufman's screenplay for *Being John Malkovich* are, as we shall see, perfect examples of classic story form. However much they hate it (and their anger I think betrays them), they can't help but follow a blueprint they profess to detest. Why?

All stories are forged from the same template, writers simply don't have any choice as to the structure they use and, as I hope to show, the laws of physics, of logic and of form dictate they must all follow the very same path. What that template is and why writers follow it; how and why we tell stories is the subject of this book.[9]

Is this therefore the magic key to storytelling? Such hubris requires caution – the compulsion to order, to explain, to catalogue, is also the tendency of the train-spotter. In denying the rich variety and extraordinary multi-faceted nature of narrative, one risks becoming no better than Casaubon, the desiccated husk from *Middlemarch*, who turned his back on life while seeking to explain it. It's all too tempting to reduce wonder to a scientific formula and unweave the rainbow.

But there are rules. As the creator of *The West Wing*, Aaron Sorkin, puts it: 'The real rules are the rules of drama, the rules that Aristotle talks about. The fake TV rules are the rules that dumb TV execs will tell you; "You can't do this, you've got to do that. You need three of these and five of those." Those things are silly.'[10] Sorkin expresses what all great artists know – that they need to have an understanding of *craft*. Every form of artistic composition, like any language, has a grammar, and that grammar, that *structure*, is not just a construct – it's the most beautiful and intricate expression of the workings of the human mind.

It's important to assert that writers don't need to understand structure. Many of the best have an uncanny ability to access story shape unconsciously, for it lies as much within their minds as it does in a nine-year-old's. This isn't a book advocating its conscious use. Its aim is to explore and examine narrative shape, ask how and why it exists, and why a child can write it effortlessly – why they can follow the rules.

There's no doubt that for many those rules help. Friedrich Engels put it pithily: 'Freedom is the recognition of necessity.'[11] A piano played without knowledge of time and key soon becomes wearisome to listen to; following the conventions of form didn't inhibit

Beethoven, Mozart and Shostakovich. Even if you're going to break rules (and why shouldn't you?) you have to have a solid grounding in them first. The modernist pioneers – Abstract Impressionists, Cubists, Surrealists and Futurists – all were masters of figurative painting before they shattered the form. They had to know their restrictions before they could transcend them. As the art critic Robert Hughes observed:

> With scarcely an exception, every significant artist of the last hundred years, from Seurat to Matisse, from Picasso to Mondrian, from Beckmann to de Kooning, was drilled (or drilled himself) in 'academic' drawing – the long tussle with the unforgiving and the real motif which, in the end, proved to be the only basis on which the real formal achievements of modernism could be raised. Only in that way was the right radical distortion within a continuous tradition earned, and its results raised above the level of improvisory play . . . The philosophical beauty of Mondrian's squares and grids begins with the empirical beauty of his apple trees.[12]

Cinema and television contain much great work that isn't structurally orthodox (particularly in Europe), but even then its roots still lie firmly in, and are a reaction to, a universal archetype. As Hughes says, they are a conscious distortion of a continuing tradition. The masters did not abandon the basic tenets of composition; they merely subsumed them into art no longer bound by verisimilitude. All great artists – in music, drama, literature, in art itself – have an understanding of the rules whether that knowledge is conscious or not. 'You need the eye, the hand and the heart,' proclaims the ancient Chinese proverb. 'Two won't do.'

This isn't a 'how to write' book. There are enough gurus already. Ostensibly it's about *dramatic* structure – about how TV dramas, plays and films work – though journalism, poetry and the novel are all called on at different times to illustrate salient points. If there is a preference for film examples it is simply because they are either well known or easily accessible, but the principles cannot be specific to that medium because they're merely the more recent technological manifestations of a far older process. The beauty of exploring film and television is not just that it lends itself to an easily accessible analysis, but that such analysis acts a bit like a barium meal: used correctly it illuminates not just all story structure, but all narrative – fictional and otherwise; it breaks open and reveals the very way we perceive and render all experience. So the structures of film and television drama are the bedrock of this book, but the implications, and the lessons these mediums reveal to us, are wider.

Storytelling is an indispensable human preoccupation, as important to us all – almost – as breathing. From the mythical campfire tale to its explosion in the post-television age, it dominates our lives. It behoves us then to try and understand it. Delacroix countered the fear of knowledge succinctly: 'First learn to be a craftsman; it won't keep you from being a genius.' In stories throughout the ages there is one motif that continually recurs – the journey into the woods to find the dark but life-giving secret within. This book attempts to find what lurks at the heart of the forest. All stories begin here . . .

Act I
Home

I

What is a Story?

'Once upon a time . . .'

Immediately you read that opening phrase, you know you're going to encounter a setting, and in that place a series of events will occur – almost certainly to an individual. In basic terms that's about it – the very best definition of a story: 'Once upon a time, in such and such a place, something happened.' There are far more complex explanations, of course, most of which we will touch on, but none that are so simple yet all-encompassing.

What an archetypal story does is introduce you to a central character – the protagonist – and invite you to identify with them; effectively they become your avatar in the drama. You live the experience of the story vicariously through them: when they're in jeopardy, you're in jeopardy; when they're ecstatic, you are too. Watch children as they view *Transformers* or *Hannah Montana* – it's extraordinary to see the process by which their feelings are sublimated and they become inextricably linked with the fortunes of their fictional counterparts.

So you have a central character, you empathize with them, and something then happens to them, and that something is the genesis of the story. Jack discovers a beanstalk; Bond learns Blofeld plans to take over the world. The 'something' is almost always a problem, sometimes a problem disguised as an opportunity. It's usually something that throws your protagonist's world out of kilter – an explosion of sorts in the normal steady pace of their lives: Alice falls down a rabbit hole; *Spooks* learn of a radical terrorist plot; Godot doesn't turn up.

Your character has a problem which they must solve: Alice has to

3

get back to the real world; our spooks have to stop a bomb going off in central London at 2 p.m.; Vladimir and Estragon have to wait. The story is the journey they go on to sort out the problem presented. On the way they may learn something new about themselves; they'll certainly be faced with a series of obstacles they have to overcome; there will likely be a moment near the end where all hope seems lost, and this will almost certainly be followed by a last-minute resurrection of hope, a final battle against the odds, and victory snatched from the jaws of defeat.

You'll see this shape (or its tragic counterpart) working at some level in every story. It might be big and pronounced as in *Alien* or *Jaws*, it might be subtler as in *Ordinary People*, or it might represent a reaction against it (Jean-Luc Godard's *Weekend*) – but it will be there, just as it is in the work of del Toro, Kaufman and Hare. It reveals itself most clearly in the framework of the classic crime or hospital drama. A murder is committed or someone gets sick; the detective or doctor must find the killer or make their patient well. Such tales are literature's heroin – storytelling with all impurities removed; a hit of pleasure; minimum effort for maximum reward. That's why detective fiction is so popular; the unifying factors that appear at some level in all stories are at their most accessible here.

But if the problem and the search for its answer provide the framework for stories, what elements are they actually built from?

The Essential Building Blocks

The protagonist

The protagonist is the person around whom the story revolves. Normally it's as obvious as that. It's Batman, it's James Bond, it's Indiana Jones. If it's difficult to identify a protagonist then maybe the story is about more than one person (say *EastEnders* or Robert Altman's *Short Cuts*) but it will always be (at least when it's working) the person the audience care about most.

But already we encounter difficulties. 'Care' is often translated as 'like', which is why so many writers are given the note (often by non-writing executives) 'Can you make them nice?' Frank Cottrell Boyce, a graduate of *Brookside* and one of Britain's most successful screenwriters, puts it more forcibly than most: 'Sympathy is like crack cocaine to industry execs. I've had at least one wonderful screenplay of mine maimed by a sympathy-skank. Yes, of course the audience has to relate to your characters, but they don't need to approve of them. If characters are going to do something bad, Hollywood wants you to build in an excuse note.'[1]

We don't *like* Satan in *Paradise Lost* – we *love* him. And we love him because he's the perfect gleeful embodiment of evil. Niceness tends to kill characters – if there is nothing wrong with them, nothing to offend us, then there's almost certainly nothing to attract our attention either. Much more interesting are the rough edges, the darkness – and we love these things because though we may not consciously want to admit it, they touch something deep inside us. If you play video games like *Grand Theft Auto* or *Call of Duty: Modern Warfare* (and millions do), then you occupy literal avatars that do little but kill, maim, destroy, or sleep with the obstacles in your path. We are capable of entering any kind of head. David Edgar justified his play about the Nazi architect Albert Speer by saying: 'The awful truth – and it is awful, in both senses of the word – is that the response most great drama asks of us is neither "yes please" nor "no thanks" but "you too?". Or, in the cold light of dawn, "there but for the grace of God go I".'[2]

The key to empathy, then, does not lie in manners or good behaviour. Nor does it lie, as is often claimed, in the understanding of motive. It's certainly true that if we know why characters do what they do, we will love them more. However, that's a symptom of empathy, not its root cause. It lies in its ability to access and bond with our unconscious.

Why are so many fictional policeman – and, indeed, doctors – mavericks? Laziness on the writer's behalf possibly, but can that really account for the widespread prevalence of one particular character trait? Why did so many find themselves irresistibly drawn to Sarah Lund in *The Killing*? Like her pulp-fiction counterparts, she broke the rules, ignored her bosses and went behind their backs; like them she was told by her bosses the Danish equivalent of 'you've got 24 hours or I'm taking you off the case'. Why did she – and why do all mavericks – prove so popular? Largely because that's how many of us feel at times too. Haven't we all at some time felt we're surrounded by idiots, by overly bureaucratic managers who don't understand us, by uncreative colleagues capable of managing only upwards and unable to see the truth in front of their eyes?

If empathy is about entering the mind of a fictional character, then it helps if that mind contains feelings similar to our own. When we watch Sarah Lund rejecting her bosses, we think, 'I wish I could do that'; when we watch Miranda Hart's Chummy in *Call the Midwife*, we bleed for her clumsiness, recognizing her own inability to fit in within ourselves. There is something immensely attractive in living through a character who *does* obtain revenge, who is proved to have value or – like the Danish detective – is finally proved right. The attraction of wish-fulfilment, benevolent or masochistic, can't be underestimated – what else can explain the ubiquity of *Cinderella* or the current global dominance of the *Marvel* franchise? Isn't there a Peter Parker in most of us longing to turn into Spider-Man? Our favourite characters are the ones who, at some silent level, embody what we all want for ourselves: the good, the bad and ugly too. We may recoil at the idea of empathizing with Adolf Hitler, but as *Downfall* attests we can and do. A good writer can force us to connect with anyone.[3]

The moment the audience is caught in the conspiracy of story is the most magical in all of drama; you'll know it well from live theatre – it's the point at which the protagonist has burrowed inside and taken over the spectator, the moment the coughing stops. There will be more on empathy later, but for now it's worth noting that we sanction the slaughter in *Modern Warfare* because the character is *us*, and we are on a mission to save the world.

The mission part is important – you can tell a huge amount about a character from their goals and desires. We will know much of a character if we know they want to save the lost Ark from the Nazis, or are willing to run from the police to Mexico but won't take the easiest route through Texas, the state in which they were raped.

Indeed, all archetypal stories are defined by this one essential tenet: the central character has an active goal. They desire something. If characters don't then it's almost impossible to care for them, and care we must. They are our avatars and thus our entry point: they are the ones we most want to win or to find redemption – or indeed be punished if they've transgressed, for subconsciously we can be deeply masochistic in our desires. Effectively they're us.

The antagonist

So something happens to a central character that throws them off the beaten track and forces them into a world they've never seen. A beanstalk grows, a patient collapses, a murder is committed. All of these actions have consequences, which in turn provoke obstacles that are commonly dubbed[4] forces of antagonism – the sum total of all the obstacles that obstruct a character in the pursuit of their desires. These forces accumulate from this initial moment as we head towards the climax of the story.

In the simple detective story they're catalysed by the murder; in the medical drama the patient. They are the problem or obstacle the protagonist has to overcome. If there's a killer or an evil mastermind bent on planetary domination then they are, obviously, the antagonists; the patient may not behave antagonistically, but they effectively embody the illness that will be the true enemy in the drama. The antagonist is thus the thing or person the protagonist must vanquish to achieve their goal.

The detective and 'monster' templates illustrate this well, but antagonism can manifest itself in many different ways – most interestingly when it lies *within* the protagonist. Cowardice, drunkenness, lack of self-esteem – all will serve as internal obstacles that prevent a character reaching fulfilment; all, for reasons we will discover, make the person more real. While antagonists can be external (James Bond), internal (*The Diving Bell and the Butterfly*) or both (*Jaws*), all have one thing in common, which Hitchcock summarized succinctly: 'The more successful the villain, the more successful the picture.'[5] The best James Bond films are the ones with the best baddies; the more effective the forces of antagonism, the greater the story.

In the simple thriller form the antagonist is marked out by their desire to control and dominate the lives of others. They don't follow the moral codes of the community; more often than not they're an embodiment of selfishness. They are also, historically, often marked by physical or mental deformity. Le Chiffre's maladjusted tear duct in the film of *Casino Royale* is the modern equivalent of *Dr No*'s missing hands or Scaramanga's third nipple in *The Man with the Golden Gun*. In a more politically correct age, the physical flaw (clearly an outer manifestation of inner damage) has been scaled down to a level society finds acceptable. If the antagonist is internal, the same principles apply: the enemy within works in opposition to the host's better nature – it *cripples* them. It stands in opposition to everything they might be. It is this that starts to hint at story structure's deeper function.

What do Bond and Blofeld, Sarah and the Terminator, Sam Tyler and Gene Hunt, Fiona and Frank Gallagher have in common? 'We're not so very different you and I,' says Karla to Smiley in *Tinker Tailor Soldier Spy*. 'We both spend our lives looking for the weaknesses in one another's systems.'

They're all opposites.

As the Joker, displaying an uncharacteristic grasp of story structure, says to Batman in *The Dark Knight*,[6] 'You complete me'. We will look at the reason for this later, but for now it's enough to note that all forces of antagonism embody the qualities missing in their protagonist's lives.

The desire

If a character doesn't want something, they're passive. And if they're passive, they're effectively dead. Without a desire to animate the protagonist, the writer has no hope of bringing the character alive, no hope of telling a story and the work will almost always be boring. Aaron Sorkin put it succinctly, 'Somebody's got to want something, something's got to be standing in their way of getting it. You do that and you'll have a scene.'[7]

At its most basic, that's all story is. The Russian actor, director and theoretician Constantin Stanislavski first articulated the idea that characters are motivated by desire.[8] As in real life, so in character: we are all motivated by objectives, however small, however inconsequential, for most minutes of every day. If we weren't, we wouldn't get out of bed. The Knights of the Round Table only come alive when they learn of their Grail, and so it is with all characters. To find Nemo, to put out the Towering Inferno, to clear their name, to catch a thief – purpose must be bestowed and actively sought, or a character is dead. Why do characters in *EastEnders* offer up the mantra, 'It's all about family'? Because it gives them something to fight for; it gives them a goal – it animates them. 'Tell me what you want,' said Anton Chekhov, 'and I will tell you what manner of man you are.'[9]

Inevitably there are caveats. It's not always enough for a hero to want love or happiness; it's too nebulous, too intangible. The most popular works embody desire in an object. Protagonists want 'Juliet'; they want 'Godot'; they want 'the lost Ark'. In film and television in particular, desires tend to be simple, tangible and easily stated: a trophy, something that can be seen or held. In *Raiders* only the lost Ark will save the world; in *Notting Hill*, love can be found in Anna Scott; *Citizen Kane* is built on a reporter's mission to explain 'Rosebud', *Apocalypse Now* on Captain Willard's desire to kill Colonel Kurtz. In television series the goal will change weekly but it will almost always be a physical embodiment of the protagonists' mission to save, preserve or enhance their world.

Whether simple (kill the shark) or profound (return the key in Channel 4's *The Promise*), the underlying 'grail quest' structure is clear. Cops want to catch the killer, doctors want to heal their patient; in truth it doesn't actually matter what the object is, its importance is bestowed by those in pursuit. In *North by Northwest*, everyone is simply chasing microfilm of an unspecified variety. Again, Hitchcock says it best: '[We] have a name in the studio, and we call it the "MacGuffin". It is the mechanical element that usually crops up in any story. In crook stories it is almost always the neck-lace and in spy stories it is most always the papers.'[10]

So a grail can be any object, but there's another caveat too. Almost all successful plays, films and novels are about primal human desires: success (*Legally Blonde*), revenge (*Falling Down*), love (*Notting Hill*), survival (*Alien*) or the protection of one's family or home (*Straw Dogs*). Why else would we consume a story so ravenously? Love, home, belonging, friendship, survival and self-esteem recur continually because they're the subjects that matter to us most. The American cable series *The Walking Dead*, in which a small gang of survivors battle a world taken over by Zombies, embodies all these elements very clearly. There's one overriding desire – to survive and prosper – yet each episode contains its own sub-goal – to get off the roof, to get the guns, to find the family or the missing girl. As in all drama, we watch as the characters seek security and vanquish any-thing that threatens it, just as we'd like to believe we would do ourselves.

When 'something happens' to a hero at the beginning of a drama, that something, at some level, is a disruption to their perceived security. Duly alarmed, they seek to rectify their situation; their 'want' is to find that security once again. They may often, however, choose to find that security in the wrong place. What a character thinks is good for them is often at odds with what actually is. This conflict, as we shall see, appears to be one of the fundamental ten-ets of structure, because it embodies the battle between external and internal desire.

External and internal desire

Hollywood blockbusters can be visceral and exciting experiences. Tantalizing in their promise, easy and effortless to digest, they glit-ter seductively, promising the vicarious pleasures of sex, violence, romance, vengeance, destruction and earned glory. Technically brilliant, occasionally profoundly moving but . . . why do they so often feel like an empty experience? Why do so few linger in the mind? Why so often does one leave the cinema slightly dejected, uneasy, stuffed with a surfeit of sugar?

The answer appears to lie, like everything else, within structure. Blockbusters are, with one or two exceptions, two-dimensional. It's a world where desire is simple: the hero wants something – to 'kill Bill' or find the secret of the Unicorn. In pursuit of that goal the multiplex hero *doesn't* change.

The cynic might well say that's because of the demands of the franchise – we want James Bond to be the same in every film. But Bond is a particular kind of character; he is the refined, simplified, hydrogenated bastardization of a deeper archetype.[11] He is white bread: impurities removed, digestion eased; a product of the demand for the thrill of story, minus its more troubling and disturbing elements – the offspring of our desire for simplicity and repetition. Bond is two-dimensional *because* he doesn't change; he has a dimension removed so we may repeatedly enjoy him. Bond just *wants*; he is an embodiment of pure desire. Three-dimensional characters, however, *do* change; their purchase is deeper. They have both a want and a need, and they are not necessarily the same thing.

When we first meet Thelma and Louise, they are living in darkness, mortgage-holders on a conservative American society. In *The Lives of Others*, Hauptmann Wiesler is a Stasi agent, the product of a world where empathy doesn't exist. In such terrain he can flourish – his power and steel are terrifying.

Thelma, Louise and Wiesler are all flawed characters, and it is this concept of 'flaw' – or of something lacking – that is absolutely critical in three-dimensional storytelling. Wiesler cannot care; the women are unknowingly repressed. These internalized characteristics are what each character needs to conquer. In order to become fully realized, they need to go on a journey to overcome their weakness, their flaws within.

Flaw or need isn't the same as their want or desire. Wiesler *wants* to punish the dissident couple he has been sent to spy on; Thelma and Louise *want* to escape the police and get to Mexico. Both sets of characters go on a journey to recognize that what they want stands in direct opposition to what they *need*. Going to Mexico or imprisoning dissidents will not make them complete.

The Russian Formalist Vladimir Propp coined the rather beautiful term 'lack' for what a protagonist is missing in the initial stages of any story, and it's this lack that three-dimensional stories exploit. A character seeks what they want and in so doing realizes instead their need. Their lack is lacked no more; they have overcome their flaws and become whole.

While it's possible for characters to get what they want *and* what they need (certainly that's what happens in *Aliens* or *Star Wars*), the true, more universal and more powerful archetype occurs when the initial, ego-driven goal is abandoned for something more important, more nourishing, more essential. In *Rocky*, *Cars*, *Saving Private Ryan*, *Little Miss Sunshine*, *Midnight Run* and *Tootsie*, the heroes find a goal they weren't aware they were looking for. Why this shape should be more truthful, we will discuss later, but we shouldn't judge the more simplistic archetype too harshly.

Detective or crime fiction – indeed any world where 'the Mountie always gets his man' – will always be popular. After all, if the protagonist is us it's comforting to be told by proxy that we're right, that we're surrounded by idiots and that everyone else is wrong. Perhaps, however, we shouldn't be told that *too* often. Films that work on a three-dimensional level, in which characters don't get what they initially want, affect us more profoundly and it is this that explains their deeper purchase; they are wholemeal grain to the two-dimensional, processed white-bread world of the blockbuster. Fun as they are, it's hard to derive much sustenance from repeated viewings of *War of the Worlds*, *Independence Day* or *The Day After Tomorrow*.

Characters then should not always get what they want, but should – if they deserve it – get what they need. That need, or flaw, is almost always present at the beginning of the film. The want, however, cannot become clear until after the inciting incident.

The inciting incident[12]

All stories have a premise – 'What if . . .?'

> A stuttering monarch takes instruction from a colonial maverick . . .
>
> A slum dweller from Mumbai is accused of cheating on *Who Wants To Be A Millionaire?* . . .
>
> A junk-collecting robot is whisked away from his home planet . . .

This 'What if' is almost always the inciting incident and inciting incidents are always the 'something' that happens in every story. Once upon a time, in such and such a place, something happened . . .

In *The Long Good Friday* Harold Shand is a gangster, planning to develop London's then derelict docklands. He's invited the Mafia to London to secure their investment when, without warning, one of his gang, charged with taking Harold's mother to an Easter service, is blown up in his car outside the church.

Harold's world is literally blown out of shape. That's the inciting incident – or part of it, because what the inciting incident must also do is awaken a desire. We go back to our story shape: a problem occurs; a solution is sought. Harold's solution is to track down the perpetrators and destroy them: 'I'll have their carcasses dripping blood by midnight,' he mutters. That's his 'want', and that's the film.

An inciting incident is always the catalyst for the protagonist's desire. In *Casualty* or *Monroe*, it will be the patient presenting themselves for treatment. In *Luther* or *Waking the Dead*, it will be the corpse begging the question 'Who did this to me?' Technically, 'Once upon a time, in such and such a place, something happened . . .' is a premise, 'and because of that I'm going to do *this* . . .' is a story.

We will explore the more detailed structure of inciting incidents later. For now, though, it's perhaps interesting to note that the first attempt to codify them was by A. W. Schlegel in 1808, who called them 'first determinations'.[13] It might be useful to see them as the subject of a film's trailer: it's the moment the journey begins.

The journey

In *Terminator 2*, James Cameron's enormously successful and groundbreaking sequel, the writer/director made two significant changes to Schwarzenegger's character. Arnie was turned from villain into hero, arguably helping position him as a 'family-friendly' star, but the far more significant adjustment was the upgrade the character underwent. The new model Terminator, the T2, unlike his predecessor, was now programmed to learn from his surroundings and experience. Cunningly, his ability to undergo internal change was actually built into the script.

As we've noted, change within seems to make the characters more interesting and give the work more bite. Compare *From Russia with Love* with *Casino Royale* and *Terminator* with *Terminator 2*: the former in each case are brilliantly slick products, but the latter have a far greater depth and resonance. As the heroes pursue their goals, their journeys in the latter films move us beyond visceral thrill to touch not just our senses but something deeper inside. In both sequels, the protagonists' superficial wants remain unsated;[14] they're rejected in favour of the more profound unconscious hunger inside. The characters get what they need. Expecting one thing on their quest, they find themselves confronted with another; traditional worldviews aren't reinforced, prejudices aren't reaffirmed; instead the protagonists' worldviews – and thus ours too – are realigned. Both literally and figuratively we are moved.

Cameron pulled a similar trick in *Aliens*.[15] When his heroine Ripley is rescued from deep space, she awakens from hyper-sleep to learn that the daughter she left behind on Earth (before the first film) has died from old age. Wracked with guilt (she promised to be back for her eleventh birthday), her nominal quest is to return to the planet to destroy aliens, but her underlying one, formulated when she adopts Newt, the orphan child she finds there, is to prove herself a mother once again. Her external desire may not deviate, but in its pursuit something important but unexpected is learned. Just as it was a rarity before *Alien* to see a female action hero (this was long before *Lara Croft*), it's still unusual to see a protagonist of a Hollywood blockbuster undergo such an internal transformation.

The quest is an integral ingredient of all archetypal stories. Change of some kind is at the heart of this quest, and so too is choice, because finally the protagonist must choose how to change. Nowhere is this more clearly embodied than in the crisis.

The crisis

The crisis is a kind of death: someone close to the hero dies (*The Godfather*), the heroes themselves appear to die (*E.T.*), but more commonly all hope passes away. Some US TV drama series refer to it as the 'worst case',[16] and in BBC continuing drama, 'worst point' has become an almost ubiquitous term. Not for nothing; it's the point of maximum jeopardy in any script, the moment the viewer should be shouting 'Oh no!' at the screen, the moment where it seems impossible for the hero to 'get out of that'. The crisis is also, in self-contained stories, almost always the cliffhanger before the last commercial break and, for reasons we shall see, the ending of every episode of *EastEnders*, of the 1960s *Batman* TV series and every American serial film of the 1940s from *Superman* to *Flash Gordon*.

The crisis occurs when the hero's final dilemma is crystallized, the moment they are faced with the most important question of the story – just what kind of person are they? Finding themselves in a seemingly inescapable hole, the protagonist is presented with a choice. In *Star Wars* Luke, reeling from the death of Obi-Wan Kenobi, must choose between the computer and the force. In *Casablanca* Rick must let Ilsa go or (by implication) destroy the world; in

Aliens, Ripley must seemingly save Newt or save herself. Even Bond can choose *not* to do battle with Dr No.

This choice then is the final test of character, precisely because it's the moment where the hero is forced to face up to their dramatic need or flaw. In the Pilgrim's Progress-type structure that underlies *Star Wars*, Luke's choice is between being a boy and being a man; in *Casablanca* Rick has to confront and overcome his selfishness ('I stick my neck out for no man') and in *Aliens* Ripley learns, by choosing to save Newt, that she can be a mother once again. You see exactly the same design in television: in the very first episode of *Glee*, Finn must choose whether to join either the glee club or the football team, and Will Schuester must choose between his club and his career. In all you can see the cleverness of the structural design – the external antagonists are the embodiments of what each protagonist fears most. To overcome that which lies without, they must overcome the chasm within.

Hence the stench of death – every crisis is the protagonists' opportunity to kill off their old selves and live anew. Their choice is to deny change and return to their former selves, or confront their innermost fears, overcome them and be rewarded. They can choose death, or they can choose to kill who they were in order to be reborn. When Gary sings, 'Am I a man or a Muppet?' at his crisis point in 2011's *The Muppets*, he's actually articulating the quintessential dilemma all protagonists face at this crucial structural point. Being a 'man' is the road less travelled – it's the much harder choice.

Like Henry V the night before Agincourt, the crisis is always the moment before the final battle in the war against impossible odds – the dark night before the climax.

The climax

The climax is the stage at which the protagonist finds release from their seemingly inescapable predicament. It's the final showdown with their antagonist, the battle in which the hero engages with their dramatic need and overcomes their flaw. Historically it is sometimes referred to as the 'obligatory scene'[17] (a term coined in the nine-teenth century by French drama critic Francisque Sarcey), though, as we shall see, a better term might be 'obligatory act'.[18]

When Thelma and Louise shoot the rapist and decide to run from the law, there's one essential sequence that has to happen: they must do battle with the law. The story demands it and instinct tells us the tale can't be over until that confrontation takes place. Once Elliot has adopted E.T. and saved him from the faceless hordes of government, there's one scene/sequence/event/act that has to take place – he has to face the 'villains' he's hidden him from.

During each film, we watch as Thelma, Louise and Elliot develop the skills they need to overcome their flaws; the two women to believe in themselves and each other; Elliot to find the tenacity and selflessness within. And here, in the climax, they apply them. Both are classically structured films – the flaws of the protagonists are embodied in the characterization of the antagonists so that in *E.T.*, when Elliot overcomes his external obstacle, his internal need is liberated, and when the women renounce society they become (we are led to believe) emancipated and whole as well.

Both the novel and film of *The Kite Runner* are constructed on a very similar and clear externalization of inner guilt. Indeed, the incit-ing incident – a phone call that tells the hero 'there is a way to be good again' – is a literal quest presented to the protagonist with atonement (embodied in saving the child) as its very clear grail; by overcoming the external obstacle, the protagonist can be healed inside.

A climax can be subverted (the Coen brothers' *No Country for Old Men* kills its protagonist at the crisis point, but it's very much an exception) but the effect is akin to Bond running from Blofeld. Unless it's part of a wider schematic plan it feels wrong – the writer has set up something and then refused to pay it off.

So the inciting incident provokes the question 'What will hap-pen' and the climax (or obligatory act) declares – 'this'. When Macbeth kills Duncan we immediately want to know what will hap-pen, and what happens is that the forces loyal to Duncan grow in number and strength until they are finally ready to confront

Macbeth and take revenge. Indeed, *Macbeth* provides the perfect illustration of how story structure works. When Macbeth kills the King of Scotland, one by one his colleagues flee to England. The English camp grows stronger and stronger until Birnam Wood is able to march to Dunsinane and Macbeth, in the last act, is confronted with the consequences of his regicide.

Inciting incidents therefore create the question that will be answered in the climax. They arouse the antagonist, or massed ranks of antagonism, and, like a snowball at the top of a mountain, these forces continue to grow in size, thundering down the mountain until they finally, directly, confront the protagonist. And that's really what the climax is – the point at which the protagonist and antagonist slug it out. If all stories are about the battle between protagonist and antagonist, physics demands not just beginning and middle, but also end, which is why storytelling feels wrong if it's either omitted or underplayed. That's why the battle is commonly termed 'the obligatory scene', though the showdown between two opposites, as we shall see, is more complex than one scene can allow.

In Bond or Hitchcock the climax is particularly easy to identify. Apart from the fact it almost always takes up the last twenty-five minutes of a film, it also tends to be the biggest and most iconic sequence. It's often set in a unique location, and almost always on territory alien to the hero of the tale.

The climax, then, is the peak of the drama: everything builds to this end, all the strands, all issues, all themes square up. Protagonist faces antagonist – all come together to fight it out and be resolved.

The resolution

The denouement of any story is where all is brought to light, feelings are finally expressed and 'rewards' for behaviour bestowed. 'Denouement' is a derivation of *dénouer*, meaning 'to untie', and that's what it is – the knots of plot are undone and complications unravelled. But it is also a tying up of loose ends – in a classically structured work there must be a pay-off for every set-up, no strand left unattended or forgotten.

The resolution is the final judgement after the battle. If the heroes have overcome their demons, they are rewarded. 'Hugh Grant' learns to be assertive, James Bond saves the world – both get the girl.[19] Often the story ends in some kind of sexual fulfilment – although even in mainstream cinema there are some interesting anomalies. In *Star Wars* Luke really should end up with Princess Leia, but she turns out to be his sister – his reward for vanquishing evil is fame instead.[20] Such a subversion may go some way to explaining the film's phenomenal success: its very sexlessness makes it digestible to children of every age – but perhaps its placing of fame on a pedestal above love says something too about the values of the society that both spawned it and still continues to nourish its success.

Traditionally stories always ended happily ever after, with all action resolved – either the tragic hero died or the romantic couple got married. As the journalist and author Christopher Booker has observed, a number of significant changes took place as a result of the Industrial Revolution in the way we tell stories – endings are just as likely now to consist of an 'open ending', partly to add an air of uncertainty and partly because in a godless universe death doesn't mean what it once did. As Shakespearean scholar Jan Kott noted before him, 'Ancient Tragedy is loss of life, modern Tragedy is loss of purpose'.[21] Characters nowadays are just as likely to drift into meaningless oblivion as to die (*The Godfather II*); just as likely *not* to marry as to find themselves at the altar (*Four Weddings and a Funeral*).

Archetypal endings can also be twisted to great effect. *The Wire* found an extremely clever way of subverting the normal character arc – by brutally cutting it off at an arbitrary point. The death of Omar Little at the hands of a complete stranger works precisely because it's so narratively wrong; it undercuts the classic hero's journey by employing all its conventions up to the point of sudden, tawdry and unexpected death. Effectively saying this is a world where such codes don't operate, such subversion also has the added bonus of telling us just how the cruel and godless world of Baltimore drug-dealing really works.

Putting it all together

These building blocks are the primary colours of storytelling. To a greater or lesser extent they either occur in all stories, or else their absence (the missing bit of Omar's arc in *The Wire*; the early death of the hero in *No Country for Old Men*) has an implied narrative effect.[22] In archetypal form these are the elements that come together to shape the skeleton of almost every story we see, read or hear.

If you put them all together, that skeleton structure looks like this:

> Once upon a time a young friendless boy called Elliot discovered an alien in his backyard. Realizing that unless he helped the creature home it would die, he took it on himself to outwit the authorities, win over sceptics and in a race against time, in a true act of courage, set his friend free.

It sounds very simplistic, and in some senses it is, but like the alphabet or the notes on a musical stave, it is an endlessly adaptable form. Just how adaptable starts to become clear when we see how it lends itself to conveying a tragic tale.

Dark Inversions[23]

When we first meet Michael Corleone in *The Godfather* he's in an army uniform, campaign honours proudly displayed on his chest. Every inch the war hero, he explains the nefarious deeds of his father and his brothers to his fiancé, before mollifying her: 'That's my family, Kay, that's not me.' Macbeth bears an uncanny resemblance. As he emerges from the mists of battle, Duncan cannot help but be impressed: 'So well thy words become thee, as thy wounds:

They smack of honour both.' Both, as far as we can tell, are honourable men.

Michael Corleone and the heroic Scottish soldier – both flawed, but their faults are not what are traditionally described as tragic flaws or blind spots. They are, instead, good qualities: selflessness and bravery, and it is this that provides the key to how tragic story shape really works.

Tragedies follow exactly the same principles as *Jaws* or *E.T.* but in reverse order. In *Jaws*, Chief Brody learns to be a hero; in *Macbeth* the protagonist's heroism is corroded. In dark inversions, a character's flaw is what conventional society might term 'normal' or 'good' – a goodness that characters overturn to become evil in their own way.

This isn't to contradict Aristotle's premise[24] that each character will have a small germ of ambition or nihilism (their 'tragic flaw') within them – indeed it reinforces his observation. Historically, critics have focused on the Aristotelian definition of a fatal malignant flaw to describe tragic heroes (Macbeth's is ambition; Othello's jealousy), but it is just as instructive, I would argue, to chart how their goodness rots. It's a common trope of liberal American movies – in both *The Good Shepherd* and *The Ides of March* idealistic patriots find their morals slowly eaten away – but it's equally apparent in *Snowtown* (the grimly brilliant story of how a schizophrenic teenager is sucked into the world of Australia's most notorious serial killer) and in Hilary Mantel's *Wolf Hall*, where Thomas Cromwell undergoes a similar corruption. It is Cromwell's goodness that corrodes him, his loyalty to Cardinal Wolsey that fixes him on the same tragic trajectory as both Macbeth and Michael Corleone. Furthermore, as we shall see, it's a goodness that is corroded according to an absolutely archetypal pattern. From *Line of Duty* to *Moby Dick*, *Dr Faustus* to *Lolita* ('good' is a relative concept), there's a clearly chartable pathway the characters follow as, in pursuit of their goal, their moral centre collapses. The initial goals can be good (*The Godfather* or *Line of Duty*), seemingly innocuous (*Carmen*, *Dr Faustus*), but the end-result is the same: the characters are consumed by overwhelming egotistical desire. The dark hero's journey is not one from selfish to selfless like *Casablanca*'s

Rick, but in the opposite direction. It's a trajectory that's largely been avoided by television, certainly in drama series; nevertheless it's rich and fertile ground.

'The goal was to turn him from Mr Chips into Scarface,' said creator Vince Gilligan of Walter White, the hero of AMC's *Breaking Bad*.[25] 'It's a Wolfman story; it's a Jekyll and Hyde story, it's a story about a guy who is a caterpillar and we're turning him into a butterfly – a meth-cooking butterfly.' It took five seasons to turn a mild-mannered chemistry teacher into a drug-dealing psychopath – a radical departure in TV series terms, yet in its rich journey of greed and moral consequence it is one with its roots firmly embedded in the bloody Scottish soil of *Macbeth*.

Breaking Bad illustrates just how the archetype works – a flaw at the beginning of a story produces its opposite at the end: bad will become good; good will become bad. Most commonly, dark inversions are used to tell the tale of good turned to evil, but as the film *Like Crazy* illustrates, with its story of how a young girl's idealistic love grows stale, the shape has a wider application.

It seems impossible to understand how, with only eight notes in an octave, we don't simply run out of music, but just as tones give rise to semi-tones and time-signatures, tempo and style alter content, so we start to see that a very simple pattern contains within it the possibility of endless permutations. Feed in a different kind of flaw; reward or punish the characters in a variety of ways; and you create a different kind of story. When Songlian embraces the darkness in *Raise the Red Lantern*, she is punished with madness. *King Lear*, *Richard II* and *Romeo and Juliet* tell stories of emotional growth – archetypically the characters should be rewarded, but instead, by punishing them, the sense of tragedy is brutally enforced. In *Taxi Driver* and *The King of Comedy*, the dark protagonists *are* rewarded, twisting the archetype to make a darkly ironic comment on a sick society. In the twisted worlds of *Moby Dick* and *Frankenstein* the heroes seem somehow worse than the monsters, and in *The Scarlet and the Black* (and the uncannily similar *Room at the Top*), we are left dangling, unsure as to whether the heroes or their societies are to blame for their tragic demise. *Elite Squad* plays on a terrible ambiguity in which the hero has both grown and diminished at the same time, while *Rise of the Planet of the Apes* embraces the shape to illustrate just how easily societies create the seeds of their own destruction. *Bad Lieutenant: Port of Call – New Orleans* goes further, celebrating the character's collapse into rotten, foetid corruption. Even Ibsen's play *An Enemy of the People* can be interpreted as a dark inversion. Traditionally hailed as a cry for freedom from mob tyranny, it's equally possible (particularly if you read the Penguin Classics translation of 1964) to see the story as one man's descent through the propagation of eugenics,[26] into misanthropy and borderline madness. This certainly wasn't Ibsen's intention (we know from his letters that he was absolutely on the hero's side), but the fact that it is possible to read the work as the journey of an altruist as he becomes consumed by loathing for 'the people' illustrates just how wafer-thin is the line between the hero's journey and its darker cousin – and just how easy it is to manipulate act structure to create numerous, if not infinite permutations.[27]

The protagonists' battles against their antagonists, their journey to victory through crisis, climax and resolution; these are the building blocks of every story. But how are they assembled? In drama the traditional approach – and certainly the most advocated – is a three-act structure. This simple paradigm has come to dominate all talk of dramatic form. But what is it – and why is it so ubiquitous? It works so well that very few people have stopped to question it. It's a shame, because what it reveals is something applicable far beyond drama itself; it tells us much about perception, about narrative and about the workings of the human mind.

2

Three-Act Structure

I smacked my little boy. My anger was powerful. Like justice. Then I discovered no feeling in the hand. I said, 'Listen, I want to explain the complexities to you.' I spoke with seriousness and care, particularly of fathers. He asked, when I finished, if I wanted him to forgive me. I said yes. He said no. Like trumps.

'The Hand' is a chapter in a short story, 'Eating Out,' by the American miniaturist Leonard Michaels; it's also in effect a complete story in itself. If all stories contain the same structural elements, then it should be relatively easy to identify within 'The Hand' the building blocks with which we should now be familiar.

Protagonist – the narrator
Antagonist – his son
Inciting incident – awareness of no feeling in hand
Desire – to explain his action
Crisis – 'He asked . . . if I wanted him to forgive me'
Climax – 'I said yes. He said no'
Resolution – 'Like trumps'.

'The Hand' is, of course, not drama, but nonetheless it contains our building blocks, but how are they assembled? In what order? By what rules? And if there are rules, why do they exist?

What is Structure?

When Alan Plater first began writing for television, he asked his agent, the legendary Peggy Ramsay, exactly what 'this structure thing' was. She replied: 'Oh darling, it's just two or three little surprises followed every now and again by a bigger surprise.'[1] Superficially glib, it's actually a brilliantly pithy analysis – pinning down firmly the essential structural ingredient of drama: the act.

Acts are a unit of action bound by a character's desire. They have their own beginning, middle and end, the latter of which spins the narrative off in a new and unexpected direction; this of course being 'the surprise' Ramsay prescribed. It's something the Greeks called *peripeteia*, a word most commonly translated as 'reversal'.

In simple terms, a character is pursuing a specific goal when something unexpected happens to change the nature and direction of their quest. While minor reversals can occur in every scene, bigger ones tend to divide the work into specific acts. On returning from a visit to his friend Obi-Wan Kenobi, Luke Skywalker finds his step-parents have been murdered – that's a reversal. Seeking vengeance, Luke now has a new quest and a new act to perform it in.

One-act plays can be traced back as far as Euripides' *Cyclops*; sitcoms tend to be told in two (*Seinfeld* displayed a complete mastery of the two-act form[2]), but when the duration of a work reaches an hour or more – certainly in television – it's rare to see less than three. Partly this is to do with the need for commercial breaks, but it also ensures there are regular gripping hooks or turning points whether there are adverts or not. It's important to remember that there is no limit to the number of acts a story can have – *Raiders of the Lost Ark* has seven – but the central archetype that governs modern screenwriting, and on which so much of storytelling is built, is three.

The Three-Act Form

Three-act structure is the cornerstone of drama primarily because it embodies not just the simplest units of Aristotelian[3] (and indeed all) structure; it follows the irrefutable laws of physics. Everything must have a beginning, middle and end. The American screenwriting teacher Syd Field first articulated the three-act paradigm, breaking act structure down to these constituent parts: set-up, confrontation and resolution, with a turning point towards the end of the first (the inciting incident) and second (the crisis) acts.

ACT ONE	ACT TWO	ACT THREE
turning point	turning point	

It's a model that lies behind all modern mainstream film and TV narratives. Contrary to the perception of many, though, it wasn't invented by Field. One only has to read Rider Haggard's novel *King Solomon's Mines*, written in 1885 and so clearly an antecedent of *Indiana Jones*, to see the structural prototype of the modern movie form.

The articulation of this structure began with the world's very first screenwriting manual: *The Technique of the Photoplay* by Epes Winthrop Sargent, a valuable and still entertaining book written during the gold-rush period of the silent movie industry in 1912. Sargent, should he have wanted it, has some claim to the title of first film 'guru'. He doesn't specifically mention act structure, but every example of story he gives ('The story must not only have a start, but an object point [and] end or climax') contains it in embryo form.

In his history of American screenwriting, *What Happens Next?*, Marc Norman charts the development of this 'growing dependence on an archetypal narrative pattern, introduced into film by [Edwin]

Porter and [D. W.] Griffith but preceding them, arcing back to the Greeks'.

> The classic movie narrative was structurally simple but capable of countless variations, applicable to drama or comedy . . . a protagonist is introduced with a goal, a desire with which the audience can easily sympathize, and then an antagonist is introduced, as an individual or a representative of an opposing force, standing in his or her way. The movie becomes their conflict, and its sequences become the more or less linear escalation of that struggle, the cowboy with the gunfighter, the lovers with parents opposing, as predictable as much of classical music . . . This seamless conflict built to a third-act confrontation – the climax – and ended with a resolution that fit the mode, death in a tragedy and marriage, most typically, in a comedy.[4]

But why do we have to tell stories in three acts? When Charlie Kaufman says of the three-act form, 'it doesn't really interest me', he's implying it's a lazy, conventional and conservative form. Yet all his films embody it.* The same tropes of a flawed individual cast off into an alien world to find themselves irrevocably changed are as standard in his work as they are in that of Richard Curtis. Why can he not help but practise what he condemns? The endless recurrence of the same underlying pattern suggests psychological, if not biological and physical reasons for the way we tell stories. If we don't *choose* to tell them that way, perhaps we are compelled to.

In simplistic terms, human beings order the world dialectically. Incapable of perceiving randomness, we insist on imposing order on any observed phenomena, any new information that comes our way. We exist; we observe new stimuli; and both are altered in the process. It's thesis, antithesis, synthesis. Students encounter something of which they're unaware, explore and assimilate it, and by merging it with their pre-existing knowledge, grow. Every act of

---

* For a full analysis of *Being John Malkovich*, see Appendix III.

perception is an attempt to impose order, to make sense of a chaotic universe. Storytelling, at one level, is a manifestation of this process. As David Mamet says: 'Dramatic structure is not an arbitrary – or even a conscious – invention. It is an organic codification of the human mechanism for ordering information. Event, elaboration, denouement; thesis, antithesis, synthesis; boy meets girl, boy loses girl, boy gets girl; act one, act two, act three.'[5]

If you strip the three-act structure down you can see this inevitable and inescapable shape at work:

Act One: Thesis
Act Two: Antithesis
Act Three: Synthesis.

The 'Hollywood' archetype, then, is dialectics in its most simplified form.[6] Take a flawed character, and at the end of the first act plunge them into an alien world, let them assimilate the rules of that world, and finally, in the third act, test them to see what they have learned. Or, in simple terms:

Act One: Establish a flawed character
Act Two: Confront them with their opposite
Act Three: Synthesize the two to achieve balance.

You can see the same pattern endlessly recurring. All stories involve characters being thrown into an alien world – a place that represents everything outside their previous existence. In *Beowulf, Gulliver's Travels* and *Heart of Darkness*, the flawed protagonists are confronted with an unrecognizable universe, one that embodies all the characteristics they themselves lack. Here, in this forest, they must find themselves anew. It's a pattern that's most readily visible in film: in *Cars* the selfish, brash, speed jockey Lightning McQueen is thrown into a 1950s backwater; in *Jaws*, Chief Brody's sleepy Amity life is torn apart by threat, fear and moral panic; and in both book and screen adaptation of *Brideshead Revisited*, suburban self-loathing Charles Ryder finds himself in a world of unimagined luxury and confidence. If one accepts this notion of entering a new world (finding oneself in the head of John Malkovich would be a particularly good example), then the story archetype and its ingredients all slip neatly into focus.

The 'surprises' that Peggy Ramsay talked about are more commonly referred to as 'subversions of expectation' – a sudden twist both surprising yet plausible which throws the story in a new direction. Tending to occur towards the end of every act (as in the attempted rape and shooting in *Thelma & Louise* or the explosion in *The Long Good Friday*), they are even more pronounced in films built around twists such as *The Disappearance of Alice Creed* or *The Sixth Sense*. It's easy to dismiss such fireworks as gimmicks, yet these subversions of expectations are nothing of the sort – they're profoundly important structural devices that underlie all storytelling, for they are the portal that invites a protagonist into their new world. A subversion is not a modern invention but *peripeteia* itself; it is the tool that catapults the hero into the opposite of their present state – from thesis to antithesis, from home to a world unknown.

That's what inciting incidents are too – they are 'explosions of opposition', structural tools freighted with all the characteristics the characters lack; embodiments, indeed, of everything they *need*. Cliffhangers, inciting incidents and crisis points are essentially the same thing: a turning point at the end of an act; the unexpected entry point for the protagonists into a new world; bombs built from the very qualities they lack which explode their existing universe, hurtling them into an alien space of which they must then make sense.

Storytelling, then, can be seen as a codification of the method by which we learn – expressed in a three-act shape. The dialectic pattern – thesis/antithesis/synthesis – is at the heart of the way we perceive the world; and it's a really useful way to look at structure. A character is flawed, an inciting incident throws them into a world that represents everything they are not, and in the darkness of that forest, old and new integrate to achieve a balance. We cannot accept chaos; we *have* to order it. If a story involves the invasion of chaos and its restoration to order (and all archetypal ones do), then it cannot help but take the form of the three-act shape.

In Bernhard Schlink's novel *The Reader* (and in David Hare's subsequent film), those three stages can be seen exceptionally clearly; indeed, the work is divided into three parts. In part one, fifteen-year-old Michael falls in love with Hanna, an older woman, who one day disappears. Seven years pass until part two. Michael has become a law student and, observing a war crimes trial, he finds the woman he loved in the dock, accused of war crimes committed while a guard at Auschwitz. Hanna is found guilty of the mass murder of 300 Jewish women, and in part three Michael attempts to reconcile the woman he loved with the monster presented to the world. Finally, through understanding of, in this case, her illiteracy, he reaches some kind of accommodation with 'truth'. Three parts (and later three acts) enact love, hate and understanding; thesis, antithesis and synthesis.

ACT ONE SET-UP	ACT TWO CONFRONTATION	ACT THREE RESOLUTION
turning point	turning point	
Inciting Incident	DESIRE	Obligatory Act
FLAW/ NEED	FORCES OF ANTAGONISM	FINAL BATTLE
INCITING INCIDENT	THE JOURNEY	CRISIS CLIMAX RESOLUTION

In the first act of any story a character is presented with a particular flaw or need. An inciting incident occurs towards, or at, the end of that first act, and the protagonist 'falls down a rabbit hole'. In the second act, the character attempts to return to the world from which they came, whilst slowly learning that another equally important world awaits them where valuable lessons may be learned. At the end of this section, at their lowest ebb, the protagonist must choose whether to confront the enemies ranged against them by calling on lessons they have learned, or to return, sheepishly, to their old self. It's at this crisis point that they almost always choose to engage in the biggest battle (or climax) of their life, to test and then assimilate their new skills, before being finally rewarded (the resolution) for their travails. It's there in David Hare's films *Wetherby* and *Licking Hitler*; it's there in Charlie Kaufman's *Eternal Sunshine of the Spotless Mind*; and it's there in 'The Hand', when the omnipotent narrator is thrown into a world of guilt and shame. All these stories contain the same DNA: a hero meets their opposite, assimilates it and is changed.

But if the three-act form allows us to access the root structure of storytelling, why does so much of theatre prior to the twentieth century (particularly Shakespeare) use five acts? It's tempting to see the five-act form as an historical idiosyncrasy, but by exploring how it evolved, the reasons for its longevity and its underlying structural traits, we shall find that it reveals itself as something far more important than that – and in so doing provides a vital clue as to how all narrative really works.

3

Five-Act Structure

Some time towards the end of the first century BC the Roman lyric poet Horace laid out the principles of act structure in his treatise *Ars Poetica*. In doing so he defined a model that would profoundly influence the dramas of Seneca the Younger, and then, thanks to its later rediscovery, the future course of drama. 'Let no play', he proclaimed, 'be either shorter or longer than five acts, if when once seen it hopes to be called for and brought back to the stage.'[1]

In 2007 the journalist Rafael Behr published in the *Guardian* his satirical version of the then very-much-in-vogue 'Yummy Mummy Lit':[2]

CHAPTER ONE: I woke up to the sound of a baby vomiting. My husband, who shows no interest in having sex with me any more, is pretending to be asleep. Didn't I used to have an exciting career in media and be fancied by men? Where did it all go wrong? (Except for my children, of course. I love them.)

CHAPTER TWO: I went on the school run and was intimidated by a woman in a 4×4 with expensive shoes. My bossy mother-in-law came round and made me feel inadequate. I accidentally sent a text message to Man I Have A Crush On (MIHACO).

CHAPTER THREE: MIHACO texted back. I am thrilled. Does this make me an adulterer? I think it is OK because my husband has gone off me. I think it is OK if I say 'post-feminist' a lot.

CHAPTER FOUR: I snogged/slept with/very nearly slept with MIHACO. It was great. But I feel guilty. I love my husband and my kids. Meanwhile I have come to appreciate that there is more to my mother-in-law than I thought. My dad is my hero, by the way.

CHAPTER FIVE: I went to a party with everyone I know. It was very dramatic. My adultery dilemma reached crisis point. I had to choose between an imperfect real life and a delusional fantasy. I realized MIHACO is an arse so chose my current family. My husband, who I thought was boring but turns out to be reassuringly stable, forgave my infidelity. He is my new hero. Although he will never replace my dad.

Two thousand years after Horace's proclamation, Behr's parody marks a staging post in a long journey. His pastiche unknowingly follows – to an uncanny degree – the five-act pattern practised by Terence, articulated by Horace, assimilated via Ben Jonson and practised by Shakespeare himself, a writer of such profound influence he affects so much of what we write, what we read and what we say.

Three-Act and Five-Act Structure

It's important to underline that a five-act structure isn't really different to a three-act structure, merely a detailed refinement of it, and historically of course both forms can be traced back to the ancients. How does it work? Polanski's film of *Macbeth* has a classic three-act shape, but it carries within it Shakespeare's five (see diagram overleaf).

Simply put, five acts are generated by inserting two further act breaks in the second act of the traditional 'Hollywood' paradigm. The first and last acts remain identical in both forms.

But how does that help us understand stories? In his monumental

		SHAKESPEARE	POLANSKI
Inciting Incident	Witches' prophecy/Decision to murder Duncan	Act One	Act One
	Macbeth becomes king	Act Two	Act Two
	Banquo murdered/ Fleance escapes/ Macduff defects	Act Three	
Crisis	Lady M goes mad/ Macbeth abandoned (worst point)	Act Four	
Climax	Final Battle	Act Five	Act Three
Resolution	Macbeth killed		

study of Shakespearean act structure,[3] the American scholar Thomas Baldwin traced the first use of five acts back to Terence (190–159 BC), noting[4] that all his plays shared a similar underlying shape:

> The first act relates the necessary preparatory information leading up to the resolution or resolutions of the characters which occasion the impending struggle . . . The second act presents the preliminary moves and countermoves preceding the main battle. In the third act, the forces opposing the young men make their chief assault, and seem to have the victory. In the fourth act the General for the young men marshals his forces in defence or counterattack; and at the end of the act the opposition has really lost, but the young men have not yet officially won. In the fifth act, they win.

If one overlaid our 'Yummy Mummy' story, Behr's chapters would fit almost exactly. Is that a coincidence, or the suggestion of a deeper connection? Baldwin said of Terence:

> [His plays have] been constructed in five, clear-cut, fully and completely demarcated stages. Terence must have been conscious of them and must purposely so have distinguished them. The carefully and closely balanced structure cannot mean anything else . . . Whether Terence himself did or did not mark these five stages as acts, he certainly did construct his plays in these five clearly marked units.[5]

The resurgence of classical ideas during the Renaissance inevitably led to a major revival of this long-forgotten form. The template Terence established became the standard for French and Elizabethan playwrights as they mined the classics for ideas. Seneca, whose plays all consisted of five parts (each separated by a chorus[6]), was a particularly strong influence, and Ben Jonson, widely perceived to be the first playwright to popularize the structure in England, not only fully embraced the form in his own work but produced the first English translation of *Ars Poetica* by a major poet, opening up Horace's structural musings to a new, hungry and literate generation.

Was Shakespeare aware of the five-act form? As Terence and Horace were part of his grammar-school curriculum, then almost certainly, in addition to which, by the mid sixteenth century it was becoming an ever more popular mode of presentation. Did he practise it? There are considerable (and very entertaining) academic arguments as to whether later editors imposed the structure,[7] though by the time the King's Men occupied the Blackfriars Theatre in 1608 the simple technical demands of trimming candles (each candle lasting the duration of an act) had certainly led to its imposition. The question is to all intents and purposes an irrelevance; what is significant is that the pattern first found in Terence fits the work of Shakespeare to a striking degree. Even if Shakespeare either refuted or knew nothing of act structure, his work naturally assumes the shape common to both Terence and Jonson. And if that is so, it underlines the idea further that storytelling has a naturally occurring pattern.

But what exactly is the shape and how does it work? To answer this, we must once again journey back to the past.

Freytag's Pyramid

The first person to properly codify Terence's pattern – as it appeared in Elizabethan drama – was the German novelist Gustav Freytag. In 1863, in his epic *Technique of the Drama*, he gave the world 'Freytag's Pyramid'. Taking a long hard look at form, he detected an underlying shape:

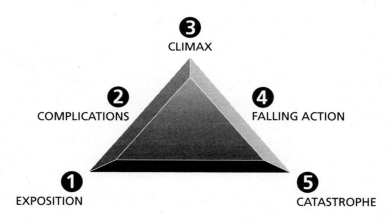

There were five stages in every tragedy, he declared:[8]

1. EXPOSITION. We meet the *dramatis personae*, and time and place are established. We learn about the antecedents of the story. Attention is directed toward the germ of conflict and dramatic tensions.

2. COMPLICATIONS. The course of the action becomes more complicated, the 'tying of the knots' takes place. Interests clash, intrigues are spawned, and events accelerate in a definite direction. Tension mounts, and momentum builds up.

3. THE CLIMAX OF THE ACTION. The development of conflict reaches its high point, the Hero stands at the crossroads, leading to victory or defeat, crashing or soaring.

4. FALLING ACTION. Reversals. The consequences of Act 3 play out, momentum slows, and tension is heightened by false hopes/fears. If it's a tragedy, it looks like the hero can be saved. If [it's not], then it looks like all may be lost.

5. CATASTROPHE. The conflict is resolved, whether through a catastrophe, the downfall of the hero, or through his victory and transfiguration.

At first Freytag's act definitions can appear confusing. Intuitively one feels the climax (the apex of the ladder) should really be in part five not part three. But Freytag is right. For the first time he articulates something deeply significant – the moment most commonly now referred to in structural study as the 'midpoint'.

The Midpoint

What does Banquo's murder in *Macbeth* have in common with the laser torture in *Goldfinger* or the sex on the piano in *Pretty Woman*? Banquo dies in Act III, scene 3. It's the heart of the play, bang in the middle, and, just as in the torture of Bond or the seduction of Vivian Ward, it marks a massive escalation in jeopardy.

Occurring almost exactly halfway through any successful story, the midpoint is the moment something profoundly significant occurs. In *Titanic* the ship hits the iceberg; in *Fatal Attraction* Dan learns his mistress is pregnant; and in *Alien* the eponymous creature bursts out of Kane's unsuspecting stomach.

Shakespeare's work fits the archetype precisely. Halfway through *Hamlet* the prince becomes certain of Claudius's guilt; in *King Lear* the hero learns his true state in the storm on the heath. It's here that Richard II discovers Bolingbroke has usurped his kingdom ('let us sit upon the ground and tell sad stories of the death of kings') and in *Othello* it's the moment the Moor swallows Iago's bait. Mark Antony turns the crowd into a mob exactly halfway through *Julius Caesar*,[9] just as Leontes learns the judgement of the Oracle of Delphi in *The Winter's Tale*. *Macbeth* too is absolutely archetypal: when Banquo is murdered and his son Fleance escapes, Macbeth is fully aware that something profound has changed. Shakespeare even spells it out:

> I am in blood
> Stepp'd in so far, that, should I wade no more,
> Returning were as tedious as go o'er.

It's Act III, scene 4, and for Macbeth – for all of them – there can be no return to how life was before.

So why do Thelma and Louise swap characters straight after experiencing sex with their loved ones? Why does Jason Bourne learn the truth about his predicament halfway through *The Bourne Ultimatum*? Why are midpoints so important in producing an emotionally satisfying story shape?[10] Do writers who are entirely unaware of story theory write them subconsciously? What is it that tells them an action of life-changing significance should occur halfway through their work?

Christopher Booker, in his encyclopaedic exploration of storytelling, *The Seven Basic Plots*,[11] argued that all stories could be broken down into five distinct sections. In my own – very brief – summary:

Call to Arms
Dream Stage
Frustration Stage

Nightmare Stage
Thrilling escape from death and resolution.

He is saying, in effect (I have paraphrased below), that these five stages follow a simple pattern – exactly the same one we first saw in Terence:

1. Set up and call to action
2. Things go well, initial objective achieved
3. Things start to go wrong as forces of antagonism gather strength
4. Things go really badly wrong, precipitating crisis
5. Crisis and climax. Final battle with antagonist. Matters resolve for good or ill.

So what happens if you apply each stage to an act? It *does* feel absurdly reductive, but as a simple catch-all synopsis Booker's pattern fits Shakespeare's act form incredibly well – be it *Macbeth*:[12]

1. Witches' prophecy and decision to murder Duncan
2. Macbeth becomes king
3. Macduff defects
4. Lady M goes mad, Macbeth abandoned. (worst point)
5. Final battle. Macbeth killed

or *Romeo and Juliet*:

1. Romeo and Juliet meet
2. Romeo and Juliet marry in secret
3. Juliet discovers she's to be married to Paris as Romeo is banished for killing Tybalt. She pretends to agree, but resolves to kill herself
4. Friar tells Juliet to give consent to marriage and gets her to take a potion faking death. Romeo hears of her demise and misses her explanatory letter by seconds (worst point)
5. Romeo rushes to tomb and kills himself. Juliet awakens, sees her lover dead, then kills herself too.

From Horace to Shakespeare and Jonson, Scribe to Molière and Racine, each stage fits snugly into this form. Take any James Bond film, the *Alien* movies, Pixar's films – indeed, any successful movie or TV drama – and you'll see the same thing: the shape that Terence adopted and Horace articulated imposing itself on the work.[13]

Hollywood movies aren't traditionally thought of as five-act pieces, so it's striking just how beautifully films built on a three-act template fit the five-act form.[14] Five acts help to illuminate not only how the second act in three-act dramas actually works, but in the process highlight the nature of dramatic structure itself. The midpoint shows us, in combination with the second and fourth act breaks, a very clear shape.

While Booker saw that shape, he failed to notice the underlying detail. In the third act, things don't go wrong immediately and continuously.[15] Rather, action peaks in the middle of the act before fortunes reverse in the second half. If we plot a graph of how turning points reflect the characters' fortunes in each act, not only is the apex of the graph – the midpoint – revealed as an extremely important moment in the drama, it's also possible to see a very clear illustration of a familiar verbal trope, the 'dramatic arc'.

The Dramatic Arc

ACT ONE	ACT TWO	ACT THREE	ACT FOUR	ACT FIVE
		MIDPOINT		
	INITIAL OBJECTIVE ACHIEVED		THINGS START TO GO WRONG	
CALL TO ACTION				VICTORY OR DEFEAT

Everyone who works in drama has at some point stumbled upon

the concept of character arcs, whether to demand or decry them. But they do exist and the underlying symmetry of their shape hints at something deeper and more meaningful – much of which we will touch on later. Too simplistic? Charlie Kaufman, in attacking classic structure, certainly thinks so. 'To me, it's kind of like saying, "Well, when you do a painting, you always need to have sky here, the person here and the ground here." Well, you don't. In other art forms or other mediums, they accept that it's just something available for you to work with.'[16]

Kaufman's analogy is a false one. A cursory knowledge of art history will tell you that even if you dismiss the Renaissance idea of perfect scientific proportion or 'golden mean', art is still about finding order and balance of some kind; even Jackson Pollock and the Abstract Expressionists found shape within chaos. So when Lotte commits adultery by climbing inside the head of John Malkovich to have sex with her friend Maxine, Kaufman is not bucking a fashion. It happens exactly halfway through the film and it raises the stakes by turning her husband into an enemy. It's a classic midpoint. Kaufman mistakes content for form; the study of five-act structure reveals the underlying journey characters – and certainly those in *Being John Malkovich* – happily tread.

So why, then, is three-act structure so ubiquitous? Five-act structure was the dominant theatrical form for over two centuries. What made it so, and if it really was so important, what led to its demise?

Five Acts versus Three Acts

Aside from the creative impulse there are two main catalysts responsible for the development of any artistic form: biology and technology. It's likely that five-act structures became commonplace not simply because they created a dramatic template that allowed writers to access successful stories. The inability to stand for too long and the capacity of the human bladder in all likelihood also played a significant role in the demand for frequent breaks. When you consider too that the candles used to light night-time and interior performances had a finite duration – for some or all of these reasons five acts became the most acceptable way of framing stories.

The five-act form arguably reached its apotheosis in the work of Eugène Scribe (1791–1861), the French master who developed, indeed arguably created, the *pièce bien faite* or 'well-made play'. Scribe's prolific output (he 'wrote' over 400 works collected in no less than seventy-six volumes) is largely explained by his employment of a team of juniors who followed a formula he honed to perfection – much as an author like James Patterson does today.[17] Scribe constructed his works around the classic Shakespearean form with each act ending in a turning point or reversal of fortune. He insisted on topical subject matter and demanded an ending where 'there is an equitable distribution of prizes in accordance with poetic justice' – one which was seen to reinforce 'the morals of the day'.[18]

Though the topicality of his plays means his work has dated, Scribe is an important figure, arguably the first to articulate a template for mass production. The writers' fear of orthodoxy and an understandable desire to place oneself above such pecuniary devices has meant that his reputation has suffered, obscuring the fact that his works were incredibly well structured, full of dashing rhetorical devices and – in their time – great fun. His success, popularity and focus on the primacy of entertainment made him, even in his own time, a subject of mockery. George Bernard Shaw disparagingly questioned: 'Why the devil should a man write like Scribe when he can write like Shakespeare or Molière, Aristophanes or Euripides?'[19] – but his influence is underrated and arguably profound.

A young Ibsen directed twenty-one of Scribe's plays,[20] and Scribe's impact on the giant of nineteenth-century theatre is clearly apparent. Ibsen's five-act *An Enemy of the People* follows the archetype to an almost uncanny degree, as do his four-act (*Hedda Gabler*) and three-act works (*Ghosts*) too. Indeed, as Professor Stephen Stanton has noted,[21] Ibsen 'founded a new school of dramatic art' largely by employing Scribe's structure and merely substituting 'serious discussion for the conventional unravelling of situation in the last act.'[22] Shaw, too, is disingenuous – not only was he aware of Scribe's influence on Ibsen,[23] there are uncanny similarities with his own work.

Without Scribe, then, there would have been no Ibsen or Shaw (at least not in quite the same form). It speaks volumes that the term 'well-made play' became a kind of shorthand abuse in the 1960s[24] – banishing, amongst others, Terence Rattigan from the English stage. It's a mindset that still lingers today – the suspicion that somehow craft must be the enemy of authenticity. It's a shame both for drama and for Scribe, whose influence not just on Ibsen and Shaw but on successive generations of playwrights from T. W. Robertson to Oscar Wilde, Bulwer-Lytton to J. B. Priestley, suggests that however dated his work a greater acknowledgement of his pivotal position is overdue.

The nineteenth-century revival of three-act drama wasn't a reaction against Shakespearean form, but instead coincided with developments in comfort and technology. No longer did the storm in *The Tempest* need to be conjured by words alone – now you could sit on a velvet seat in a heated room and indulge yourself in the magic of stagecraft with all the wizardry of stage machinery and sophisticated lighting at your disposal. Suddenly a trip to the theatre was an altogether friendlier proposition; and even without gaudy spectacle (which must have felt much like the advent of widescreen or 3-D did to us) less frequent intervals had become an altogether more comfortable experience – one with far fewer extra-curricular distractions. Three acts resurfaced, which is why, coinciding as it did with the birth of cinema, film structure and consequently TV structure owe their evolution to the theatre – it was simply the most convenient reference point to start from.

As we've seen, successful three-act works mimic the shape of the larger structure; indeed, the shape of the protagonist's journey in the former is more clearly marked out by the demands of the five-act form. Writers who struggle with the Hollywood paradigm often find the five-act shape gives them the control over their middle section they otherwise find hard to deliver. Used wisely, it imposes a much stronger structure, creates regular gripping turning points that increase narrative tension and in turn eliminates one of the most common problems new screenwriters are heir to: the 'sagging', disjointed, confused and often hard-to-follow second act.

But five acts do something else too. As we dig deeper, the five-act form allows us to uncover the most extraordinary – and intricate – underlying pattern.

4

The Importance of Change

He locates the gun behind the toilet cistern, composes himself and moves towards the washroom door. In the small Italian restaurant, Sollozzo and McCluskey sit impatiently. He makes his way back to the table. He takes his seat, a subway train rumbles above but he hears nothing but the sound of his own heart. Diners talk on obliviously, the train screams past, he rises, pulls the gun, pauses and then in a moment plants a bullet in the forehead of both his guests. A mist of blood, a table upended, and Michael Corleone's life is changed for ever.

Michael's murder of a corrupt police captain and his gangster friend is a justly iconic Hollywood scene. But it's iconic not just in terms of *The Godfather*. Take a look at Michael's face. Note the eyes, and behind them the conflict between the loyal, law-abiding war hero and the murderer he's about to become; between the son whose future lay outside the family business and the act that will link him to their criminal trade for ever. From the moment he pulls the trigger, Michael's destiny is assured. The conflict between the person that was and the person that will be, and the act of will it takes to pass from one state to the other, are captured perfectly.[1]

In truth it's a scene that exists in every movie. Al Pacino, in this one moment, depicts the essence all drama is built on: change, and the internal struggle a character must undergo in order to achieve it.

We've seen that in three-dimensional stories the protagonist goes on a journey to overcome their flaw. They learn the quality they need to achieve their goal; or, in other words, they change. Change is thus inextricably linked to dramatic desire: if a character wants something, they are going to have to change to get it.

In Aaron Sorkin's movie *A Few Good Men*, Lt Kaffee (Tom Cruise) sets himself the goal of bringing down the corrupt Colonel Jessup (Jack Nicholson). Kaffee is a smug, superficial, rather spoilt boy, who has built his fledgling career on avoiding courts and plea-bargaining his clients' fates. But he wants to bring Jessup, the supremely powerful army chief, to book for bullying a raw recruit to death. Unless Kaffee grows up, overcomes his flaws and dares to take Jessup on in the courtroom unaided and man-to-man, he will not achieve his desire. His flaw is he's a child in a man's world; his want is justice. To get it he's going to have to change – to become a man. That, in one particular manifestation, is the dramatic archetype, one entirely built on change.

Walter White, the fictitious anti-hero of *Breaking Bad*, puts it well. Attempting to explain chemistry to his uninterested science class, he declaims:

> 'Well, technically it's the study of matter. But I prefer to see it as the study of change. Now just think about this. Electrons, they change their energy levels. Molecules? Molecules change their bonds. Elements, they combine and change into compounds. Well, that's all of life, right? . . . It's solution then dissolution, over and over and over. It's growth, then decay, then transformation.'[2]

Change is the bedrock of life and consequently the bedrock of narrative. What's fascinating is that like stories themselves, change too has an underlying pattern. In every archetypal tale a template (or its shadow) can be found; an unchanging paradigm that can help us unlock the mysteries of structure.

What is this pattern and how does it work?

The Change Paradigm

It's possible to break down Ridley Scott and Callie Khouri's film *Thelma & Louise* into five distinct stages.

1. Two women set off on a camping trip. Louise is uptight and repressed and Thelma an innocent, living in a brutal marriage which she believes is happy. Stopping off at a bar, starting to let go, Thelma is subjected to an attempted rape. Louise confronts the attacker and shoots him dead. (INCITING INCIDENT)

2. Louise immediately decides to run from the scene of the crime and head to Mexico. Thelma is desperate to hand herself in and go back to her husband Darryl, but, after a phone call in which for the first time she sees him in his true repressive colours, she agrees to join Louise. Fugitives from justice, Mexico is in their sights.

3. The two women start to relax and enjoy themselves. On Thelma's instigation they pick up a handsome boy (Brad Pitt) and Louise contacts her boyfriend (Michael Madsen) for the first time, asking for help. That night in a motel both women have sex. The next morning Louise says a final goodbye to her man and Thelma, discovering her beau has robbed her, takes charge. On the run, with no income and no source of help, she holds up a supermarket. The police, already looking for them for the murder, have the first clear lead as to their whereabouts.

4. The police start to close in. Louise's insistence that they can't travel through Texas reveals that she herself was raped there many years ago. With their goal almost impossibly far away and their woes increased by the pursuit of a lecherous tanker driver, they drive through the night,

toying with the idea of handing themselves into the police. Instead, accidentally, they give their specific whereabouts away. (CRISIS)

5. With nothing left to lose, they turn on the tanker driver, lure him into a trap and then blow up his load. Cornered by the police they face the might of the authorities or . . . The two hold hands, accelerate and drive off the cliff into the canyon beyond.

Two ordinary women, oppressed by a brutal patriarchal society, find fulfilment beyond this petty bourgeois life in what, we are told, is not suicide but something more graceful, something with grandeur. With all the skills the writer, cast and director can muster, we are to believe that this ending – with the protagonists' flaws overcome – is some kind of ascension, some kind of reward.

Structure

I have no idea whether screenwriter Callie Khouri consciously wrote her script in five acts, but it's easy to see how the film can be divided into those classic archetypal stages. It's interesting to note, too, that in so doing an underlying symmetrical uniformity emerges. The 'third act' lasts forty minutes, bisected by a midpoint, while the duration of each other section is twenty minutes long.

The film charts the growth of Thelma from a dependent little girl to a liberated woman, while Louise goes on a similar journey, but from a different direction – from repressed to liberated too. Thelma learns self-determination; Louise, the ability to share. They are on equal and opposite roads of travel. In addition, if we agree on the central characters' flaws – that Thelma is an innocent, and Louise a world-weary cynic – it's possible to see not only that the underlying architecture of the story is built around opposites, but that both characters overcome their flaws and achieve self-realization in the same way.

What's more significant for now, however, is that they change according to an identical underlying pattern. This pattern is built around the characters' central flaws or needs. If we remember that at the beginning of every story these elements are unconscious, then it's possible to chart how those flaws are brought into the conscious mind, acted on, and finally fully overcome:

THELMA — LOUISE

ACT 1

Naïve — Cynical
Eyes open — Eyes open
New world — New world

ACT 2

Wants to call police — Wants to run
Prevaricates — Prevaricates
They agree to go to Mexico together

ACT 3

Singing in car/Thelma bonds with JD/Louise contacts Jimmy
Sex with boyfriends
Thelma takes charge – Louise lets go – Robbery

ACT 4

Fear of future
Regression to old selves
Do we embrace new selves or don't we?

ACT 5

Assertion of new selves
Blowing up of tanker
Suicide/ascension

Most of the significant points are shared – albeit approached from different directions; as Thelma learns greater self-confidence, Louise learns to let go. Their equal and opposite reactions complement each other until finally both find the balance within themselves to become complete.*

If you take any three-dimensional film and plot the way characters change in each act – how they become aware of and finally overcome their flaws – you will find a similar design. It's a pattern that is in effect a roadmap of change, one that charts a growing knowledge of a protagonist's flaws; their gradual acceptance, prevarication and final total rebirth. In essence, it looks like this:

THE ROADMAP OF CHANGE

ACT 1
No knowledge
Growing knowledge
Awakening

ACT 2
Doubt
Overcoming reluctance
Acceptance

ACT 3
Experimenting with knowledge
MIDPOINT – KEY KNOWLEDGE
Experimenting post-knowledge

ACT 4
Doubt
Growing reluctance
Regression

* For the same pattern applied to *Hamlet* and others, see Appendix II.

ACT 5
Reawakening
Re-acceptance
Total mastery

Or graphically:

ACT ONE

Total mastery — No knowledge

Re-acceptance — Growing knowledge

Reawakening — Awakening

ACT FIVE — **ACT TWO**

Regression — Doubt

Growing reluctance — Overcoming reluctance

Doubt — Acceptance

ACT FOUR — **ACT THREE**

Experimenting post-knowledge — Experimenting with knowledge

THE 3-D ROADMAP OF CHANGE

MIDPOINT
(Breakthrough) Key knowledge

Seinfeld deftly parodied the great clichés of screenwriting with its mantra 'No hugs, no learning' and many a writer will roll their eyes when a script editor dares to ask, 'What does your character learn?' As the paradigm illustrates, however, learning is central to *every* three-dimensional story: that is *how* the characters change; they learn to overcome their flaw and, what's more, they appear to learn according to a pattern. Their unconscious flaw is brought to the surface, exposed to a new world, acted upon; the consequences of overcoming their flaw are explored, doubt and prevarication set in before, finally, they resolve to conquer it and embrace their new selves.

You see the same design in *Strictly Ballroom*, in *Attack the Block* and in *The Lives of Others*; you see it not just in David Hare's *My Zinc Bed*, but at some level in all his work. The films are different because the flaw is different; in *Strictly Ballroom* Scott has to learn courage; in *Attack the Block* Moses battles his own cowardice and in *The Lives of Others* Wiesler masters empathy. At the beginning of *E.T.* Jack scolds his younger brother Elliot for upsetting their mum: 'Damn it,' he says, 'why don't you grow up? Think how other people feel for a change.' That's Elliot's flaw – he has to learn to empathize, he has to embark on a journey that finally allows him to let his closest friend go. Each act is a different stage in that struggle. He overcomes this flaw gradually, sequentially, following the same pattern as Thelma and Louise.[3]

Reverse the pattern and you have *Macbeth* and *The Godfather*; their goodness corrupted to the very same design. In the archetype every character has a flaw; the 'roadmap' illustrates how they overcome it.* Too far-fetched? It *does* appear simplistic, but try examining almost any movie from *Casablanca* to *Iron Man*; *Juno* to *Bringing Up Baby*; *The African Queen* to *Casino Royale*. It's there too in Shakespeare, just as it is in Hare's *My Zinc Bed*, Kaufman's *Being John Malkovich* and del Toro's work too.

But why? How can such uniform structure possibly exist?

Christopher Vogler and the Hero's Journey[4]

It's 1973 and *American Graffiti* has just become, dollar for dollar, the most successful movie of all time. George Lucas, its begetter, begins to ponder on the nature of stories. Where, he asks, are the big

---

* See Appendix V for illustration.

mythological tales? Where are the westerns of today?[5] Discovering the work of the anthropologist Joseph Campbell, who had studied rights-of-passage stories across cultures, he realizes there are similarities between Campbell's Jungian interpretation of myth and one of his own nascent works. He fuses the two together with extraordinary results.[6] *Star Wars* is born, but so too is a monster that threatens to engulf the entire film industry.

The early 1970s were an extraordinarily vibrant time for American cinema. Any era that can produce *Five Easy Pieces*, *Taxi Driver* and *Chinatown* is a healthy one; but with a few (monumental) exceptions the movies weren't works that concentrated on what Hollywood does best – making vast amounts of cash. So when a hungry industry saw *Star Wars* become insanely popular and then learned it was built from a template and could thus be replicated, all hell broke loose. It was a gold rush. Suddenly there was a 'map', and if you didn't follow the map it was much harder to get your work made. However, it wasn't an easy map to read, and like many a prospector found, a short cut was hard to resist.

Which is where Christopher Vogler, a young script analyst at Disney, came in. He boiled down Campbell's epic study of mythology, *The Hero with a Thousand Faces*, into a seven-page memo[7] which, in time, was to give birth to a book, *The Writer's Journey*, and a template that was to influence a generation of film-makers and film executives. It was here that the ire of purists was incubated, and many writers began to feel that if you didn't follow what was rapidly becoming a philosopher's stone, your work simply wouldn't get produced: to them, Vogler was reducing the muse to a flat-pack plan. It wasn't true, but as the journey structure of films from *Star Wars* to *The Lion King* really did seem able to transmute base metal, many felt it was.

So what did Vogler articulate? If you were being cruel you'd call it 'Campbell for Dummies'. The principles are simplistic, reductive, but contain the kernel of something extremely important – something of which even the author himself does not appear to have been aware. Vogler created a structural model based on Campbell's belief, formulated in 1949, of a *monomyth*.[8]

Campbell argued that within all the traditional stories of ancient cultures (normally supernatural ones concerning themselves with either aspects of human behaviour or origins of natural phenomena) there could be found one underlying identical pattern. This monomyth was fairly simple: 'A hero ventures forth from the world of common day into a region of supernatural wonder: fabulous forces are there encountered and a decisive victory is won: the hero comes back from this mysterious adventure with the power to bestow boons on his fellow man.' What Campbell found in all myths was a quest to find a magic elixir, and the ensuing battle to return it to the homeland.

I first came across Vogler's (and thus Campbell's) work when I was a young script-reader myself and I dismissed it fairly abruptly. I was working on *EastEnders* and simply couldn't see how a hero's journey could apply to Pauline Fowler in the launderette. When I started to explore structural theory more seriously, I went back to it again. It *is* flawed and simplistic,[9] but it is useful in helping to prise open some key elements of structural design. Vogler's model consists of twelve key stages:

1. Heroes are introduced in the ordinary world where . . .
2. they receive the call to adventure.
3. They are reluctant at first or refuse the call, but . . .
4. are encouraged by a mentor to . . .
5. cross the threshold and enter the special world where . . .
6. they encounter tests, allies and enemies.
7. They approach the inmost cave, crossing a second threshold . . .
8. where they endure the supreme ordeal.
9. They take possession of their reward and . . .
10. are pursued on the road back to the ordinary world, undergoing a spiritual death before . . .
11. they cross the third threshold, experience a resurrection and are transformed by the experience.
12. They return with the elixir, a boon or treasure to benefit the ordinary world.

Part of the reason I was so quick to dismiss it was because, like Freytag, it suggested the biggest point of drama, the supreme ordeal, was in the middle of the film – implying a backward journey in which the forces of antagonism didn't build. Equally, I couldn't understand how there could be two different screenwriting paradigms. Surely there could only be one or none at all?

Two simple actions were, however, able to unlock the conundrum. The first was to attempt to fit both paradigms together – to give Vogler's work an act structure. Vogler himself suggests how it fits into a three-act shape, but the five-act pattern is, once again, far more revealing:

ACT ONE
1. Heroes are introduced in the ordinary world where . . .
2. they receive the call to adventure.

ACT TWO
3. They are reluctant at first or refuse the call, but . . .
4. are encouraged by a mentor to . . .
5. cross the threshold and enter the special world where . . .

ACT THREE
6. they encounter tests, allies and enemies.
7. They approach the inmost cave, crossing a second threshold . . .
8. where they endure the supreme ordeal.
9. They take possession of their reward and . . .

ACT FOUR
10. are pursued on the road back to the ordinary world, undergoing a spiritual death before . . .

ACT FIVE
11. they cross the third threshold, experience a resurrection and are transformed by the experience.
12. They return with the elixir, a boon or treasure to benefit the ordinary world.

The second action was to apply it to an existing work – to actually feed in a character flaw.[10]

In Baz Luhrmann's *Strictly Ballroom*, Scott Hastings is a great dancer but he's crippled emotionally – a narcissistic, workaholic loner. He's desperate to win the Pan-Pacific ballroom championship but is unaware of his own more desperate need for intimacy. That's his flaw – and if you substitute the word 'elixir' for 'intimacy', something interesting happens.

ACT ONE

We meet ambitious, headstrong, emotionally stunted Scott in his limited world, a man obsessed with winning on his own terms.

He meets Fran, an amateur dancer, who dares to ask him to dance with her – he gets the call to be brave.

ACT TWO

He is reluctant at first, refusing the call, but is encouraged by her strength of character to . . . cross the threshold and dance with her in competition.

ACT THREE

By continuing to dance/flirt with her, he incites the ridicule of his peers, undergoing tests, winning allies and provoking enemies . . . until he crosses a second threshold where, finally brave enough to stand up to the dance authorities who have condemned them as a couple, he endures the supreme ordeal and casts them aside.

He takes possession of Fran – his reward, and shows her his vulnerability. He learns to dance with his heart, experimenting with a new way of seeing the world, but . . .

ACT FOUR

. . . is pursued on the road back to the ordinary world by doubts, insecurities and uncertainties as he finds it harder than he thought to deal with the pressures his newfound bravery brings, those of peer pressure and the risk of failure. Worried he won't ever win a competition with Fran, he rejects her, facing spiritual death.

ACT FIVE

Scott must choose between winning and experiencing the intimacy of true love. He crosses a third threshold, experiencing a resurrection – finally and irrevocably standing up to his tormentors and dancing with Fran in the final competition – forgoing the rules – to the rhythm of his heart.

Transformed by the experience he returns with the elixir – a boon or treasure to benefit the ordinary world.

What you see – in clear, equal act divisions – is that the elixir, the elusive treasure that the hero or homeland needs, is exactly the same element the protagonist needs to cure their flaw. The story becomes the hunt for the key to overcoming Scott's unique problem instead.

It's the same with Thelma, who learns to take control, and for Louise, who learns to let go: the story shape is structured around how they find, retrieve and finally master the quality in their life that has eluded them. They start flawed, they find the elixir, learn how to use it, and end complete.

It's to Vogler's credit that he first detected Campbell's principles in modern movie-making and started to excavate the idea of common structures. His work is frustrating however, partly because Vogler himself makes no attempt to dig deeper than noting its resemblance to the 'monomyth'; partly because his own elucidations are often confused and partly because there's no real attempt (apart from some quasi-mystical mumbo jumbo) to understand why.[11]

Contrary to the hosannas that greeted its arrival, Vogler's paradigm is in essence nothing more than a three-act structure viewed from the protagonist's point of view; it's no more complex or original than that. It's most significant contribution may be as a tool that helps us answer the all-important question 'why?' It's a question we get closer to resolving by looking in more depth at the one key feature it shares with 'traditional' structure: the 'midpoint' or 'supreme ordeal'.

The Importance of the Midpoint

We know that the midpoint in *The Godfather* is when Michael shoots the policeman and his life changes for ever; we know it's the moment the *Titanic* hits the iceberg. But what exactly is it? How does it unite the traditional Hollywood three-act archetype, Vogler's work and the Shakespearean five-act structure? Indeed, why does it exist at all?

The midpoint in our change paradigm corresponds to the moment of Vogler's 'supreme ordeal'. It's the point at which, in the 'Hero's Journey', the protagonist enters the 'enemy cave' and steals the 'elixir'; it is – in our paradigm – the moment of 'big change'.[12] It isn't necessarily the most dramatic moment, but it is a point of supreme significance. As *Macbeth* illustrates, it's the point from which there's no going back. A new 'truth' dawns on our hero for the first time; the protagonist has captured the treasure or found the 'elixir' to heal their flaw. But there's an important caveat . . . At this stage in the story they don't quite know how to handle it correctly. The 'journey back' is therefore built on how the hero reacts to possessing the 'elixir' and whether they will learn to master it in a wise and useful way.

In *The African Queen*, Humphrey Bogart and Katharine Hepburn play a river boatman and a missionary thrown together by a German massacre in the heart of Africa. Despite their antipathy, they resolve to venture down a perilous river to blow up the enemy's battleship. Exactly halfway through the film they must navigate past a heavily fortified fortress, an act which will quite probably lead to their deaths. Against the odds, however, they succeed, and giddy with their good fortune they embrace and kiss for the first time.

As in *Thelma & Louise*, the two protagonists are clear opposites – he, crude and worldly; she, refined and repressed. Emotionally the scene marks the point at which they overcome their flaws fully for the first time: he shows tenderness; she expresses sexual feeling. Their immediate reaction is to appear embarrassed and deny anything has happened. They want to return to their old selves but they can't; the die is cast and both must live with the consequences of their kiss. In addition, the film adds further jeopardy – the Germans are now aware of their presence; our two heroes must learn to assimilate their newfound intimacy while at the same time being pursued down-river by an angry and ruthless foe.

The midpoint, then, is the moment the protagonists are given a very powerful 'drug' but not the necessary knowledge to use it properly. How they develop that knowledge forms the underlying subject matter of the second half of the film. A well-designed midpoint has a risk/reward ratio: a character gains something vital, but in doing so ramps up the jeopardy around them. It's an obstacle that can dramatically raise the stakes and in the process force the heroes to change to overcome it. That change marks the point of no return for the protagonists; it's the end of the outward journey to find their 'solution' and the beginning of their journey back.

There's a very literal example in Mel Gibson's *Apocalypto*, where the whole story is built around an outgoing and return journey. The hero, Jaguar Paw, is a young warrior captured and taken hundreds of miles to be sacrificed while his pregnant wife is left behind to die. Exactly halfway through, at the moment of sacrifice, he escapes (fully asserting his courage for the first time) and races home, wounded, to rescue his partner pursued by the murderous, vengeful tribesmen he's humiliated. He starts the story a boy, lacking courage. He ends it, of course, a man. It's a suitably dramatic illustration of the change paradigm and significantly the biggest change seems to lie directly at the heart of the story.

This is as true in television as it is in film. The first three series of *Prime Suspect* were all two-parters, and at the end of each first part – effectively each story's midpoint – you are left screaming warnings at Jane Tennison as she faces a new obstacle that changes the tenor of the whole investigation. Midpoints occur simply too often to be coincidences. They're not. Understanding their true significance unlocks a door, behind which lies the reason stories are the shape they are.

5

How We Tell Stories

'*Tom Jones* . . . has 198 Chapters, divided into eighteen Books, the first six of which are set in the country, the second six on the road, and the final six in London . . . Exactly in the middle of the novel most of the major characters pass through the same inn, but without meeting in combinations which would bring the story to a premature conclusion . . . Symmetry,' says author and critic David Lodge, 'matters more to writers of fiction than readers consciously perceive.'[1]

E. M. Forster's *A Passage to India* centres around an ambiguous incident in the Marabar Caves between a local doctor and an Englishwoman abroad. Everything in the novel leads first into then spirals out from this moment: an encounter, shrouded in mystery, in a dark cave that occurs exactly halfway through the book. The ubiquity with which such symmetry occurs in fiction suggests something structurally important is going on. Why is Homer's *Odyssey* separated into twenty-four books, with Odysseus arriving in Ithaca to reclaim his kingdom almost exactly halfway through? Why is Virgil's *Aeneid* arranged so similarly? 'The artist,' said Mondrian, 'spontaneously creates relationships in equilibrium – complete harmony [is] the goal of art.'[2] Again, we must be careful of oversimplification, but the existence of such a thing as a 'midpoint' suggests that stories tend towards a symmetrical nature, and that the centre of each may have a unique and specific importance.

It may seem counter-intuitive, but by looking at how midpoints work in other forms of story – in both two dimensions and with multiple protagonists – it's possible to find important clues as to something more than coincidence is occurring.

The 'Midpoint' in Two Dimensions

We've established that change is at the root of all drama, but at the same time noted that in two-dimensional stories protagonists don't change. But drama cannot exist without change; arguably it *is* change, so in a world where detectives stay constantly the same, what fuels the dramatic engine?

In a classic episode of *Columbo* or *Inspector Morse*, the protagonist seeks the 'truth' that lies behind the crime they're investigating. While the internal protagonist goes on a journey to discover who they really are and in doing so heals themself, the purely external protagonist learns the true nature of the crime they are investigating and in catching the perpetrators heals the world. They may not change inside – their knowledge *of* a situation changes instead.

Rather than a flaw, these characters have a deficiency of knowledge, which improves as the story progresses. Morse knows nothing of the killer at the beginning of his journey – but everything by the end. There is a pattern to this change, too. In the finale of series three of *Spooks* (by Ben Richards),[3] Adam, our hero, learns that his wife Fiona and Danny, a fellow agent, have been kidnapped. Again, it's possible to break the story down into the traditional five-act shape:

ACT ONE
Adam tells Fiona he 'wouldn't swap her for the whole world'. Fiona, on a routine mission with Danny, is kidnapped by North African terrorists. (Inciting incident)

ACT TWO
The kidnappers demand the British government immediately withdraw all forces from Iraq – the Prime Minister must announce it at a summit that evening. Fiona and Danny scramble to get an SOS to their colleagues. Adam finally learns of their capture but at the cost of being captured by Khatera – another kidnapper – himself.

ACT THREE

MI5 become suspicious and begin a systematic search for their missing colleagues. Exactly halfway through the episode they manage to plant a bug on Adam and Khatera. MI5 now have knowledge of who the terrorists are. (Midpoint)

Danny and Fiona attempt to escape but are captured again. Danny is murdered trying to save Fiona, while Adam is forced to listen in horror down the phone.

ACT FOUR

Khatera insists Adam take her to the government conference to see the PM's announcement. Adam attempts to 'turn' her, but not quickly enough, and with the clock ticking he discovers something even worse. The terrorists aren't interested in a government announcement. Khatera has a bomb stitched inside her stomach, and has double-crossed Adam to lead her to the PM. (Crisis)

ACT FIVE

Adam learns Khatera's true motivation, talks her down and gets her to reveal Fiona's whereabouts. In a last-minute chase he saves the day, his wife and the country.

Not only does the story follow a classic structure, it should be possible to see that the gang's 'knowledge *of*' changes in much the same way as it would in three dimensions. At the beginning of the story Adam knows nothing; at the end of act two he has a first inkling of his adversaries; at the midpoint the identities of the kidnappers are revealed; and at the end of act four, he discovers that both he and the PM are standing next to a human bomb. (It is shown in graphic form overleaf.)

The midpoint in two dimensions, then, is the moment the protagonists start to really understand the nature of the forces ranged against them – the moment MI5 realize and identify who Adam, Fiona and Danny's kidnappers are. It's the 'moment of truth'.

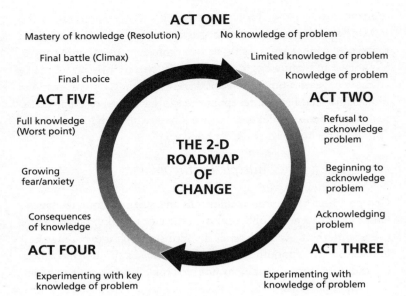

ACT ONE

Mastery of knowledge (Resolution)   No knowledge of problem

Final battle (Climax)   Limited knowledge of problem

Final choice   Knowledge of problem

ACT FIVE   ACT TWO

Full knowledge (Worst point)   Refusal to acknowledge problem

THE 2-D ROADMAP OF CHANGE

Growing fear/anxiety   Beginning to acknowledge problem

Consequences of knowledge   Acknowledging problem

ACT FOUR   ACT THREE

Experimenting with key knowledge of problem   Experimenting with knowledge of problem

MIDPOINT
(Breakthrough) Key knowledge

It's the same point at which James Bond – finding himself imprisoned with a laser beam rising between his legs – discovers Goldfinger's true nature,[4] or when Mitch McDeere realizes his firm of lawyers (*The Firm*) is actually a Mafia front. It's often the moment when the protagonist holds the solution to the mission in their hands. It can be the object of their chase (the Lektor decoding machine in *From Russia with Love*) or the subject of the chase (Javier Bardem's Silva in *Skyfall*).[5] In detective films, it's the piece of information that changes the story completely and offers the first tangible clue to the real perpetrator; and in the works of Agatha Christie it's often the murder itself, which is not, as might be assumed, the inciting incident – an honour reserved instead for the moment when Poirot's suspicions of foul play are first aroused.

It's the halfway stage of the thriller – the end of the outward journey to achieve the protagonist's goal, and the beginning of the journey back. From this moment the protagonist's adventure can never be the same again. What it has in common with its 3-D equivalent is deeply significant. It's the moment of *truth* in both.

But what about other kinds of stories? Can the multi-protagonist films of Robert Altman, or Tarantino's form-shattering *Pulp Fiction*, really follow this model too?

Multiple Protagonists

George Lucas's *American Graffiti* tells the story of four teenagers, Curt, Steve, Toad and John, over one night in 1962. It's shortly before the death of J. F. Kennedy and, the film seems to imply, American innocence itself. Set in the small town of Modesto, California, where Lucas himself grew up, the narrative is built around Curt's sudden decision not to go east to university with his best friend Steve. With a backdrop of contemporary rock 'n' roll, it's a film that drips with nostalgia while prefiguring the tragedy yet to come; Toad (we learn in a powerful postscript) will be reported missing in Vietnam, while John will meet his fate at the hands of a drunk driver.

Each character has their own call to action, and each is thrown into the woods, both metaphorically (super-cool John Milner has to babysit a twelve-year-old girl; super-safe Curt finds himself committing a night's worth of crime) and literally (Toad and Steve find themselves abandoned in a forest exactly halfway through the film). Confronted with their opposites, each learns and changes in their own way; Curt, who was planning to stay in their small American town, decides to leave for college, and Steve, who was planning to go, decides instead to stay.

Though the characters are bound together by world and time scheme, each has their own story, each has their own inciting incident, turning points, crisis, climax and resolution. Each character will play out their own first act before the film moves on to the collective act two – and so on to the end of the work. And the midpoint? John talks to twelve-year-old Carol in the town's car graveyard, not just a memento mori, but the first time any of the characters utters a word that doesn't try and project a fake persona – John speaks truth. One character's midpoint effectively embodies every other character's too; and from this point on the four teenagers must acknowledge their own truth in their own way. It's a touching scene that anchors the film beautifully. What does it tell us about our model?

Having multiple protagonists can seem complicated because individual stories can be connected in an array of different ways – by subject matter (*Parenthood*), by precinct (*Diner*), by character interaction (*Short Cuts*), by theme (*Babel*) or, indeed, any permutation of all of them. In its most sophisticated form – the television gang show of which either *The West Wing* or the very first episode of *ER* would be a good example – the work appears to have a fragmented, disjointed, episodic approach. But look closely and the same structural rules apply. All the key story components are there from inciting incident to resolution, but each is carried by a different character – the storytelling baton is passed from one to another as their individual vignettes pass by: the inciting incident will affect Dr Greene, the midpoint Nurse Hathaway and the climax Dr Benton. Thus different fragmented characters come together to create our recognizable story shape.

Even in a novel aspiring to explore economic policy in different parts of the Soviet Union (Francis Spufford's *Red Plenty*) you see the same – very sophisticated – version of this principle. The various protagonists, each with their own story and their own section, are pieced together to create a picture of the creation, rise and destruction of the Russian economy, and thus of communism itself. What appears arbitrary is in fact fixed and certain. It seems impossible to depart from the classic story shape.

Pulp Fiction by Quentin Tarantino and Roger Avary tells three separate stories: Pumpkin and Honey Bunny hold up a diner; Vincent has to take his boss's girl Mia out for dinner; and Butch fails to throw a boxing match. It appears to scorn narrative convention by ordering events non-chronologically, but a closer look at its structure reveals something very familiar:

PROLOGUE – Honey Bunny and Pumpkin decide to hold up the diner in which they are seated.

ACT ONE
Jules and Vincent perform a hit for their boss Marsellus. A reluctant Vincent reveals he has been asked to take Marsellus's wife Mia out for dinner. (Inciting incident)

ACT TWO
Butch receives money to throw a fight. Vincent takes Mia to Jack Rabbit Slim's. They dance – and bond.

ACT THREE
Vincent goes back to her house. Mia ODs and, with the stakes raised to breaking point, Vincent takes a huge risk and plunges a giant syringe of adrenalin into her heart. (Midpoint)

Butch double-crosses Marsellus and not only fails to throw the fight; he beats his opponent so hard he kills him. His getaway is scuppered when he realizes he's left a watch – with massive sentimental value – behind. He returns to find Vincent waiting to avenge Marsellus, kills him, only to then run into Marsellus himself.

ACT FOUR
Marsellus and Butch are imprisoned by 'Zed', who sodomizes the former while the latter looks on. Butch saves him, and is thus free to return to his girlfriend. It's her questioning that elicits the immortal riposte to 'Who's Zed?' – 'Zed's dead' (Crisis)

ACT FIVE
We are back to the diner of the prologue. Pumpkin and Honey Bunny pull their guns, only to be seen off by Jules and Vincent. Jules

overcomes his flaw in an act of redemption; Vincent is resurrected to fight another day.

Pulp Fiction reorders narrative chronology to specifically create a 'Hero's Journey'. It hands the baton between the protagonists (most particularly Butch and Vincent) and by moving Vincent's death to before his showdown and victory in the diner, Tarantino and Avary create a classic call-to-action, adventure, death and rebirth structure. Each protagonist has their own clear three-act story, but by intercutting and reordering them, the writers create an overall five-act 'master shape' – the same shape as every other tale. At its heart lies one iconic scene: Vincent plunging adrenalin into Mia's heart, echoing the truth the film embraces – the triumph of life over death. This is of course the opposite of a death-dealing hitman's world, and it leaves the audience on their own particular high; a midpoint fittingly foreshadowing the achingly clever happy end.

The paradigm, then, provides the skeleton of two-dimensional, three-dimensional and multi-protagonist modes, whether told in genre or art-house form, and in each the 'truth' of every tale confronts the protagonists halfway through.

The Story Shape

Take any Shakespeare play, or indeed any film we've mentioned, and compare act one and act five, act two and act four, and both halves of act three. All form at least approximate mirror images of each other; each side of the midpoint reflects opposite mental states; each point of the outward journey is mirrored in its return. Now look at the change paradigm and note how act one and act five are mirrored too. It's hard to ignore the aspiration for symmetry.

In all the stories we've looked at or mentioned, whether two- or three-dimensional, there have been a striking number of elements in common:

- 'home' is threatened
- the protagonist suffers from some kind of flaw or problem
- the protagonist goes on a journey to find a cure or the key to the problem
- exactly halfway through they find a cure or key
- on the journey back they're forced to face up to the consequences of taking it
- they face some kind of literal or metaphorical death
- They're reborn as a new person, in full possession of the cure; in the process 'home' is saved.

What this would suggest is one underlying structure. There is, and it's very simple:

JOURNEY THERE; JOURNEY BACK

Often this shape can be literal and easy to spot: it's *Orpheus and Eurydice* – the descent into the Underworld to retrieve the object of supreme importance and return it to the land of the living. It's a shape that abounds in myth, from Persephone to Jason; it's also the story of Buster Keaton's foray into a Unionist stronghold to steal back his locomotive – *The General*; and it's familiar too from the earliest days of childhood:

> Jack is poor, goes up a beanstalk, finds giant and goose that lays golden eggs, heads back with goose, defeats giant, no longer poor.

> A dragon captures a princess. One man ventures out, kills the beast and returns with the princess, only to discover that the dragon isn't quite dead after all . . .

Boiled down to its essence, the shape becomes:

- there is a problem
- the protagonists go on a journey
- they find the solution

- they return
- the problem is solved.

Cinderella finds love with her prince and brings it back home. Hansel and Gretel find courage in outwitting the Witch and bring that back home too. Theseus slays the Minotaur; Perseus the Gorgon. A community needs fire . . . a man needs a woman . . . a woman is looking for love . . . the pattern in which something missing is found halfway through a story endlessly recurs. Even if the protagonists don't literally have to slay a dragon or steal fire from the gods, they always have to leave their home to solve the problem they find there, then bring that solution back home. Journey there; journey back.

There are some stories that don't appear to fit this shape: *Saving Private Ryan*, *Apocalypse Now*, *E.T.: The Extra-Terrestrial* and *The Godfather* are all structured around the protagonists getting what they want at the end, not halfway through their films. Why do they, and many others, conclude at the end of the outward journey?

The answer is simply that the archetypal 'journey there; journey back' structure is buried within the more obvious outward journey. Halfway through *Saving Private Ryan* the team learn of Ryan's whereabouts and that going on would be suicidal. They resolve to continue as hope and courage prevail. Halfway through *Apocalypse Now*, Chief insists they carry on with their normal duties and search a sampan. Willard shoots an innocent passenger and overrules him. At the midpoint of *E.T.*, E.T. phones home, and in *The Godfather*, as we've seen, Michael commits bloody murder right at the heart of the movie.

What all these incidents have in common should now be clear: we know the midpoint of each film is the moment when each protagonist embraces for the first time the quality they will need to become complete and finish their story. It's when they discover a *truth* about themselves. In an archetypal script, that truth will be an embodiment of everything that's the direct opposite of the person they were. The protagonist will embrace that truth and attempt to assimilate and understand it in the second half of the tale.

So in a three-dimensional drama the midpoint is where a character learns what they are capable of, and in a two-dimensional drama the truth about the adversary (or whatever the character's predicament is) is revealed. Often you will see both at the same time. In *The Godfather II* Michael discovers Fredo's betrayal at the midpoint, and takes the decision then (though we only learn this much later) to kill him.

All stories at some level are about a search for the truth of the subject they are exploring. Just as the act of perception involves seeking out the 'truth' of the thing perceived, so storytelling mimics that process. The 'truth' of the story, then, lies at the midpoint. The protagonist's action at this point will be to overcome that obstacle, assimilate that truth and begin the journey back – the journey to understand the implications of what that 'truth' really means.

Thus the 'journey there; journey back' structure exists in all archetypal stories. It's either literally presented (*Jack and the Beanstalk*), hidden underneath the literal story as part of an internal change (*E.T./The Godfather*) or embodied as knowledge sought, retrieved and acted upon (*Spooks*).

In all it should be possible to find some semblance of this familiar shape:

- a protagonist has a problem
- they leave their familiar world
- they go on a journey
- they find the thing they're looking for
- they take it back
- the consequences of taking it pursue them
- they overcome the consequences and solve their problem.[6]

We've already explored how stories involve characters being thrown into a world that represents the opposite of everything they believe and stand for – how an inciting incident embodies all the characteristics the protagonist lacks. The midpoint in every example we've used appears to contain the very essence of that missing quality – the opposite of their initial state. It's the 'truth' of what they're looking for, or, as Joseph Campbell would put it, the elixir hidden in the enemy's cave.

The story shape allows individuals to find, possess and assimilate that which is missing within them. In two dimensions it's the vital clue that reveals the path to catching the crook or healing the patient; In both two and three dimensions it is an embodiment of truth that the protagonist must learn. The novelist Hilary Mantel was writing specifically about fairy tales when she wrote of the archetypal journey 'into the woods':

> The journey into the wood is part of the journey of the psyche from birth through death to rebirth. Hansel and Gretel, the woodcutter's children, are familiar with the wood's verges but not its heart. Snow White is abandoned in the forest. What happens to us in the depths of the wood? Civilization and its discontents give way to the irrational and half-seen. Back in the village, with our soured relationships, we are neurotic, but the wood releases our full-blown madness. Birds and animals talk to us, departed souls speak. The tiny rush-light of the cottages is only a fading memory. Lost in the extinguishing darkness, we cannot see our hand before our face. We lose all sense of our body's boundaries. We melt into the trees, into the bark and the sap. From this green blood we draw new life, and are healed.[7]

Mantel's words reach far beyond her intended meaning to encompass the shape of all stories: the enduring pattern of how someone is found by being lost. All tales, then, are at some level a journey into the woods to find the missing part of us, to retrieve it and make ourselves whole. Storytelling is as simple – and complex – as that. That's the pattern. That's *how* we tell stories.

We must dig deeper though, into the microstructure – the smaller and seemingly unrelated aspects of storytelling. Here we will find that structure isn't just a clever and adaptable repeatable pattern, as intricately structured as a snowflake, but is the root of character, dialogue, theme, genre: everything. 'Screenplays are structure,' said the writer of *Butch Cassidy and the Sundance Kid*, William Goldman,[8] but it's not just screenplays; it's all narrative. By discovering how and why this is so, perhaps we may be able to answer *why* we tell stories too.

Act II
Woodland, Day

6

Fractals

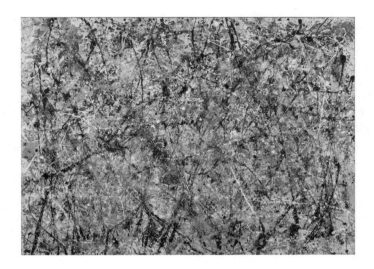

Art is born out of as well as encapsulates the continuing battle between order and chaos. It seeks order or form, even when portraying anarchy. It's a tension visible in both Greek statuary[1] and the colour field paintings of Rothko and Newman, stopping off at every conceivable artistic movement in between. It's a tension that arises from our natural urge to reconcile opposites.

When Friedrich Nietzsche declared in *The Birth of Tragedy* that 'art owes its continuous evolution to the Apollonian–Dionysian duality', he was implicitly declaring his belief that the tensions between form and content, head and heart, discipline and desire were the building blocks of dramatic structure.

Jimmy McGovern, the godfather of British screenwriting, once said, 'You write a script twice. The first time you pour out all your passion, anger, energy, and frustration. Then you go back and write it with your head.'[2] Lose the heart and you end up with little more than an instruction manual; lose the conscious shaping of the intellect and you get *On the Road*. Both, some will claim, are art of a sort, but Truman Capote's famously waspish dismissal of Kerouac's work, 'That is not writing, that is typing' is as true of one extreme as the other. Great art needs both.

So where does that leave Jackson Pollock and 'action painting'? At first glance, Pollock's Abstract Expressionism appears to be chaotic, but dig deeper and it's possible to detect an underlying structure there too. Pollock's paintings are 'fractal'; tiny sections of the work mimic the structure of the whole; simple geometric patterns are repeated in different magnifications. Imagine looking at a photograph of the branching of a tree: remove any knowledge of scale or context and it would be impossible to tell whether you were looking at twig, branch or trunk; each unit replicates both a smaller and a larger one.

And so it is with drama. Stories are built from acts, acts are built from scenes and scenes are built from even smaller units called beats. All these units are constructed in three parts: fractal versions of the three-act whole.[3] Just as a story will contain a set-up, an inciting incident, a crisis, a climax and a resolution, so will acts and so will scenes.

The most obvious manifestation of tripartite form is in beginning, middle and end; set-up, confrontation and resolution. It's a story that's been told a thousand times: boy meets girl, boy loses girl, boy gets girl again; it's *Four Weddings and a Funeral*, *When Harry Met Sally*, *Notting Hill*. What's fascinating is that micro versions of the very same structure are performing exactly the same function on a cellular level. Stories are formed from this secret ministry; the endless replication of narrative structure is going on within acts, and within scenes.

By looking first at acts, then analysing how the order they come in affects their purpose, and then digging further into the microscopic study of scenes, we should get a much clearer idea of how this fractal structure works, and thus reveal the extraordinarily ordered world that lies just underneath the appearance of freedom and chaos – and indeed of artistic whim.

7

Acts

Raiders of the Lost Ark has a classic story structure, constructed from seven clearly defined stages. In the first act, Indiana Jones's rivalry with the Nazi archaeologist Beloq is sown; in the second he is tasked with finding the Ark of the Covenant. In the third he bonds with former girlfriend Marion and they agree to hunt for it together; in the fourth he finds the Ark, then loses it to his adversary. The fifth act sees him recapture it, only to lose it in the sixth where – worse – Marion is kidnapped. In the seventh he saves both it and her; Beloq is vanquished and Indy is rewarded with his girlfriend's love.*

The 'into the woods' shape is very visible, with a clear and archetypal midpoint, the discovery of the Ark, in (perhaps coincidentally) a very dark cave. This midpoint, coming exactly halfway through the fourth act, gives the story a classic symmetrical structure, a structure confirmed by the mirroring of the inciting incident – the set-up of the rivalry with Beloq – and the crisis point – Beloq stealing both the Ark and Marion from under Indy's nose. A clear and contained unit of action binds each act, mostly built from the gaining, losing and regaining of the biblical treasure in different locations.

A cursory search on the internet reveals five possible act structures claimed for Spielberg's epic – each completely different. I am unaware whether the screenwriter Lawrence Kasdan planned seven acts, and they certainly aren't marked on any script I've seen. So how do we know these are acts? The answer hinges on an important structural question: how do you define an act?

---

* For a more detailed breakdown of the structure, see Appendix I.

An act is discernible because of the three-part structure that mimics the overall story shape. We've already noted that acts are bound by dramatic desire, with a turning point spinning the character off in pursuit of a new goal. In addition, fractal theory dictates that every act will contain all the essential elements of story: protagonist, antagonist, inciting incident, journey, crisis, climax and – occasionally – resolution. A course of action, defined by one single desire, will be completed, whether successfully or not. Take the first act of Kasdan's script:

> It's 1936, and archaeologist Indiana Jones is in the Peruvian jungle seeking a golden idol hidden inside a booby-trapped temple. He finds the idol, exits the temple only to be confronted by arch rival archaeologist René Belloq, who steals it from him and leaves him for dead. Indy escapes in a waiting seaplane.

All the critical ingredients of story are present:

Protagonist – Indiana Jones
Antagonist – Beloq
Inciting incident – Discovering the temple
Desire / journey – To retrieve the golden idol
The crisis – Beloq surprises him
The climax – Beloq steals the idol
Resolution – Indy escapes with his life.

In addition one can include a midpoint: the retrieval of the idol from the inner heavily fortified temple; an echo of 'into the woods' once again. It's a very simple tripartite unit that mimics completely the overarching story shape. It's a fractal, a smaller unit repeated continually within the structure to build the larger whole – much like a Pollock painting or, indeed, molecules and atoms (see opposite).

The first act of *The King's Speech* is striking in its similarity. There are three very distinct stages: Bertie's terrible speech at Wembley; his wife's pursuit of a cure; and the first meeting between the future king and Logue. It's an entire movie in miniature – it has its own

PART ONE	PART TWO	PART THREE
TURNING POINT1	TURNING POINT2	

inciting incident (the speech); its own crisis (Bertie's choice whether or not to go); its own climax (the battle with Logue) and its very own clear midpoint – the moment where Elizabeth seeks out, in the darkened basement, her potential Australian cure.

In the last act it's the same – the King goes to Logue's house to ask him back, they rehearse in Westminster Abbey and then the King performs the final gut-wrenching speech. In addition there's the midpoint, again appropriately: 'I have a voice!'

So acts are fractal building blocks of the whole. Once that becomes clear, numerous other structural elements begin to swim into focus, built as they are from the same tripartite form. What are they, and why?

Questions and Answers

In a three-act drama, the first and second turning points broadly correspond to the inciting incident and crisis points, with the first act being the set-up of the story and the last act its climax. Inciting incident and crisis points are thus directly related to each other. But how? A crisis point always embodies the worst possible consequence[1] of the decision taken when the initial dramatic explosion occurred.

In a well-structured story, this decision inexorably brings the character face to face with their worst fear: the obstacle that is going to force them to face up to their underlying flaw. If a character is wary of commitment, then the crisis will force them to face losing someone they love (*Casablanca*); if a character is selfish, they are brought face to face with what they might lose by being so (*Toy Story*); if a character is timid they will have to face up to what timidity might cost (*Notting Hill*).

This is how the archetype works: structure at the level of scene, act and story conspires to bring the protagonist face to face with their darkest fear, or weakest link – and at the crisis point, forces them to confront it. When *Toy Story* begins, Woody is selfish and terrified of abandonment even as he masquerades as a selfless leader. Buzz arrives and, though it's partly accidental, Woody is responsible for pushing him out of the window, catalysing a journey into exile (into the woods) that only ends when at the crisis point he must choose whether to enlist the cooperation of others. If he doesn't change and become truly selfless (as opposed to just appearing so), the crisis 'tells him', then he'll lose his friends for ever.

Sometimes it's easier to think of the structure in question-and-answer form. Q: What are the worst possible consequences of Macbeth's decision to kill the King of Scotland? A: The massed ranks of his former allies will march upon him seeking revenge. Good structure will deliver a crisis point that forces the protagonist to choose between their old and new selves. Remember, Macbeth's flaw is actually his humility (the story is a dark inversion) and, by the last act, he overcomes this flaw through the wholesale adoption of arrogance, i.e. his belief that 'none of woman born' shall harm him. From modest war hero to omnipotent tyrant, Macbeth completes his journey and, because it's a tragedy, he dies.

The question-and-answer structure not only binds stories together, it appears within every act. In *Thelma & Louise* the worst possible consequences of two women stopping at a roadhouse without male company (the mini inciting incident) are that one of them will be victim of an attempted rape and the other will shoot the perpetrator (the mini crisis). In the final act of the film, the worst possible consequence of blowing up someone's petrol tanker is that the police will pursue you to a point of no escape. In both acts, the second turning points work as typical crisis points, presenting the protagonists with a classic choice: will they hand themselves in or go on the run? In both, the protagonists' final choice is to escape the law.

Once this tripartite structure is understood, two more things become apparent. All acts have the same underlying shape but take on a different purpose depending on the *order* in which they appear in any story. The tripartite shape placed at the beginning of a story will resolve itself into an inciting incident; in the middle it will form the foundations of a midpoint; and at the end, a climax. Such is the beauty of dramatic form; simply structured cells merge together organically to build units of striking complexity.

8

The Inciting Incident

LUCAS: Your mission is to proceed up to Nung River in a Navy Patrol boat. Pick up Colonel Kurtz's path at Nu Mung Ba, follow it, learn what you can along the way. When you find the colonel, infiltrate his team by whatever means available and terminate the colonel's command.

WILLARD: Terminate? The colonel?

. . .

CIVILIAN: Terminate with extreme prejudice.

Apocalypse Now by John Milius and Francis Ford Coppola

In *Apocalypse Now* Captain Willard, a shell-shocked casualty of the Vietnam War, is called to HQ and given a mission: to head downriver and assassinate a rogue colonel. If all stories are a quest, then the inciting incidents are like this – an invitation to begin the journey. They say to the protagonist: 'This is your goal'.

If a story is 'once upon a time something happened', then the inciting incident is the 'something' that kick-starts a story. But is it always this simple?

In Peter Weir's 1985 film *Witness*, an Amish boy witnesses a murder in a railway station restroom. Detective John Book (Harrison Ford) is assigned to the case, and much to his horror discovers that McFee, his boss, is the killer. When McFee learns his dark deed has been uncovered, he attempts to kill Book, forcing him to flee the city with the boy and his mother to take refuge in the Amish community.

Screenwriting manuals tend to suggest the inciting incident is simply one explosion that blows a character's world apart, but if that's so, which part of *Witness* is the fabled 'call to action'?

★

First acts, as we've noted, exist in tripartite form, mimicking the greater structural whole:

1. Set-up (including mini inciting incident)
2. Confrontation (conflict ending in crisis point)
3. (Climax and) Resolution.

In *Star Wars*, Princess Leia flees from the forces of Darth Vader, dispatching 3PO and R2D2 with a distress call. Meanwhile on the Planet of Tatooine, Luke Skywalker is finding life frustrating – no one takes him seriously. Luke discovers the distress call but does nothing. Only when his step-parents are brutally murdered does he resolve to leave his planet and seek revenge.

In *Some Like It Hot*, two musicians, Jerry and Joe, find themselves in a speakeasy raided by police. Strapped for cash and attempting to borrow a car to get to another gig, they accidentally witness the St Valentine's Day Massacre. Realizing their lives are in danger, they decide their only hope is to join a girl-band – as girls – and flee to Miami.

In both of these films, it's possible to detect three clear stages. In every first act:

- The protagonist will be alerted to a world outside their own.
- They will make a decision on how to react to this and pursue a course of action that will precipitate a crisis.
- This will force them to make a decision propelling them into a whole new universe.

The fractal story structure is immediately apparent – a pattern very clearly at work in *Witness*. The first stage of act one ends when Detective Book takes on the case of the Amish boy who saw the murder. The second stage culminates when McFee is revealed as the killer. In classical terms then – if we wish to pin down one specific moment in the first act as an inciting incident – it is simply the crisis point (the second turning point) of the first act.[1] Like all good crisis points, it's a subversion of expectation, a cliffhanger, an antithesis to what's gone before. It's the moment that presents Book with a choice: whether to take a first big step outside his own limited world into the woods of new experience. Fractal structure reveals its mystery once again.

It's worth observing just how closely this follows the 'Roadmap of Change' we explored in Chapter 4. If act one of the paradigm moves from 'no awareness', via 'growing awareness' to 'awareness' (all of a new world) then the structural *function* of the inciting incident – to blow the protagonist into an alien world – should be even more apparent.

It's identical in *Thelma & Louise*. As the film starts, the two women are embarking on a camping trip. Stopping off at a roadside bar is a very clear step into a world different from their own. As they both start to let their hair down, they begin to shed more of their former selves – but this is drama; every action has a consequence. Thelma attracts the attentions of a local redneck who brutally assaults her. The crisis is precipitated. Given the choice to kill him or warn him off, Louise – provoked – shoots him in the head and they flee from the scene. Both are thrown into a completely alien world – into the woods again.

Sometimes an inciting incident isn't immediately clear because an audience isn't always aware from the start what the character's journey is going to be. Robert Redford's film *Ordinary People* tells the story of how teenager Conrad Jarrett, traumatized by the death of his brother, seeks psychiatric help. The journey into the woods – and thus the moment that kick-starts it – only becomes apparent when one realizes it's a journey towards healing. What catalyses that journey? The first stage of the first act ends when Conrad is thrown into a new trauma by his mother trashing his breakfast before him; this in turn sparks a journey of introspection, culminating in a flashback of his brother's death. For Conrad, it's a choice – continue to suffer, or seek help.[2] If the inciting incident is the *what*, then the flashback is clearly Conrad's motivation for seeking help, the *how* that will eventually enable him to find peace. In truth, all three parts are related – as they should be – but question and answer, the root of all structure, is inherent in the crisis and climax of the act.

In this formulation an inciting incident gives us two elements. The act one crisis point poses a question: will the protagonists make a break with their old selves? And, as we've already noted, for the story to really kick off, the protagonist is now required to make a decision how to respond. The 'explosion' and the desire it creates often occur in the first act, embodied in crisis and climax. It can be useful to look at these points as the *what* and the *how*. The crisis becomes the *what* – 'What's the problem?' And the climax the *how* – 'This is how I'm going to deal with it'.

Often that decision is made simply and quickly. In *Apocalypse Now* it's very clear that Willard – by accepting a proffered cigarette – has answered his call to action. In tripartite terms this decision is the third stage – the climax of the first act. However, it's not the only way of telling a story. The beauty of act structure is, as we've seen, that it's as infinitely adaptable as music. The most common adaptation – and I would argue the most misunderstood – was termed by Joseph Campbell the 'refusal of the call'. Once again its true nature becomes clear when viewed through the prism of the five-act form.

The Deferred Call

In *Raiders of the Lost Ark*, Jones's antipathy to Beloq is ignited in act one but lacks direction until he's given his mission at the end of act two. We know he detests Beloq by the end of the first act, but at this point that doesn't elicit a story. They only become rivals when Jones begins his quest for the Staff of Ra in the second act, for only then are they both engaged in the main action of the film. Technically Jones's action is a deferred response – antipathy is awoken in the first act but not given direction until the end of the second. *Erin Brockovich* has a similar pattern: the first act revolves around Erin's desperation to get a job, but the true story of the film, the exploration of the chemical crime, doesn't achieve focus until the end of the second stage. It's a very popular technique – in the BBC's *Life on Mars* it was actually part of the format: a crime would take place in the first act and either Sam or

Gene would refuse to join in the investigation until motivated by a further turning point that became the end of act two.

Why this long delay? The 'Roadmap of Change' illustrates the underlying pattern. In the second act, the protagonist moves from 'refusal to change' to 'acceptance'.[3] In *Thelma & Louise*, Thelma initially refuses to accompany her friend to Mexico. Only after a patronizing, misogynistic phone call from her husband forty minutes into the film does she commit to the journey.

In three-dimensional drama it's quite common for a protagonist to begin their journey at the end of act one, but not the process of underlying change until the second act turning point – if you like, a *buried* 'refusal of the call'. In *Witness*, John Book flees into the Amish community at the end of the first act, but only when he hands his gun to Rachel twenty minutes later does the underlying journey from selfishness to selflessness really begin. It's a particularly common device in Shakespeare: Macbeth gets the idea to kill the king at the end of act one, but he prevaricates until the end of act two; Hamlet's ghostly father demands revenge at the end of act one, but only at the end of the second act does his son resolve on a plan ('the play's the thing') to entrap Claudius, and in *King Lear*, the first act ends with Lear walking out on Goneril, but it's not until the end of the second act that he finds himself rejected by both daughters and thus begins his true journey to the heart of the storm on the heath.[4]

Inciting incidents, then, are not the simple 'explosions' of screenwriting lore – they're manifestations of structure, a product of the way we order the world. Like every other act, they consist of thesis, antithesis and synthesis – a tripartite form containing a complete structure within themselves. If in doubt about story structure, it is always useful to refer to fairy tales for validation – they contain the DNA of almost every story we tell. Take *Jack and the Beanstalk*:

1. Down to their last penny, with father dead, Jack's mother sends him to market to sell Daisy, their cow.
2. On the way to market Jack succumbs to a mysterious stranger who offers to swap the cow for some magic

beans. Jack's mum is furious and throws the beans out of the window

3. Overnight a massive beanstalk grows right up into the sky.

Which part is the inciting incident? If one is forced to highlight one single aspect, then inciting incidents are the invitation to leave home and venture into the forest; to reject the thesis of the first stage for the synthesis of the new world. This is where the journey into the woods (or up the beanstalk) begins. But the incidents don't always have to be 'an explosion' either – there are no explosions in *Fawlty Towers*, merely an ever-growing complication. Hollywood tends to extremes; it's perfectly possible for a story to start with a guest turning up whom Basil doesn't like. They need not all begin with big bangs – they can simply be the first crack that allows the daylight in.[5] If one pursues this line of thought, it's possible to argue that inciting incidents are simply the first important choice the protagonist makes in any story.

What the study of inciting incidents reveals to us is the ubiquity of the fractal story shape. Every act has two turning points within it, the latter of which acts as an explosion that invites the protagonist into an alien world. In the first act, that second turning point is called an inciting incident; if it's the penultimate act, it's called a crisis point. Structurally they're the same thing – a choice that presents itself to the protagonist, their name and function changing only according to their position in the story. In the first half of any tale, they lead further into the forest; in the second half they signpost the return.

All crisis points, like all choices, are invitations to venture into a different world. The inciting incident is merely the first invitation. But not only does this invitation occur across an overarching story and *within* acts; the fractal pattern continues and is replicated within the basic building blocks of drama – in the microstructure of scenes.

9

Scenes

'Drama is life with the dull bits cut out.'

Alfred Hitchcock

Jack Crabb is 121 years old. The film that tells his story from birth to death lasts 139 minutes. Even with its longer than average duration, the writers of *Little Big Man* have only just over sixty seconds to cover every year of his life.[1]

They don't of course, because that isn't a writer's job (there were five screenwriters credited on the film incidentally, including its stars Dustin Hoffman and Faye Dunaway, which may go some way to explaining its inordinate length). A writer's task is to distil the story they're telling into a comfortable running time, normally an hour or ninety minutes, by choosing to focus on the most important or significant moments. They will seek out these moments; they will distil and concentrate; they will chisel and hone. Out of less they will attempt to capture a *whole* and present it – normally in a linked chain of cause and effect – in a manner dependent on the type of tale and genre they wish to employ.

All dramatic structure is built on the chassis of change. Complete change, as we've seen, is commonly referred to as a 'dramatic arc'. Just as stories are made from acts and acts are built from scenes, so each of these units represents a different kind of change. Stories as a whole illustrate complete change; acts show major change and scenes minor, individual moments. It's in the latter – the single cells of the organism – that a writer's effort is concentrated, for each is a unit of change. Select and build these units correctly and you will create a plausible, thrilling, moving work that in portraying a tiny fraction of a life captures the essence of its whole.

But how do scenes work? What does drilling into the substrata tell us, not only about how change works on a microscopic level, but what that in turn may reveal about broader dramatic form?

Like complete stories or acts, scenes are internally structured. They move from set-up to conflict to crisis, before building again to climax and resolution. Scenes, like acts and like stories, have their own three-act structure, and mimic exactly an archetypal story shape.

Just as in every story a protagonist battles an antagonist in pursuit of a goal, so scenes replicate that structure. It's not enough for Lauren Branning in *EastEnders* to want a drink or President Bartlet in *The West Wing* to get out of bed. Drama demands conflict on a scene-by-scene level. If Lauren wants a drink, then Kat must not serve her; if President Bartlet wants to get out of bed, then his wife must forbid him. For drama to occur, a protagonist must be confronted with an equal and opposite desire. The goals of protagonist and antagonist in every scene are in direct conflict – opposites once again.

So protagonist and antagonist each have their objective, and just as in a complete story only one person can win. If Lauren or Mrs Bartlet wish to win, they require a turning point. How well these turning points are executed is, like the mastery of exposition, a tell-tale sign of a writer's ability. They are a vital structural tool; how they work in scenes will help us understand how they work in all drama – indeed, in all story.

Turning Points

Every scene has a turning point for one simple reason – scenes exist *because* they have a turning point. It is why a writer selects them to tell their story: turning points are the units of change, the key moments from a character's life.

The following scene is from *EastEnders* by Tony Jordan. Two sisters, Kat and Zoe, have been arguing: Zoe wants to go to Spain; Kat doesn't want her to go. A furious argument has developed in an Indian restaurant after Zoe has told her family that she's planning to emigrate with her Uncle Harry. Kat has reacted badly, forbidding her to go, and fuelled by drink the row has burst out into Albert Square:

SCENE 33/60. BRIDGE STREET. EXT.
NIGHT. 23.30.

(ZOE *storms out of restaurant with* KAT *in pursuit*.)

KAT: Zoe, come here!

ZOE: No! I'm fed up with you picking on me all the time!

KAT: I'm not picking on you.

ZOE: Embarrassing me in front of everyone.

(KAT *catches her up in Bridge Street, rowdy noise coming from Queen Vic*.)

KAT: Just listen to me, will you?

ZOE: I'm going and there ain't nothing you can do about it.

KAT: D'you wanna bet? We'll go and ask Dad together, shall we, see who he listens to?

ZOE: Why don't you just leave me alone?

KAT: Because you're not going to Spain!

ZOE: Yes I am.

(*As* ZOE *moves to stride away*, KAT *grabs* ZOE's *arm*; ZOE *spins and pushes* KAT *away*.)

ZOE: Get away from me!

KAT: No!

ZOE: You don't rule my life.

KAT: You're not going to Spain and that's that.

ZOE: Why not?

KAT: Because I said so, alright?

ZOE: And I have to do everything you say, do I?

KAT: No . . . but . . .

ZOE: (*Cuts in*) You can't tell me what to do, you ain't my mother!

(ZOE *turns again, this time striding away.*)

KAT: (*Shouts after her*) Yes I am!

(ZOE *stops dead in her tracks and looks back at* KAT.)

FADE OUT.

Although scenes are the main building blocks of any script, they can be broken down into even smaller units, commonly known as beats. Tony Jordan's scene – all scenes in fact – are made up of a series of actions and reactions, each one constituting an individual 'beat':

KAT: Just listen to me, will you?
ACTION

ZOE: I'm going and there ain't nothing you can do about it.
REACTION

KAT: D'you wanna bet? We'll go and ask Dad together, shall we, see who he listens to?
ACTION

ZOE: Why don't you just leave me alone?
REACTION

Both characters are pursuing equal and opposite desires. One character does (or says) one thing and the other character responds. And this continues throughout the scene until one crucial moment:

KAT: You're not going to Spain and that's that.
ACTION

ZOE: Why not?
REACTION

KAT: Because I said so, alright?
ACTION

ZOE: And I have to do everything you say, do I?
REACTION

KAT: No . . . but . . .
ACTION

ZOE: (*Cuts in*) You can't tell me what to do, you ain't my mother!
REACTION

(ZOE *turns again, this time striding away.*)

KAT: (*Shouts after her*) Yes I am!
UNEXPECTED REACTION

All scenes proceed on the basis of action/reaction/action/reaction until the moment when they suddenly hit an unexpected reaction: the moment when one character achieves their goal and the other loses it. That's what a turning point is.

If scenes are microcosms of dramatic structure, then scene turning points correspond to the moment of crisis in both act and story. Like any crisis point, they demand of the protagonist a choice. The answer to the question posed by that choice – 'What are they going to do?' – will form the set-up for the next scene. Once again, three-act structure is reproduced at a cellular level.

But why does it force a change? Simply because turning points bring a character face-to-face with the consequences of *not* changing. Just as in the macro structure of *A Few Good Men*, Daniel Kaffee will not bring down Colonel Jessup unless he grows up, so here Kat is presented with the prospect of losing Zoe unless she tells the truth. Kaffee's final act crisis is either to stay a boy and plea-bargain his client's verdict or go head-to-head in court with Jessup as a man. Kat's scene crisis is whether to be honest or continue to incur her daughter's wrath. The choice presented on both macro and micro levels, for Kaffee and for Kat, is whether to kill off their old selves and be born anew. The road the characters should take must be the harder one – by making the *right* choice, both stand a far greater chance of losing everything. Kaffee might lose and throw away any chance of prosecution, whilst Kat has a darker secret to reveal – not only is she Zoe's mother, but (and not even the audience know this) the sainted Uncle Harry is a paedophile who many years before raped Kat to become Zoe's dad. By choosing the harder course, she may be forced to reveal her biggest, most traumatic secret.

Come in Late, Get out Early

William Goldman once said, 'I never enter scenes until the last possible moment . . . and as soon as it's done I get the hell out of there.'[2] Most screenwriters are familiar with the maxim 'Come in late, get out early'; as a writing device it creates great narrative momentum but it has an interesting side-effect too – it makes scene structure harder to uncover because, if done well, it removes the elements that allow its detection.

If they are structurally correct, there are three things in every scene that can be – and often are – eliminated: the set-up, which can be implicit from the previous scene; the climax and the resolution, both of which can be played out in the following action. Indeed, it's possible for each scene to consist solely of the period of confrontation. Done well the drama is then built around confrontation/crisis in a sequence that never seems to stop moving; like a French language elision the unnecessary letters are removed. It's a technique used endlessly by the creator of TV series *The Street*, Jimmy McGovern, in the UK, and to dazzling effect in Aaron Sorkin's *The West Wing*. For a particularly good example try 'In the Shadow of Two Gunmen', Part Two, Act One. The first scene ends with the revelation that the president has been shot, and it just gets more and more dramatic from there.

It's a technique some call 'top-spin' as it creates an extremely powerful narrative drive. Every scene ends on a question – partly 'Where did that come from?' but more importantly 'How are they going to get out of that?' By cutting away at the crisis point, a writer thus creates a sequence in which question is followed by (delayed) answer, which is followed by a question once again.

Why does it work?

'Story as such', said E. M. Forster, 'can only have one merit: that of making the audience want to know what happens next. And conversely it can only have one fault: that of making the audience not want to know what happens next.'[3] By cutting away at the crisis point, each scene ending requires an explanation, and thus creates curiosity and anticipation, defers gratification and keeps people watching. The thriller writer Lee Child puts the art of narrative drive succinctly: 'You ask or imply a question at the beginning of the book and you absolutely self-consciously withhold the answer. It does feel cheap and meretricious but it absolutely works.'[4] It's the skeleton of detective and medical narratives once again.

Previously we defined an inciting incident as a question to which the crisis point provides the answer, but in fact all story relies on the repetition of question and answer. Child isn't being meretricious at all; he just has a very good understanding of narrative. The technique of 'come in late, get out early' simply accelerates this process, forcing every scene to cut off at the 'worst point' of a scene.

Ashley Pharoah, the co-creator of *Life on Mars* and one of the most successful writers on British television, learned his craft on *East-Enders*. Explaining how he mastered writing for the show, he said, 'I didn't know how to write *EastEnders* until I started to imagine the drums at the end of every scene.'[5] Without consciously articulating it, Pharoah had inadvertently stumbled on a major structural truth. He discovered that the iconic drums marking the cliffhanger of every episode were in essence identical to the 'unexpected reaction', turning point or crisis point inherent in each and every scene. Cliffhangers *are* crisis points; crisis points *are* cliffhangers.

The 'unexpected reaction' Zoe gets when Kat tells her she's her mum is a classic subversion of expectation – an explosion that happens in the life of a character to throw their journey off-course – and it's a technique immediately familiar to a generation who grew up on either *Doctor Who*, *Batman* (the TV version) or Saturday Morning Pictures. What all scenes are built from, in essence, are mini inciting incidents, linked together to form a story. Every scene's crisis point is a mini explosion that upsets the character's life, creating within them a new plan (or want) to solve it.

So inciting incidents aren't just restricted to the opening acts of drama. In fractal form they occur not only at the end of every act, but within every scene. Subversion of expectation is an essential device in all archetypal drama: we are led down a path to expect one thing, only to turn a corner and find ourselves confronted with its opposite. It's thesis/antithesis in action.

10

Putting It All Together

It tells the story of how a deeply unfashionable man is invited into a privileged world and in so doing creates the coolest club on the planet. In the process he loses his only friend and despite inordinate rewards is still unable to get the girl. *The Social Network* is Aaron Sorkin and David Fincher's fictional account of how Mark Zuckerberg created Facebook with the help of his friend Eduardo in reaction to being dumped by his girlfriend. It's a modern tragedy, with an 'into the woods' structure: the Winklevoss twins who invite Mark into their elite WASP world represent every single quality he himself lacks. One of the most striking features of the structure, however, is the very clear and direct relationship between the first and last acts:

ACT ONE
1. Mark is dumped by Erika
2. Works on Facemash – enlists Eduardo
3. Winklevoss twins invite Mark to join them

ACT FIVE
1. Winklevoss twins sue Mark
2. Works on Facebook – sacks Eduardo
3. Tries to make 'friends' with Erika.

They are mirror images.

Every act is an individual fractal unit consisting of the same basic ingredients. Yet when you place those fractal units side by side, something rather exciting occurs; like a living organism each takes on unique characteristics to support the structure of the greater whole. It appears that as acts are joined together, they assume an overall symmetry, each developing their own particular function to help support the larger structure. While few works attain a perfect state, writing and rewriting tend to sculpt a work so it more clearly reproduces a classical shape – one where each act plays its own key part. But what are the unique ingredients embodied in each act?

First Acts

In any first act the tripartite structure normally has a clear and defined purpose, the micro crisis point providing the catalyst for both the next act and the story as a whole. As we've seen, it will have a direct and clear relationship with the crisis point of the overall story. In *The Godfather* Michael Corleone innocently attends his sister's wedding. He has no intention of entering the family business until his father is shot. That action not only propels Michael into the second act by posing the question 'How will he react?' – it forms the spine of the whole tale. Michael must find out who betrayed his father. At the end of act one a character stands at the edge of the forest, about to begin their journey.

Second Acts

As act two begins, characters tend to pursue a short-term solution to their problem based on their initial character flaws. Michael may be aware of a new world, but he enters it desiring only to protect his father. It takes a second 'inciting incident' – the discovery that his father has been set up for a further assassination attempt – to really change him. Structurally this is the point that forces a protagonist to realize things can no longer stay the same: Thelma can't behave like a little girl; Daniel Kaffee can't behave like a little boy; and Lightning McQueen can't behave like a brat. The second act, then, contains its own call to action and crisis that will force our hero to make a choice between their old and new selves. In *The Godfather*

Michael discovers that, having fooled his father's would-be assassins, he is not scared but exhilarated. He enters the forest.

Third Acts and Midpoints

The midpoint of the story is, not unexpectedly, the midpoint of the third act too; once again, an individual act takes on the shape of the overall story. In both you see the same pattern – what a character is scared of in the first half, they now embrace with enthusiasm. Midpoints are, as we've seen, the 'truth' of the story,[1] a truth the protagonist must embrace.

'This outburst of deed from the soul of the hero, or the influx of portentous impressions into the soul; the first great result of a sublime struggle, or the beginning of a mortal inward conflict.'[2] Gustav Freytag's description of the midpoint (or, as he refers to it, 'climax') in *Technique of the Drama* may sound portentous by modern standards, but it's not inaccurate. Here, in the heart of the forest, the character embraces their new self. Knowledge is gained that can never be lost; where they have 'sought', here they 'find' and they can never go back. Michael Corleone builds up his courage, shoots the cop and then experiments with the reward that change can bring – marriage to a beautiful girl in bucolic Sicily. It's never that simple, though: change must come again. Michael's new wife is murdered – the crisis point of the third act – and like any good crisis point it forces Michael to confront his earlier actions. Once again he must choose: whether to stop and return to his former self, or drink the dark 'elixir' he has found and, with its magic working on him, head towards home.

Fourth Acts

The crisis point of act four is of course the crisis point of the story. For the protagonist it's the moment they're confronted with the decision whether to embrace change and triumph, or reject it and fail. This is the 'worst point', the moment when everything could end and failure has won the day. It's not uncommon for the stench of literal or metaphorical death to cloud the air. From *Macbeth* to *Toy Story 3* via *Kick-Ass*, *The Long Good Friday* and *The Shawshank Redemption*, death clouds everything.[3] Once again the reason is structural.

Faced with the ultimate crisis, the structure asks of the protagonist one simple question: will you revert and die, or change and live? It's the death of the old self (or the father in Michael Corleone's case) so that the new person can live. It's the protagonist's biggest test. Is Michael ready to assume his father's mantle and with the ruthlessness he's assimilated avenge his death? Is he strong enough to carry home the lessons learned within the heart of the forest?

An interesting by-product of act four is the preponderance of what is referred to in *Team America* as 'monologuing' – the moment where Blofeld or Goldfinger tells us the 'how' and 'why' of his plan or the hero explains their motivation. If dramas are journeys from darkness to light, then this speech can be seen as the final piece in the jigsaw: the moment we finally truly understand a character's motives (as in Philippe Claudel's *I've Loved You So Long*) before the final 'battle'. Some screenwriters treat the monologue with grave suspicion – for reasons we shall visit again in Chapter 14.

So Don Corleone lies dead in an orchard; and an invitation is handed to Michael. Will he accept it and, if so, what manner of godfather will he become?

Fifth Acts

The protagonist normally enters the last act with one concrete objective: to defeat the antagonist, to overcome their demons, to win the prize, to get home or to get the girl. In other words, the 'sub-goal' of the fifth act is identical to the main – original – goal of the story. They have returned from whence they came with a truth they must deliver to their tribe – and not always a truth the tribe wants to hear. If the antagonist they must now face is truly archetypal they will be an embodiment of the protagonist's flaw, making external and internal battles one and the same. Using the knowledge gained at the midpoint and tested through the trials of the fourth act, they are, against all odds, able to defeat their enemies, overcome their flaws and in doing so become complete. Michael Corleone subsumes all the evil of his enemies to become even more demonic than them. As his nephew is baptized, Michael is too – in rivers of blood. He has overcome the last vestiges of goodness in his soul and attained a particularly dark kind of completeness.

Fractal Structure and Change

If symmetry and balance is sought in a story structure, then it should be possible to detect a distinct relationship between the first and last acts of *any* drama. If there is truth to the change paradigm, then it should reveal itself here.

In every complete story there are two major turning points: one which should call the protagonist to action, while the second should show them the consequence of accepting that call. That consequence should then present itself to them as an obstacle that invites their final choice. If we accept fractal theory, it dictates that the same structure will appear in microcosm not just in first acts (which we've seen in our analysis of inciting incidents), but in last acts too. If we're right, last acts will display an identical three-part structure, a structure where:

1. Faced with the worst point, the protagonists waver, unsure how to act until there is a new 'call to action'. An opportunity presents itself, inviting them to rededicate themselves to change.
2. They make their choice, accept the call and commit themselves to a course of action that they must pursue relentlessly to its logical conclusion, which in turn leads them to . . .
3) one final choice: the most dangerous and most profound task they will need to achieve to overcome their flaw.

That's exactly what happens in *The Godfather*. Just before he dies, Don Corleone tells his son there is a traitor amongst them who will reveal himself by approaching Michael to broker a deal. Using the terminology of the roadmap of change, this is followed by three very distinct phases.

REAWAKENING – at his father's funeral, Michael is approached by Tessio, the family stalwart, who offers to broker a deal. He is the traitor in their midst. Michael resolves to act.

RE-ACCEPTANCE – Michael kills Tessio, and then, while his son is baptized, everyone else who has dared to challenge him.

TOTAL MASTERY – his wife Kay asks him whether he killed his sister's husband. Michael looks her in the eye and tells her he didn't. The lie to his wife is the biggest sin of all. Michael has mastered evil.

The first turning point in the fifth act is the presentation of the opportunity to commit to change (a mini 'inciting incident') and/or a conscious decision to do so.

In *Thelma & Louise* the fifth act begins with their knowing there is no possibility of escape. They could hand themselves in, but then they spot the tanker driver . . .

In *E. T.: The Extra-Terrestrial*, Elliot quietly mourns E.T.'s death. Then the creature's heart begins to glow . . .

In *Strictly Ballroom* Scott learns that his father always regretted not dancing his own steps. Does he want to be brave, or live his life in fear? Will he dance with Tina, or his true love Fran?

The second turning point is a mini worst point, containing the hardest choice of all.

In *Thelma & Louise* the women are cornered by the police at the Grand Canyon. They can surrender or embrace a different kind of escape . . .

In *E.T.* Elliot must choose to say goodbye to his closest friend. In *Strictly Ballroom* Scott chooses to dance with Fran against all advice. But the plug is pulled, the music stopped and they are suspended from the competition. To the sound of Scott's father, then Fran's father and grandmother, and then the entire audience clapping, Scott finally learns – without music – to dance to the rhythm of his heart.

Observe also how the final act, in its tripartite form, often mirrors, almost identically, the structure of the first act of each film:

In *The Godfather*:

ACT ONE
1. Wedding – Michael is honest with Kay
2. Celebration of life
3. Father is shot.

ACT FIVE
1. Traitor is revealed
2. Orgy of death
3. Funeral – Michael lies to Kay.*

In *Thelma & Louise*:

ACT ONE
1. Submissive to patriarchy and societal norms
2. Subjugated and terrorized by male
3. They flee scene of the crime.

ACT FIVE
1. Police locate them
2. They subjugate and terrorize a male
3. Rejection of patriarchy and societal norms.

* For further examples see Appendix VI.

In *E.T.: The Extra-Terrestrial*:

ACT ONE
1. E.T. is trapped on earth
2. Chase to escape authority
3. Elliot befriends E.T.

ACT FIVE
1. Elliot mourning
2. Chase to escape authority
3. E.T. returns home.

And in *Strictly Ballroom*:

ACT ONE
1. Scott dances his own steps selfishly
2. He refuses to dance with Fran
3. He chooses to dance with Fran.

ACT FIVE
1. He chooses to dance with Fran
2. He dances with Fran
3. He dances with Fran to the rhythm of his own heart.

The revelation of this mini story structure within each act has wider significance. If you take any archetypal story and imagine folding it over on itself at the midpoint, it's possible to see with far greater clarity just how great story's aspiration for symmetry is. Not only do the first part of act one and the last part of act five mirror each other, but act four becomes a mirror of act two, and one half of the third act, bisected at the midpoint, becomes a mirror image of the other.

In a second act, protagonists move towards and embrace commitment; while act four works the other way: faced with overwhelming odds, the commitment is tested and as the worst point nears, abandonment is considered.

Take a look at the roadmap overleaf:

ACT ONE

Total mastery   No knowledge

Re-acceptance   Growing knowledge

Reawakening   Awakening

ACT FIVE   **ACT TWO**

Regression   THE 3-D   Doubt
                    ROADMAP
Growing   OF   Overcoming
reluctance   CHANGE   reluctance

Doubt   Acceptance

ACT FOUR   **ACT THREE**

Experimenting   Experimenting with
post-knowledge   knowledge

MIDPOINT
(Breakthrough) Key knowledge

Note not only the three-part structure of each section, but also how, if you bisect the diagram (effectively placing a vertical line down the centre), one half is absolutely related to the other. Not only are the beginning and end bookends (No knowledge/Total mastery), so are both halves of act three – with acts two and four becoming opposing versions of the same journey.

Act one and act five, act two and act four and both halves of act three – all echo and mirror each other around the midpoint. Further, in an absolutely archetypal script, the crisis in act two will work like an inciting incident – directly related to its mirror image, the crisis point in act four. As in the story structure, so in its participant elements. If Darryl is the one who is slighted by Thelma at the end of act two of *Thelma & Louise*, then at the end of act four Darryl will be playing a significant role in tracking Thelma and Louise down; Rosencrantz and Guildenstern attend Hamlet in act two; in act four they die. At every level it should be possible to detect the same structural relationship. In the first half of every script, the question will be asked: 'What is the worst consequence of *this* decision?' and in the second half the answer will come: '*This* is'.

When they wrote the screenplay for *The Godfather*, were Francis Ford Coppola and Mario Puzo (who employed a very similar structure in his novel) aware of this? Certainly most writers are not. So why does such symmetry occur?

When we watch films or television, we're all aware of when something *feels* right. If it doesn't, at best we're dissatisfied; at worst bored to tears. There can be many reasons for this, but more often than not it's because a work is badly ordered. We sense something is wrong because it simply doesn't fit the structure it aspires to. Occasionally this is a conscious choice – in the Coen Brothers' work (*Miller's Crossing, No Country for Old Men*) this disorder is something of a trademark – but more often than not (*Bad Boys II, Where the Wild Things Are*) tedium is bred from a failure of form. In classic Shakespeare you see a tripartite shape occur five times – each act containing its own thesis, antithesis and synthesis. Shakespeare *feels* right. It's not surprising therefore that if he didn't prescribe act breaks, his editors were able to do so – they appear at the end of every three-part unit, part of a natural shape and rhythm.

However – and it's a vital caveat – it's perfectly possible for great works not to conform. The fractal patterns we've been discussing are ideal patterns and it's not hard to find exceptions. Some films (*Andrei Rublev, Weekend, The White Ribbon*) deliberately subvert the pattern (a subject I will return to in depth later on), but many others are structurally imperfect. Some simply don't have a second half of act three, an act four (*The Lion King*) or even a fifth act; others may have seven acts and become the fourth most successful film of all time. A script, after all, can have as many acts in its middle section as a writer likes; just as story is dependent on structure, structure is dependent on the demands of each story. Few fit perfectly, but how many works of art are completely flawless? Their strengths lie partly in their imperfections.

It's vital to stress too that most writers, very sensibly, don't think like this consciously; they don't sit down with a chart. What's fascinating is how often archetypal structures arise unconsciously. Our brains are divided into left and right hemispheres, the former concerning itself with order, structure, logic; the latter with imagination and creativity. Just as we function best when we are able to bring both sides into harmony, so stories themselves seem to gravitate towards a similar balance. Storytelling is about bringing opposites together and stilling the conflict between order and chaos within.

Inevitably this doesn't just take place in a whole story and its fractal reductions. The relationship of opposites is fundamental to the way we actually perceive drama. That's what we must look at next, for it is the key to everything.

Act III
The Forest

Showing and Telling

How do I express in a picture that she's in a mood with me?
I'm not going to say 'She's in a mood with me',
I'm going to say 'She's tapping her foot'.[1]

Mike Skinner, The Streets

The Volkswagen 'Lemon' one-sheet has a justifiable place in the history of advertising. Briefed with selling a small car built in Germany to an American nation that equated size with importance – and all this only fifteen years after the end of the Second World War – the Doyle Dane Bernbach agency catalysed what was to become known in marketing circles as the 'creative revolution'. They changed the face of advertising, and they did it by showing, not telling.

Take a look at the advert and ask yourself: 'What does my mind immediately try to do?' It attempts to make sense of the relationship between the image and the strapline. It probably asks, 'How is the car a lemon?' followed shortly perhaps by another question, 'Why would they say that about their own product?' It's a basic narrative technique which forces you to read the copy underneath in the hope that it will explain such a superficially strange juxtaposition. The advert sucks you in; it impels you to do the work. As such, its structure – because it generates conflict and the desire for its resolution – is fundamentally dramatic.

The Pixar screenwriter and director Andrew Stanton was a movie buff who had seen every single David Lean film except *Ryan's Daughter*. It's 1992, LaserDiscs are all the rage and he finally gets to watch the work of his idol. 'It was like the clouds parting,'[2] he said, and one sequence in particular – a cut between two scenes – unlocked for him the mysteries of dramatic structure. In the first scene, the unhappily married Rosy Ryan tries to tell her priest that she's sexually frustrated; there has to be more to life. This is pre-war Catholic Ireland, however, and the priest has harsh words of warning. 'Rosy, don't nurse your wishes. You can't help having them, but don't nurse them, or sure to God you'll get what you're wishing for.' Immediately the film cuts to the arrival of a tall handsome stranger disembarking from a bus, lit in striking silhouette against the sea. Stanton got exactly the message Lean intended – 'this man is exactly what Rosie wishes for, and he's going to bring trouble'.

The film doesn't *tell* you that connection. Stanton worked it out, as any viewer would – it *showed* you. And this was the moment that he started to understand one of the most basic but important tenets of dramatic construction. Screenwriting is showing not telling; structure is the presentation of images in such a way an audience are forced to work out the relationship between them. Stanton had stumbled upon what is known amongst film theoreticians as the 'Kuleshov Effect'.

The Kuleshov Effect

In the early years of the twentieth century the Russian director Lev Kuleshov filmed a Russian matinee idol staring in turn at a bowl of soup, a coffin and a girl. Audiences raved about the actor's ability to effortlessly evoke hunger, grief and desire. What they didn't know was that he used the same shot of the actor each time – just cut to each different object.[3]

Kuleshov discovered that the extraordinary new medium of film took advantage of the human need to impose order on the world. If an audience is presented with disparate images they will assemble them into a meaningful order. It's a truth on which all film grammar is based.

Stanton, together with his co-writer of *Finding Nemo*, Bob Peterson, coined a phrase for the underlying structural importance of this juxtaposition, 'the unifying theory of two plus two'. As he puts it:

> Good storytelling never gives you four, it gives you two plus two . . . Don't give the audience the answer; give the audience the pieces and compel them to conclude the answer. Audiences have an unconscious desire to work for their entertainment. They are rewarded with a sense of thrill and delight when they find the answers themselves.[4]

It's a statement of profound importance, and not unique to the moving image.

Gary Davies appeared to ask whether we were ready to boogie before urging a big Wembley welcome for Kim Wilde ... [And] there she was, waving a red scarf and bending over a lot so that the cameras could catch the cleavage. 'It's great to be here,' she said. After a song or two a discussion developed in our row about the catering staff, who were dealing out the lager and cold dogs in what seemed to be Motherwell colours. We reached no important conclusions.[5]

When the DJ and journalist John Peel reviewed Kim Wilde (supporting Michael Jackson) at Wembley in 1988 he illustrated the difference between showing and telling. It's easier to write *diegetically*, 'Kim Wilde was boring'; indeed, in journalism (particularly the tabloid variety) it might be preferable, but it's less deep, it's less involving. Instead Peel dramatizes the boredom through the juxtaposition of images, and in so doing he forces the reader to become involved. He writes *mimetically*, forcing the reader to bridge the gap between Kim Wilde and the catering staff and thus draw their own vivid picture of the event. Peel is using the language of film.

In its infancy, television turned its back on such language in favour of a more 'proscenium arch' approach: the camera was part of the audience; the action observed, separate, on the stage. It ignored the work of Kuleshov and Eisenstein (the father of the montage, effectively the Kuleshov Effect in action), partly because such theories were still relatively obscure but also because the technology simply didn't exist to capture the fast-cutting juxtapositional language of film economically.

Though technology has changed, it's surprising how many people assume TV drama to be diegetic. While American cable drama has largely been liberated from this tyranny (helped by larger budgets and technology), it's still not uncommon to find screenwriting manuals that insist story be carried in dialogue. The same belief underlies the plaintive cries of critics who bemoan the lack of theatre on television, claiming it's a natural fit.[6] But they are wrong; it's not there for one simple reason – it doesn't work. It's boring and turgid and painful because it's not written for the medium. Television drama, like film, relies on the juxtaposition of images to convey a mental state. Theatre, much more a diegetic medium, doesn't. The very way theatre operates should make this obvious: there are no close-ups; there is little or no fragmentation of either time or space; and we rely, for example, on the soliloquy to convey the feeling that a great film-maker can create through the manipulation of pictures. Theatre isn't worse or inferior to television – its potency simply lies in live performance.[7]

Film, then television, liberated mimesis – and exploited its potential ruthlessly. In doing so, it changed entirely the way the world heard stories about itself. The development of the moving image was akin to the discovery of molecular science; it ushered in art's atomic age. Take a look at the following painting by Willem de Kooning, one of the pioneers of Abstract Expressionism.

Again, monitor yourself as your brain absorbs it, tries to order and make sense of the shapes within. Are they faces? Naked bodies? Women? Then when you learn its title is *Excavation*, ask how you reassess and reorder your thoughts to render sense. The act of interpretation – of fusing the disparate together – creates the picture in your head.

When Marcel Duchamp placed, with questionable genius,[8] a urinal in an art gallery and called it *Fountain* he was simply extrapolating this process – making the gallery itself the frame of the work.

The *Fountain*'s power grows from its environment; from the fact it simply *doesn't* belong. Two opposites are placed side by side; art is rendered from juxtaposition. That interpretation *is* the art.

It's a process open to abuse and obfuscation; as the worst of modern art attests, you can of course juxtapose anything. Exploiting the human desire to fuse opposites can be a profitable business, but when it's done with skill and insight it can be a meaningful one too. When the shapes coalesce and evoke a truth from their association, the observer is rewarded with an overwhelmingly powerful experience.

Good dramatists know this, which is why they exploit it to the full. The moving image by its very definition cannot deal with what we cannot see. There are two ways round this for a writer. Their work can *tell* us or it can render complex emotional experience into pictures.

It should, of course, do the latter. As E. M. Forster said, 'In the drama all human happiness and misery does and must take the form of action. Otherwise its existence remains unknown.'[9] In pure film and television, feelings, reflections and motivation – indeed, all interior life – are expressed in action and thus inferred, by the viewer, from context. A screenwriter cannot simply write, 'David stares into the fire wondering whether to vote Labour or Conservative', as the audience have no way of inferring that. Certainly they can have him say, 'I've been pondering which way to vote', but if they write, 'David stares into the fire' and it's preceded by a scene in which the character realizes something he always thought certain about one of those parties has been found wanting, the audience will understand mimetically. They won't need to be told, and it will be far more powerful because they will have worked it out for themselves. As The Streets' Mike Skinner said, why tell us she's angry, when you can show her tapping her foot? We see her face, we see her foot, and we *know*.

A well-told film or television work thus reveals its story through its structure – the order in which images appear. Characters are revealed through behaviour and explanation of motivation is avoided; characters do things, and through doing them we understand them. As long as a character has a clear goal, the way they choose to act in achieving it will reveal them. In a strange way, a protagonist is like film itself; as they pursue their desire they project their content, their purpose, their nature onto the audience. When they cease to move, they cease to be revealed; the audience ceases to be active and so ceases to care.

Audiences *like* to work; it's the working that glues them to the narrative. In detective drama, the viewer's urge to understand is absolutely central to narrative propulsion, but it's true of all film and television. As *The Wire* creator David Simon put it:

> [A viewer] loves being immersed in a new, confusing and possibly dangerous world that he will never see. He likes not knowing every bit of vernacular or idiom. He likes being trusted to acquire information on his terms, to make connections, to take the journey with only his intelligence to guide him. Most smart people cannot watch most TV, because it has generally been a condescending medium, explaining everything immediately, offering no ambiguities, and using dialogue that simplifies and mitigates against the idiosyncratic ways in which people in different worlds actually communicate. It eventually requires that characters from different places talk the same way as the viewer. This, of course, sucks.[10]

Bad writing explains; good writing shows.[11]

Andrew Stanton noted that his theory of $2 + 2 = ?$ – of showing rather than telling – doesn't just apply to images.

> I want to get an abortion, but my boyfriend and I are having trouble conceiving.

American comedian Sarah Silverman's joke is built on a classic subversion of expectation. But take a look at any joke, or any scene in any drama: the juxtaposition of opposites, verbal or visual or both, is the central plank not just of showing rather than telling, but of all humour, all narrative. Something, confronted with its opposite, makes us recast our notion of that 'something' again. As we noted in Act II of this book, scene structure is the smallest applicable version of thesis/antithesis/synthesis; the crisis point in every scene is a microcosm of an inciting incident. It appears that this unit – of something confronted by its opposite – is of central importance to storytelling.

At its most heightened, subversion of expectation doesn't just occur to the character, but to the audience as well. In Henri-Georges Clouzot's 1950s masterpiece *Les Diaboliques*, a wife and mistress of a provincial headmaster gang up to kill him. They succeed, but the corpse first disappears then returns to haunt them. The wife, who has a weak heart, dies of shock, and we learn that the mistress and the headmaster – who isn't really dead at all – planned it all along.

In *Sixth Sense* and *The Hours* exactly the same trick is used: the audience is forced to believe the version of events presented to them, only to learn later that crucial elements are the opposite of what they appear – in both films the protagonists are dead and the audience is manipulated to think the opposite, before being exposed to reality in the final scenes.

It's the Kuleshov Effect. In all these stories the audience is presented with key facts then invited to infer a connection. It's a heightening of thesis/antithesis to make the impact more extreme; it's the mechanism of Sarah Silverman's joke. It's also a technique at the heart of dramatic construction, with a lineage that runs from Greek tragedy to the present day. In *Oedipus Rex* Oedipus sets out to discover what is causing the plague in Thebes – only to find that he is. The same DNA is in the marrow of *The Bourne Ultimatum* and *Planet of the Apes*. In Chaucer's *Pardoner's Tale*, three men plan to find Death but instead find a pile of money. Each double-crosses the other and they all end up, with perfect irony, dead; in *The Murder of Roger Ackroyd* the killer turns out to be the narrator of the story, and the novel, in hindsight, a suicide note.

Aristotle writes of this effect in *The Poetics*: 'A change to the opposite in the actions being performed . . . in accordance with probability or necessity' and cites the story of Lynceus to press his case. The hero is being led away to execution, followed by Danaus, who is planning to perform the deed; 'but, it came about as a consequence of preceding events that the latter was killed and Lynceus was saved'.[12] It's *peripeteia* again, a reversal of fortune; the world suddenly revealed as the opposite of what it appeared. To the Greeks it was always partnered by *anagnorisis* or 'discovery', in which a character's ignorance is replaced by knowledge. Aristotle argued, I think correctly, that it's a fundamental unit of dramatic construction – something is confronted by its opposite and revealed to be something else.

The use of sudden revelation, of the last-minute twist, seems a world away from the films of Eric Rohmer or Ingmar Bergman, and it's easy to dismiss it as a populist technique – possibly because it's the recurring motif of soap plots ('You ain't my mother' – 'Yes I am'). But *EastEnders* uses and exploits that technique for a reason. It's not just that cliffhangers are a direct descendant of Greek tragedy – at best nothing more than *peripeteia* in action. They are, but they're also more than that.

At the beginning of a scene characters establish themselves on fairly solid ground, pursuing a goal they believe will restore order to their world. Just when they think they might be getting somewhere, something happens to throw their world into turmoil once again. Finding themselves in the middle of an uncharted world, the characters have to start, yet again, asking the question 'How the hell do I get out of that?' Scene and story shape directly echo each other. Subversion of expectation is actually a mini journey 'into the woods'. Effectively a character goes 'into the woods' in every scene.

The 'forest', then, is an explosion of opposition: whether embodied as inciting incident or act turning point or midpoint or crisis point or scene turning point, it is the primordial building block of all drama. And those blocks create the confrontation of something with its opposite. Kuleshov stumbled on something far more than a clever editing technique: he discovered, though never fully appreciated, this simple, basic building block. Everything that follows – character, dialogue, multi-protagonism, thematic stranding, television structure – all of it flows from here. When two opposites are juxtaposed correctly, an explosion occurs, and story comes alive.

Act IV
The Road Back, Night

12

Character and Characterization

EXT. A BUILDING OVERLOOKING CAMBRIDGE CIRCUS, LONDON, 1979.
The traffic idles by.

INT. ROOM OVERLOOKING TRAFFIC.
Civil Service décor, utilitarian, drab. A Formica table with four chairs – an ashtray at its centre.

TOBY ESTERHASE, *prim, upright, well dressed, enters. He carries a folder, which he positions carefully as he sits, arranging everything just so. He checks his fob watch, and looks up impatiently.*

ROY BLAND, *unkempt, rough, and with a cigarette in his mouth, backs into the room. He coughs repeatedly, but pays no attention to* ESTERHASE. *He too sits at the table.*

PERCY ALLELINE *enters brusquely, efficiently and takes the head chair. He acknowledges no one.*

BILL HAYDON *enters, slowly, balancing a cup of tea, saucer on top, in a precarious manner. Effete. He attempts to shut the door with a back heel, but fails. He sits, unconcerned.*

ESTERHASE *gets up to shut the door. He sits again. No one speaks.*

ALLELINE *lights his pipe and, once successful, looks up.*

ALLELINE: Right. We shall start.

Tinker Tailor Soldier Spy by John le Carré.
Adapted for BBC 1 by Arthur Hopcraft, 1979

All great drama is character-based, all enduring drama is character-based, all popular drama is character-based, and all plausible drama is character-based. Without credible, vibrant, exciting, living, breathing, empathetic characters, drama simply doesn't work. But what makes great characters? And what hidden role does structure play in guaranteeing their success?

The Basic Principles

We are all identical – yet we are all different. Everyone to a greater or lesser degree shares the same basic psychological make-up – we all have the ability to love, to be jealous, to procreate, to be defensive, to be open, to be vengeful, to be kind. We all have experience or knowledge of fathers, mothers, children and love and we display these characteristics and influences in different proportions depending on who and what we are. Just as all humans look the same yet are totally different, so it is with our psychological make-up.

Everyone customizes, consciously or not, everything they do. Clothes, car, home or phone – everyone at some level displays behaviour that presents themselves in a different way. We all do similar things, yet everybody does everything in their own unique manner. If someone offered us £10 million, we'd all spend it differently. It's a standard definition of character, but it's a good one; everyone surmounts the same obstacle uniquely and in doing so leaves their fingerprints behind.

This applies to *any* obstacle: we all make coffee, eat or drive differently. The characters in *Tinker Tailor Soldier Spy* all enter the room differently. Every decision we make or action we perform when confronted with an obstacle is a choice that reveals – through action – our personality.

In every scene, remember, a protagonist is presented with a mini crisis, and must make a choice as to how to surmount it. Meeting with a subversion of expectation – a blow to their established plans – a character must choose a new course of action. In doing so they reveal a little bit of who they are. Our hero rings up his girlfriend to discuss plans for the weekend and she tells him she's leaving him: he might smash up her car or he might wish her well. Our heroine inherits a million pounds: she could become a drug addict or make ten million more. The choices they make will illustrate their character. In the opening scene of the BBC series *House of Saddam*, Saddam Hussein summons his best friend, embraces him, pulls a gun and shoots him in the head. Though the subversion of expectation is this time transferred to the viewer, the result is the same; one piercing direct action tells us, without words, the kind of man he is. He wants to show the Iraqi people he is utterly ruthless; what better method than to shoot the man he loves? If he is capable of that one action, runs his logic, he is capable of anything. Yet he is also capable of great love for his family. And in that paradox lies the truth about characterization.

Characterization

Two cowboys are trapped on the precipice of a gorge. Behind them, the posse closes in; in front of them, hundreds of feet below, lies a torrential river. Their choice is stark:

BUTCH: DAMMIT! Well, the way I figure it, we can either fight or give. If we give, we go to jail.

SUNDANCE: I been there already.

BUTCH: But if we fight, they can stay right where they are and starve us out or go for position – shoot us; might even get a rockslide started and get us that way. What else could they do?

SUNDANCE: They could surrender to us, but I wouldn't count on that. (*He watches the posse manoeuvre.*) They're goin' for position, all right. Better get ready. (*He loads his gun.*)

BUTCH: Kid – the next time I say, 'Let's go someplace like Bolivia,' let's go someplace like Bolivia.

SUNDANCE: Next time. Ready?

BUTCH: (*Looking into the deep canyon and the river far below*) No, we'll jump.

SUNDANCE: (*After looking down*) Like hell we will.

BUTCH: No, it'll be OK – if the water's deep enough, we don't get squished to death. They'll never follow us.

SUNDANCE: How do you know?

BUTCH: Would you make a jump like that you didn't have to?

SUNDANCE: I have to and I'm not gonna.

BUTCH: Well, we got to, otherwise we're dead. They're just gonna have to go back down the same way they come. Come on.

SUNDANCE: Just one clear shot, that's all I want.

BUTCH: Come on.

SUNDANCE: Uh-uh.

BUTCH: We got to.

SUNDANCE: Nope! Get away from me!

BUTCH: Why?

SUNDANCE: I wanna fight 'em!

BUTCH: They'll kill us!

SUNDANCE: Maybe.

BUTCH: You wanna die?!

SUNDANCE: (*Waving his pistol at the river far below*) Do *you*?!

BUTCH: All right. I'll jump first.

SUNDANCE: Nope.

BUTCH: Then you jump first.

SUNDANCE: No, I said!

BUTCH: What's the matter with you?!

SUNDANCE: (*Wildly embarrassed*) *I can't swim!*

BUTCH: (*Guffawing at his partner*) Why, you crazy – the *fall*'ll probably kill ya!

SUNDANCE *shakes his head as he ponders the insanity of actually jumping to escape their pursuers. He grabs a gun belt held out by Butch, jumps with him in tandem, and wails.*

SUNDANCE: Ohhh . . . s - h - i - i - i - i - i - t !

Butch Cassidy and the Sundance Kid by William Goldman

Your husband commits adultery. He is President of the United States. You are invited to comment by a voracious press.

You and your younger brother are competing for leadership of the Labour Party; you are far more experienced and everyone expects you to win. How do you feel if you lose? What do you say to him?

The conflict between how we wish to be perceived and what we really feel is at the root of all character. The Sundance Kid and Butch Cassidy 'are two sides of one personality. They are one protagonist,' said the screenwriting guru Robert McKee. What he's alluding too – though doesn't fully explore – is the central importance of internal conflict in character creation.

You only have to look at some of the towering figures of the last century to observe the dissonance between a character's image and their behaviour: Stalin professed to love his people but killed an estimated 20 million of them; Tony Blair proclaimed his socialist credentials while presiding over a massive expansion of free-market capitalism; and John F. Kennedy's democratic idealism didn't extend to his treatment of women nor to his expansion of the war in Vietnam. This isn't to condemn them; at the heart of all of us – and thus all great fictional characters too – is conflict. Steve Jobs, in the words of his biographer, 'was an anti-materialistic hippie who capitalized on the inventions of a friend who wanted to give them away for free, and he was a Zen devotee who made a pilgrimage to India then decided that his calling was to create a business'.[1]

Whether real or imagined, great characters are consciously or subconsciously at war with themselves. As the French philosopher Montaigne eloquently put it: 'We are, I know not how, somewhat double in ourselves, so that what we believe we disbelieve, and cannot rid ourselves of what we condemn.' Just as it's true of Ronald Reagan, who, while seen as 'America's friend', led, behind the scenes, an almost solitary existence, so we find the same dichotomy in fiction. From Huckleberry Finn and Jay Gatsby to Don Draper and Tony Soprano, conflict is the lifeblood of their being.

There is a contradiction within us all. We are all animals yet we are all capable of rationality. We all have our own personal survival to ensure, yet we all have to live in society. For these animal and rational instincts to accommodate each other we place restrictions on many of the things we feel or would want to say – they're simply not acceptable in company. You only have to read an internet message board or an anonymous blog to see what happens when such societal restrictions are removed: the absence of identity allows the inner animal off the leash. It's no accident that liberal websites are often home to the most offensive knee-jerk correspondence; a quick visit to www.guardian.co.uk reveals the bastions of liberal humanism only a hair's breadth away from shouting at one another, 'wanker'. Strip away an individual's need to identify themself and you reveal something akin to a Tourette's zoo. Remove the need for tolerant, understanding appearance and you unleash the true feelings of impotence, anger and rage that can lurk beneath.

No one is immune. Publicly we tend to present ourselves as models of civic virtue – in France, no one supported the Vichy regime; in South Africa, no one ever voted Nationalist. When reader Beth Druce wrote to the *Guardian* in September 2011, 'I liked Victoria Beckham's second fashion line, which she showed in New York last week, but feel a little bit icky about saying so. Am I normal?' she was merely illustrating the lengths to which we all go to manage how we're perceived by others. Our darker feelings – the rage or shame that fill our websites – can rarely be shown publicly, because most communities find it unacceptable. But of course in most of us the capability is there. 'I see and approve the better course, but I follow the worse' goes the Latin saying. As St Paul succinctly put it in Romans 7:19: 'For the good that I would, I do not: but the evil which I would not, that I do.'

We hide our dark impulses, we deplete our energy worrying about how we may be perceived; it's an anxiety that fuels fashion, music and art. Capitalism feeds off it, not only by exploiting our need to be new and get ahead, but also – rather brilliantly – the opposite too. The 'guilty pleasures' phenomenon of recent years is a clear and vivid example of the realization that it's intensely liberating to stop being cool and instead dance to Abba. But coolness, like new season trends, tends to be the main driver. The lengths we go to convince ourselves of our own superiority is remarkable. Rare is the critic who doesn't declare their preferences without one eye on fashion, but then rare is the consumer too.[2]

At the end of Oliver Stone's sporadically brilliant *Nixon*, the eponymous president stares at a picture of Kennedy and intones, 'When they look at you, they see what they want to be. When they look at me, they see what they are.' This conflict between who a character is, and who they want to be, is real life's gift to drama. Writers have always known that when their characters act in a manner they profess to disapprove of, when they lie, when they self-sabotage and generally act contrary to their conscious proclamations and beliefs, they are far more interesting, far more exciting to write, and feel far more true to life.

Two of the most successful television shows of recent times are built around this dichotomy. *Glee* is about letting go and liberating oneself from the repression of peer group pressure and expressing your inner self. *Mad Men* is its polar opposite: all human feeling is repressed for the holy grail of appearance. The shows are mirror images of each other; the same programme flipped on its head. How fascinating (and telling) that they should be products of the same society at the same time.

So why is conflict within three-dimensional characters essential? If dramatic structure is intrinsic to the human mind, it suggests, perhaps, that there could be a psychological basis for the paradoxes that inform all great drama and characterization.

The Psychological Basis of Characterization

We are animals, and our primordial instinct is therefore to survive and continue our bloodline. All of us are at some level driven by this extraordinarily powerful motor; so strong it can both dominate and overrule conscious behaviour. We may not always be aware of the impulses, but at some level they are always there.

In 1943 Abraham Maslow published 'A Theory of Human Motivation', in which he set out his analysis of man's basic primal drives. He called this his 'Hierarchy of Needs' (see diagram opposite).

Maslow is not without his detractors, but it's hard to refute that at some level these needs can and do act as a motivating force. Human beings always seek 'safety',[3] and the primal urges for food, water, sex, security, safety, self-esteem and self-actualization are fundamentally selfish manifestations of this overriding desire to survive.

Seeking safety, ironically, entails repressing these other desires, consciously or unconsciously, so that one can live within a group. Unbridled sexual desire, or a thirst for revenge, simply isn't compatible with the consensus on which societies tend to depend – if anything they will jeopardize the very security sought. Such desires therefore have to be repressed, creating a conflict between the way we want to be seen and the deeper feelings we are reluctant to admit to both in others and in ourselves.

This conflict – between our individual urge to survive and the problems that creates for co-existing with others – is, appropriately, at the centre of all the major western psychological theories. It was first expressed by Sigmund Freud, then later debated, dismissed, elucidated or expanded by his spiritual descendants. Freud saw the conflict as essentially a battle between the super-ego ('the parent')

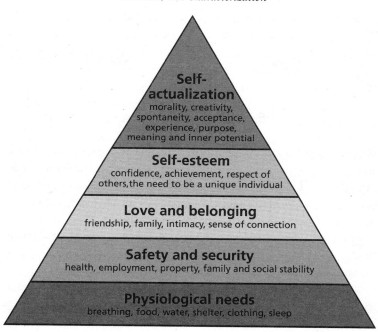

and the id ('the child'); the rational, intelligent, ordered side versus the irrational, animal, libidinous one.

Carl Jung's own philosophy (he was initially Freud's pupil) is built on a similar duality, and the same conflict is the cornerstone of his work. Jung believed that every psychological power had its opposing force, whether it was ying and yang, anima and animus or, most pertinently, between the persona (the façade one shows to the world) and its shadow (the unconscious urges that lie beneath). The heirs of Freud and Jung, be they Erik Erikson with his theory of normative conflict (which gave us the identity crisis); Alfred Adler, founder of the school of individual psychology (which gave us the inferiority complex); or Rollo May (the father of existential psychoanalysis) – all observed and built their theories on this duality of the mind.

What's striking about these theories is not so much their differences (of which there are many) but just how much they have in common. Not only do they all suggest that man lives in a conflicted, neurotic state in which primal desires are at war with socially acceptable behaviour, they also tacitly accept that these neuroses need to be integrated and overcome in order for 'happiness' to be achieved. For Freud this meant sublimating the sexual impulse into socially appropriate and personally rewarding work; for Jung that the persona must encounter and integrate the shadow.

When we remember that all archetypal stories are journeys towards completion – voyages from darkness to light – and involve the reconciliation of opposites, it's not hard to detect the connection between psychological and story theory. In our own paradigm, a flawed, conflicted hero goes on a journey to become whole, integrating the lessons he has learned from others on the way. Successful happy endings, both in fiction and in psychology, involve the individual resolving conflicts and learning to integrate and balance opposing forces. Just as all stories seek to resolve order from chaos, man seeks to still the raging conflict within. Or, as F. Scott Fitzgerald put it, 'The test of a first-rate intelligence is the ability to hold two opposed ideas in mind at the same time and still retain the ability to function.' He might just as easily have said 'a first-rate human being'. 'Blest are those', says Hamlet of his friend Horatio,

> Whose blood and judgment are so well commingled
> That they are not a pipe for fortune's finger
> To sound what stop she please.

The Importance of Paradox

'It's not a smile, it's a lid on a scream.'

Julie Goodyear

Michael Corleone is a character continually at war – not just with others, but also with himself. The midpoint image of the man who believes himself to be one thing battling a very different inner self is a universal, central image in all three-dimensional drama. When composing the soundtrack for *The Social Network*, Trent Reznor was searching for a theme that captured the fictional Mark Zuckerberg. He settled on a plangent piano motif, suffused with melancholy but underscored with an insistent throbbing electronic edge.[4] The combination of loneliness and underlying rage got him exactly.

House is a misanthrope who will go to any lengths to save a life; David Brent believes everyone in *The Office* loves him to hide the terrifying loneliness within. The more you look the more you realize the conflict between inner and outer self is absolutely central to successful dramatic characterization.[5] In *Fawlty Towers* Basil Fawlty is a man of substance, well versed in the finer things in life; a man who prides himself in his aptitude for service and a man who hates the working class. He's also a struggling philistine; a hen-pecked husband and manager of a cheap hotel in Torquay. *Dad's Army's* Captain Mainwaring is a soldier, a successful public figure and a model of respectability. He's also a figure of fun, a provincial bank manager stuck in a hopeless marriage. *Mad Men's* Donald Draper is a rich, sophisticated playboy, lord of everything he surveys, a man who has everything; but he's also dirt-poor 'white trash', a lost soul and a man who has nothing. Indeed, he's not actually Donald Draper at all.

In *Lethal Weapon*, *48 Hrs.* and every 'buddy'-based cop show, the paradox is, as in *Butch Cassidy and the Sundance Kid*, built into two characters.[6] In its most extreme form, the gap between how a character wishes to be seen and who they really are is dramatized by splitting one character into two identities. Here we enter the territory of the superhero – *Superman*, *Spider-Man*, *Captain America* and *Batman* (with *The Incredible Hulk* as the dark inversion). All are constructed around the idea of one personality hiding within another. This is, of course, the root of their success – was there ever a more ready invitation for a child's empathy? Impotent and powerless as children often feel, with parents who insist on a strict bedtime, who better to identify with than someone who looks so familiar but is secretly harbouring within them an omnipotent god?

J. K. Rowling distilled and bottled the formula and with Harry Potter took over the world. Interesting to note, too, that the most modern manifestation of the super-hero paradox is *Dexter*, a character and show bearing an uncanny similarity to the darkest versions of *Batman*. It's perhaps telling that a serial killer should be a super-hero for our times.

But no show more ruthlessly exploited the gap between who we are and who we would like to be than *The Office*. Ten years after making it, Ricky Gervais reflected, 'Being a fake documentary was so important, because without that it was just a bunch of people not doing much. But as soon as you turn the camera on . . . it explains everything.'[7] The camera gave licence to show both the characters' real selves and their façades; its very subject became how neurotic, unhappy people *wish* to be seen.[8] Gervais, with Stephen Merchant, built paradox into the very DNA of one of the last decade's most successful shows. David Brent is the Captain Mainwaring of the millennium – his desperate loneliness fuelling his desperate presentation.

Brent has a truth to him, founded on the simple fact that both in fiction and in us too (if we're honest) we are divided. But paradox isn't just the territory that basic psychological theory and characterization have in common; it's an integral part of structural design.

13

Character and Structural Design

'Relationships, easy to get into, hard to maintain. Why are they so hard to maintain? Because it's hard to keep up the lie! 'Cause you can't get nobody being you. You got to lie to get somebody. You can't get nobody looking like you look, acting like you act, sounding like you sound. When you meet somebody for the first time, you're not meeting them. You're meeting their representative!'

Chris Rock, *Bigger & Blacker* (HBO, 1999)

Ziggy Sobotka in series two of *The Wire* is the damaged and inadequate son of a respected union activist. Unable to live up to his father's reputation, he seeks to replenish his ego by attempting to convince both himself and others he's a major-league criminal. But he is as inept at crime as he is at life, and the more his felonious plans go awry the more he becomes a joke, the derision of others further aggravating his desire to prove himself. That gap, between how he wants to see himself and who he really is, creates a classic neurosis and, as he is unable to reconcile the two, his ending can only be tragic. It's an archetypal tale: a character who has to abandon his ego-driven goal for a more satisfying 'need' finds himself unable to do so, and is punished. But it tells us something, too, about characterization.

What are Facebook and Myspace but adverts for how we'd like to be seen? What are the unwatched programmes on your Sky+ but taunting reminders of who we might really like to be? A character's *want* is a superficial conscious desire for the thing they think they need in order to present themselves to the world, a projection of how they consciously wish to portray themselves. For Citizen Kane this desire is for power; for Gatsby wealth; for Tony Soprano 'respect'.

Rocky wants to win the World Championship, and Lightning McQueen the Piston Cup, because they will bolster their conscious public images, their outer shells, their masks, their super-egos – the 'character' they want others to see. They don't want to lose because they fear it will expose their weakness, their soft underbelly, the id. What they're scared of, ironically, is the part that would make them whole. The antagonist they fear, then – the 'monster' they must overcome – is the embodiment of the very thing lacking in themselves.

Fully realized characters have a façade. It's constructed of elements the character believes to be beneficial but, as we discover, will actually destroy them. Lightning McQueen is happy to be perceived as arrogant and indifferent (that's his character) but these are the very elements that land him in his predicament. William Thacker in *Notting Hill* might be the opposite of the hero of *Cars*, but his diffidence, shyness and reserve – the façade he's trapped behind – are the very things standing in the way of winning Anna Scott. It is the façade that triggers the problem. That's why Jack Baker loses Suzy Diamond in *The Fabulous Baker Boys*, just as it's Michael Corleone's compassion that leads him to avenge his father.

Conversely, the traits a character may believe to be a weakness, if indeed they are conscious of them, become the elements that offer redemption. It's Lightning McQueen's selflessness and empathy that save his soul, and (because it's a dark inversion) Michael Corleone's ruthlessness that ensures his succession.[1] The relationship between what a character wants and their outer façade, between what they need and their inner vulnerabilities – their complete character in other words – is thus inevitably linked to dramatic structure.

How is this done? In *The Fabulous Baker Boys* Jack Baker (Jeff Bridges) is a selfish, self-centred screw-up, unable to cope with intimacy or hold down any kind of relationship. However, even as we're made aware of his considerable flaws, it's also made clear he has the potential to show love. He looks after the little girl who lives upstairs, he fights passionately for his sick dog, and as the woman he sleeps with in the opening scene reminds him, he's not entirely selfish – he has 'great hands'. Michael Corleone may reject his family's credo of violence, but the steel with which he explains who they are to Kay (Diane Keaton) reveals the seeds of his future self. Internal conflict exists from the beginning of the story, like tinder, ready to be kindled into flame. It was the Hungarian critic Lajos Egri who said, 'Every character a dramatist presents must have within it the seeds of its future development.' There must be the potential for villainy at the beginning in the boy who is going to turn criminal at the end of the play.

As a story progresses and *need* supplants *want*, the traits that help a character sustain their outer appearance are slowly transformed by the 'better' angels within. *Need* becomes conscious at the inciting incident, is embraced at the end of the second act, and at the midpoint triumphs for the first time; hence Thelma's look of post-coital revelation and, on a much darker journey, the look of both pain and power on Michael Corleone's face as need triumphs over want for the first time. The subconscious has been dredged and brought to the surface to take over.

Post-midpoint the protagonist has to learn how to integrate the now dominant new self with the old one. It's not enough for them to assume an entirely new personality – they have to learn how to merge the good from the new with the good from the old.[2] Then, as the journey nears its end, the two sides are brought into balance. It's dialectics – it's thesis and antithesis, seeking synthesis once again. If one was being overtly schematic the relationship between façade and flaw would look something like this (see overleaf):

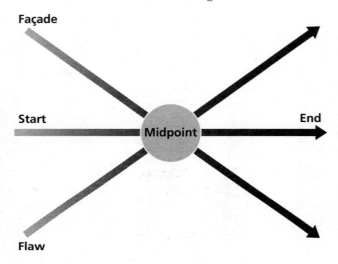

It is of course absurd to represent characters mathematically, but for ease of illustration let us say that Thelma begins her journey 25 per cent a woman and 75 per cent a little girl. As the story progresses, the proportions change incrementally to arrive finally at 75 per cent woman and 25 per cent child within. Indeed, such is the dialectical nature of act structure that in a perfectly ordered script you can see a very clear pattern to the way characters change. If we accept that at the midpoint a character's need will overcome their want for the very first time (and that's actually a rather good definition of a three-dimensional midpoint's function), then it's possible to chart graphically how a character evolves (see opposite).

Think of Macbeth and how the poison inside him grows act by act until it overwhelms him. Think of Elle in *Legally Blonde*, the dizzy airhead who finds a brilliant legal brain germinating within. As the film starts she is all pink with a loud hairdo; ninety-six minutes later and a qualified lawyer her barnet is immaculate and there's a small splash of pink on her collar. As thesis meets antithesis and the two interact, watch how in each act one side supplants the other as the nature of the internal conflict (and her costume) changes.

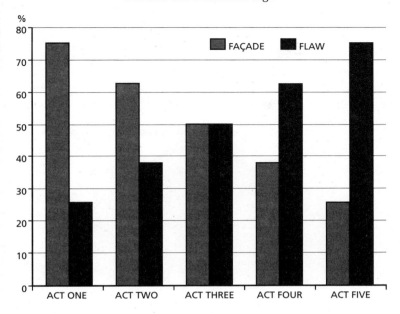

It's a grossly reductive and simplistic way at looking at character-ization – flesh and blood makes things far more refreshingly complicated – but it contains an underlying and deeply significant truth. It's a commonplace that character and story are the same thing – a character is what they do and, consequently, what a char-acter wants reveals who they are. The traits a character displays in pursuit of that goal (both conscious and unconscious ones) are, we can see, directly linked to structure. At different points in the story the traits will appear in different proportions. What appear to be random quirks of individual characterization are in fact intimately linked to a pattern, one built on the war between opposites, and seeking perfect symmetry.

In an archetypally structured story, the qualities a character dis-plays in pursuit of their goal will be the ones that sabotage their ability to achieve it, and those traits will have initially unconscious opposites that will, if redemption is the endpoint, come to their salvation. In a tragedy, the opposite occurs. Jay Gatsby creates an entirely fictitious self designed to win Daisy Buchanan; but the very impulses that create his fantasy are the ones that push her away.

Character and structure then are indivisible; one is a manifestation of the other. But if structure is really so schematic, so reducible, an immediate question arises. If all structure follows an identical archetype, then how does one account for an infinite variety of character?

14

Character Individuation

A man with a small penis builds a skyscraper; a woman who fears sex becomes a nun; a man riddled with self-loathing becomes a comic – all are familiar dramatic (if not melodramatic) tropes, but each contains a truth. People construct a public face in order to deal with the conflicts that rage inside them. So it is in drama. Jimmy McGovern's Father Greg in *Priest* is a practising homosexual; *Boardwalk Empire*'s puritanical enforcer of prohibition is a sexual deviant. Characters create façades to mask the things they fear inside – we all do.

A character's façade, then, is an outer manifestation of an inner conflict. But if it were simply the case that anyone with hidden vulnerabilities had a hard exterior then there would be very few different character types. How do we explain this apparent paradox? If properly conceived, characters not only fit into the story paradigm but are also an integral part of its design. *Witness*, *The Searchers* and *Notting Hill* all have at their centre protagonists who are terrified of intimacy – but there's a world of difference between John Book, Ethan Edwards and William Thacker. Surely story structure is too schematic to produce such variety?

The answer is reasonably straightforward: writers *dress* their characters in different ways – their behavioural quirks, felicity with language, milieu and setting all go a long way to aid differentiation. But how can four characters with the same root flaw and internal conflicts be so different if they are strapped to a structural grid? Fortunately, conflict manifests itself in many different ways.

People create a persona that will make them safe and they strive to attain the status and achievements they feel will bolster that self-image. In fictional terms, their wants are desires they mistakenly believe will make them complete and calm the conflict within. It's a familiar fictional device: Citizen Kane seeks to control a world that terrifies him; Gatsby wants wealth to hide his terrible poverty; Tony Soprano exudes violence to mask his vulnerability; and Donald Draper creates a false persona to bury the completely different person underneath. As we've seen, the façades these characters assume do not bring them happiness. Why then do they choose them, and what can that tell us about character individuation?

Ego Defence Mechanisms

Faced with extreme stress some characters will laugh, others will cry, some will intellectualize, some may punish others. It's a cornerstone of characterization, but it's a centrepiece of psychological theory too.

Freud believed the ego had defence mechanisms that were designed to deal with internal conflict. These devices were an outlet for the neuroses born from the constant tussle between the public face – the super-ego – and the id or inner rage. He argued that when id impulses (the desire to have sex or take revenge) come into conflict with the super-ego (the impulse that tells them this is unacceptable), dissatisfaction, anxiety and neuroses develop. To deal with these uncomfortable feelings, the ego creates defence mechanisms – not permanent paths to happiness, but psychological 'coping systems' that allow individuals to 'manage' on a day-to-day basis.

It was Kenneth Tynan who said 'a neurosis is a secret you don't know you're keeping'. We employ many different kinds of defence mechanism to deal with the problems these 'secrets' throw up, many recognized in the pioneering work of Sigmund Freud and his daughter Anna.[1] They're commonly grouped into four different categories:[2]

  i. Pathological (e.g. delusional projection)

  ii. Immature (e.g. passive aggression)

  iii. Neurotic (e.g. hypochondriasis)

  iv. Mature (e.g. humour/altruism).

Most of the traits will be familiar: visible in friends, colleagues and to those with self-knowledge. But they are perhaps easier to detect in those living public lives, partly because fame tends to exacerbate them, and partly because neurotics are arguably more driven to seek fame and approbation. For our own purposes, what's important is that they will also have instantly recognizable manifestations in drama:

INTELLECTUALIZATION
– concentrating on the non-emotive aspects (*Manhattan*)

REPRESSION
– repelling pleasurable instincts (*The Remains of the Day*)

REGRESSION
– to an earlier stage of development (*The Big Chill*)

SUBLIMATION
– shift of negative emotions into another object (*Chocolat*)

RATIONALIZATION
– specious reasoning away of trauma (*Leaving Las Vegas*)

ISOLATION
– separation of feeling from ideas and events (*The Searchers*)

PROJECTION
– attack others for fault within self (*The Sopranos*)

DENIAL
– refusal to acknowledge emotional trauma (*Rosemary's Baby*)

DISPLACEMENT
– shifting internal aggression etc. to a different target *(Death Wish)*

REACTION FORMATION
– believing the opposite of what one feels *(Crash)*

In simple terms, a flawed character has an extraordinarily wide range of options out of which they can construct a façade. How does a character react to their inability to be intimate? Do they . . .

Intellectualize it?	Blame their partner?
Make a joke of it?	Live in isolation?
Bury all desire?	Deny there's any problem?
Behave childishly?	Sleep with prostitutes?
Build a skyscraper?	Attack others?

Attempts are made to hide trauma (or, in our world, a character's flaw) in any number of behavioural ways. Fear of intimacy can prompt a character to don many different masks: that's why the protagonists of *The Searchers*, *Witness* and *Notting Hill* are so different yet still products of the same underlying flaw.

In story terms, ego defence mechanisms are the masks characters wear to hide their inner selves; they are the part of the character we meet when we first join a story, the part that will – if the archetype is correct – slough away.[3] If you accept this, you start to see just how deep are the psychological roots of story shape: for the characters (and us by proxy), the archetype acts as a template for resolving neurotic conflict.

What causes that neurotic conflict? The answer not only throws light onto some of the most common dramatic techniques, it raises important questions both about the nature and importance of exposition, and dramatic structure as a whole.

The Origin of Neurotic Conflict and the Rubber Duck

All three-dimensional characters, when we first meet them, are flawed. In psychological terms they are the victims of neurotic trauma: there is a mismatch between their wants and needs; they are dysfunctional, and in order to cope with that dysfunction they have adopted defence mechanisms that help in the short term, but if sustained can cause profound damage. Often this trauma has its origins in an off-screen experience that has occurred before the film, play or TV programme has begun.

In *EastEnders* it would be Kat's rape by her Uncle Harry; in *Silence of the Lambs* it would be Clarice witnessing the slaughtering of the lambs. The early death of siblings drives both *Walk the Line* and *Ray!* – one seen in the prologue, the other in flashback – but in its most common manifestation the root of trauma is not revealed until at least two thirds into, if not the end, of a story. It's the final piece of the jigsaw that magically explains who the protagonists are – and why they are the way they are.

No one has yet come up with a better term for this than film director Sidney Lumet and writer/collaborator Paddy Chayefsky. Together they christened it the 'Rubber Ducky' moment,[4] their slang for an incident in earlier life that supposedly 'explains' who that character is now. Not surprisingly, the expression is cynical in intent – it was simply too easy to explain psychopathic tendencies, they felt, by revealing that 'Someone stole their rubber ducky when they were a baby'. Their cynicism, however, has failed to prevent it from becoming a common dramatic motif,[5] and indeed it has a certain pedigree. In *Thelma & Louise* it's when Louise was raped in Texas; in *Citizen Kane* it's his separation from 'Rosebud'; in *Casablanca* it's when Ilsa leaves Rick in Paris; and in *Rain Man* it's the splitting up of the brothers as babies.

It's the foundation stone too of all films that use 'periodic' structure; films where we know absolutely nothing about the protagonist at the beginning, and which create change not from within the character but from the slow revelation to the audience of who they actually are. Change occurs not in the protagonist, but in *us*. Both in art-house (*I Know Where I'm Going!* and *Red Road*) and mainstream (*Rachel Getting Married* and *The Bourne Supremacy*), all are structured around the build to, and revelation of, the moment that tells us who the protagonists *are*. All, of course, following the change paradigm to a tee.

Most films don't reveal this moment until at least the end of the fourth act – partly to help create mystery and anticipation throughout the story, and partly because the story *is* the character's journey towards that moment. Again, story matches psychological theory: characters are taken on a journey to acknowledge and assimilate the traumas in their past. By confronting and coming to terms with the cause of their traumas they can finally move on.

The 'Rubber Ducky' moment, then, is when the split in personality originally occurred and a schism developed between the healthy individual they were born as and the damaged person they later became. It's the event that has triggered the creation of the psychological defence mechanisms – in effect, the moment that catalysed the creation of the neurosis, and consequently the character's façade.

Kane was deprived of love – so he builds an empire.

Louise is hard, aloof and controlling because of what happened to her in Texas.

Rick Blaine is rude and selfish because Ilsa abandoned him in Paris.

At its best the Rubber Ducky moment can be a strong and powerful dramatic device, but at its worst it can lead to overblown melodrama, speechifying and cliché. (Quint's speech about the shark attack on the USS Indianapolis in *Jaws* steers a very fine line between the two.) David Mamet scathingly refers to it as the 'death of my kitten' speech – that point in a play, usually three-quarters of the way through, when the writer interrupts the action with a pretty monologue. It often begins: 'When I was young I had a kitten . . .'

The writer Simon Stephens noted the same 'tendency in apprentice playwrights to write about ancient family secrets which are revealed "four-fifths through the play, often in a drunken confessional speech"'. Like Mamet, he's dismissive, describing it as 'theatrically inert'.[6] Orson Welles himself referred to 'Rosebud' as 'dime-book Freud'. Arguably the revelation of off-screen trauma works when it informs the current storyline and creates an active goal, as in *Thelma & Louise*. For a compelling modern spin, it's possible to view *The Social Network* as one long argument between the characters as to what the Rubber Ducky moment actually is. It works less well when it's back-story. But should it happen at all?

Mamet insists writers resist: 'When the film turns narrative rather than dramatic, when it stands in for the viewer's imagination, the viewer's interest is lost . . . The garbage of exposition, backstory, narrative, and characterization spot-welds the reader into interest in what is happening *now*. It literally stops the show.'[7] He's ridiculing, rightly, the culture of over-explanation that litters bad narrative and pushes the audience away, refusing to treat them intelligently enough to add 2 plus 2 themselves.

Mamet points out, as E. M. Forster did before him,[8] that our only interest should be in what happens next. We know, after twenty-three films, almost nothing about James Bond's background.[9] We don't need to – he's pure character; we know who he is. The less back-story a character has, the more readily an audience is able to identify with them – the more we can see they're like us and not like someone else. We may *want* to know more, but it's the *not* knowing that keeps us watching. It allows us to fully experience the journey ourselves and actively join in the process in which a character pursues their goal, their flaw is subsumed into their façade, their need into their want, and the goal of all drama is achieved – a rich, complex, three-dimensional character appears in front of our eyes.

There's a reason Hergé's Tintin has absolutely no discernible character while he's surrounded by an extraordinarily rich gallery of archetypes – how easy it is for a child to step into his plus fours and become the hero of the adventure, for the character is so like himself. David Fincher said of Robert De Niro's iconic character in *Taxi Driver*: 'I don't know where Travis Bickle is from or what made him do what he did. I don't know and I don't care. That's what makes him compelling.'[10] His point is simple but important. If a film is working correctly, the protagonists *are* us. The less we know about them, the more we are able – like the characters in *Being John Malkovich* – to climb into their heads and make their experiences our own.

Truly archetypal drama induces a sense of peace; the story works as a temporary balm, purging[11] our own inner distress. We heal as we watch, not because the work articulates the need for conflict resolution, but because it allows us to enact the process ourselves. Badly placed back-stories inhibit that process, disrupting our ability to empathize. That's why structurally perfect films can affect us so deeply; if character and structure are one there is no need for explanation. The profound effect of the archetype resolving itself touches us on an unconscious level far more than words ever can. It's also, of course, why we can find disrupted structure so distressing, and rightly too – for inducing a sense of peace isn't always every artist's aim.

15

Dialogue and Characterization

BOND: Do you expect me to talk?

GOLDFINGER: (*Looks back, laughing*) No, Mr Bond. I expect you to die.

Goldfinger by Richard Maibaum and Paul Dehn

Every utterance, however intangible, is at some level an expression of intent. The three most important functions of dialogue – characterization, exposition and subtext – are all, as we shall see, products of character desire. Dialogue, then, is both born out of *and* an essential component of structure.

'Show, don't tell' has long been a screenwriting maxim. David Hare argues paradoxically that 'telling, not showing' (that is, that film is as much a verbal as a visual medium) is the truer way.[1] He's right, but not for the reasons he thinks he is. Verbal felicity is important and can be dazzling – dialogue can make or break a work – but that doesn't mean that film is a verbal art.

The Jazz Singer was the first full-length feature to carry synchronized sound, and on its arrival in 1927 it changed everything. Prior to its release, audiences inferred meaning by applying a causal connection to the juxtaposition of images. With the advent of sound however, something rather extraordinary happened – the very same audience found there was a similar relationship to be established between image and dialogue. Lev Kuleshov's research was carried out at the very beginning of movie history – when it was a purely visual medium[2] – but one of the key assets of the evolution of sound was the realization that (though never articulated as such) the Kuleshov Effect applies equally to dialogue too.

Dialogue plays an essential part in the creation of a character's façade; unless their guard is down, people speak according to the way they would like to be seen. But masks have a tendency to drop; truer intent can be glimpsed behind the words, and this occurs when the Kuleshov Effect takes place – when words are juxtaposed with action. As we've already noted, when a character says and does something contradictory, drama immediately comes alive, for a gap is created in which an audience can be active. When word and action are divorced and effectively juxtaposed, the viewer is immediately more involved. If dialogue is just telling, this doesn't happen.

Good dialogue, then, is a manifestation of behaviour, not an explanation of it. Great dialogue *shows* us who our characters are. Telling *is* showing – it reveals character.

Characterization through Dialogue

Transcribe the text of an interview with a politician on TV and it will almost certainly be full of shorthand and revisions as the speaker develops new thoughts that interrupt old ones and they search for the right words and sentences – indeed, often the right argument too. Write it down verbatim and it will look a mess.

Good dialogue doesn't resemble conversation – it presents the illusion of conversation, subservient to the demands of characterization and structure. Dialogue is not narrative either; it's not there to carry the story: dialogue is the characters' responses to the narrative – their reactions to the obstacles that litter their path. Speaking, then, is another form of 'doing' – it's a tool used by characters to negotiate their way around an obstacle. Like any action, each utterance leaves a fingerprint that helps us to trace them. As the creator of *Buffy the Vampire Slayer* and director of *The Avengers*, Joss Whedon, says:

> Everybody in your scene, including the thug flanking your bad guy, has a reason. They have their own voice, their own identity, their own history. If anyone speaks in such a way that they're just setting

up the next person's lines, then you don't get dialogue: you get soundbites . . . if you don't know who everybody is and why they're there, why they're feeling what they're feeling and why they're doing what they're doing, then you're in trouble.[3]

Dialogue must make every character individual, and in order to do that it has to fully embrace the principles of characterization. Good dialogue conveys how a character *wants* to be seen while betraying the flaws they want to hide. Comedy takes this to an extreme as both David Brent and Ali G attest, though as the former seems so familiar and the latter is so closely modelled on 'Big Dawg' rap DJ Tim Westwood – the son of an Anglican bishop – the real-life antecedents are clear.

If every choice a character makes tells us something about them, then that includes their subliminal, subconscious choices too. Each character's voice will be a result of those different choices, some probably made long before the story has begun. Grammar, vocabulary, syntax, rhythm, sentence length, jargon or slang – when combined in a particular way, they all allow us to understand who a person is. Change one and the character changes. Dialogue isn't just about what someone says; how they choose to say it is important too. Every utterance reveals something of the melting pot of desire, culture, background, worldview, status, social codes, gender, subconscious fears and upbringing – the crucible from whence they came.

These choices may be subconscious, but they are still active. When any dramatic work gets reflective, concentrates on backstory or over-explains; when you hear the words 'do you remember?' or 'that reminds me of when . . .' – you know it's a piece that's in trouble. So it is with dialogue. When it fails to be an accurate, characterized reaction to an obstacle in their pursuit of a goal, it fails. Dialogue should be the character *in* action.

16

Exposition

'Happy Wedding Day, Sis.'[1]

EXT. STEPS. WESTMINSTER ABBEY

MAN A: Isn't that the Prince Regent, only son of Queen Victoria, heir to the throne and a man whom I'm told consorts with prostitutes, standing over there?

MAN B: Yes.

In the fifth century BC, the lines spoken by Man A would have been given to the Prologue. Believed to be an invention of Euripides and often taking the form of a deity, this Prologue assumed human form to impart all the information an audience required about setting, biography, character, plot and motivation in order to follow the story. In modern parlance, the Prologue was the narrator.

If Man A was the narrator, there would be nothing wrong with our snatch of television dialogue. However, as first theatre then film and television developed an increasing emphasis on realism, the idea of a character standing outside the action began to seem anomalous. While Shakespeare dabbled with various gentlemen passing by to comment on the action (*King Henry VIII*'s First, Second and Third Gentleman), by Victorian times the role of the Prologue had been handed to the two maids gossiping about their employers – tradecraft fondly known as 'table-dusting'.[2] The device went out of fashion when, with deft hand and considerable craft, it proved possible to present all the information an audience required dramatically – and thus surreptitiously – without letting them know this was being done.

Terence Rattigan has some claim to being the first absolute master of modern realist exposition. *The Winslow Boy* is a peerless example – a theft, a trial and a national scandal all seamlessly conveyed in reported action without ever leaving the drawing room. Such a skill is rare and its mastery is one of the great 'tells' of talent – bad exposition is the first thing that will betray a writer.

Why is it so difficult? Exposition is awkward to present because it rarely occurs in real life. Exposition, after all, is *telling* and drama is *showing* – form and function are fundamentally at odds. It's the easiest thing to write badly, the hardest to write well, which is why it's such a prime target for satirists. Take a look at the following:

INT. HOLBY WARD. DAY.

The door to the private room slams open. MICKIE *looks up from her patient,* JULIA, *and frowns.* WILL *and* MUBBS *enter, on a mission.*

MICKIE: I thought Connie was coming?

WILL: Er, yeah. Not this time. Looks like you're stuck with me.

(*Behind them,* BOB *scurries in, nervous, fretting, heads over to his wife,* JULIA, *on the bed.*)

BOB: Julia, what's wrong? (*To* WILL) You said this could happen. Is her heart giving up?

JULIA: No one's giving up, I just fainted.

BOB: It's her faulty valve, isn't it? The baby's putting too much pressure on her heart, like you said it would.

WILL: Echo does show some deterioration since your last visit. But Julia collapsed because her heart isn't pumping enough blood to her brain.

JULIA: The baby's okay, isn't it?

MUBBS: We'll carry out an ultrasound to make sure. (*To* MICKIE) Can you get Julia started on some fluids?

JULIA: (*Sneering, at* WILL) I suppose you still think I should've got rid of it?

WILL: We can repair the valve after you've had your baby. But you need to understand the risks of going full term with your condition.

JULIA: The fifty per cent chance I won't make it? (*Beat*) I'll take my chances.

MUBBS: What about her medication?

WILL: (*Checking notes*) It seems to be working rather too well. I'd expect a *high* blood pressure with your condition. Yours is actually extremely low.

BOB: But that's good, isn't it? You said that high blood pressure meant that she could have a stroke.

(WILL *nods, clears his throat.*)

WILL: Yeah, but . . . this is very low. Putting Julia at risk of cardiac arrest. (*He has a sudden thought*) You did switch to the calcium blockers as we discussed?

JULIA: Yes. You said the ACE inhibitors would harm the baby.

WILL: There's no way you could have exceeded the dosage?

JULIA: I'm not an idiot!

MICKIE: I'm sure Mr Curtis wasn't implying that.

It's from *Holby City* back in 2005, though it's perhaps more reminiscent of Victoria Wood's satirical *Acorn Antiques*. In its early years Continuing Drama in Britain (and I suspect worldwide) had a tendency to believe its audience weren't very bright. Writers were actively forced to explain everything, and told that only absolute knowledge of plot points, motivation and surgical technique would keep them watching. The results were, of course, mostly turgid.[3]

Most dramatic fiction demands plausibility – for characters not to say things they wouldn't say in real life. However, characters also need to impart essential information for the audience's benefit. Just as a writer has to resolve the conflict between structural demands and 'reality', so they face the same dilemma with dialogue. How do they square the circle? How do they stop it sounding like a (very old) episode of *Holby City*? The answer, once again, lies in embracing the principles of dramatic structure.

Fundamentally there are two types of exposition:

1. conveying information that neither audience nor characters know
2. conveying information the audience needs but *all* the characters know.

Conveying information other characters don't know

Doctors and policemen inhabit so much of our dramatic terrain, not just because we're interested in matters of life and death; their value lies equally in their ability to elicit important plot information. *EastEnders* began in 1985 with the murder of Reg Cox for sound dramatic reasons: not only did it provide a great hook, it allowed the audience to access the Square through the police interrogation. That's why most new series have an ingénue too, be it Carter in *ER*, Rachel in *Friends*, Sam in *Life on Mars* or any first-year student in *Casualty*. The questions they ask provide the answers the audience need to know. Tourists and students, strangers and authority figures, all perform the same function – they provide a dramatic imperative for the facts to be explained – once again, they are us.

Conveying information all other characters do know

Life becomes considerably more complicated when a writer needs to get across information of which all the characters are aware but the audience isn't. Why would a wife, for example, tell her husband that he's got a potentially fatal illness if it's something they both already know? The inexperienced writer might begin: 'Listen, you know you've got . . .', or 'You heard what the doctor said, it's . . .' The better writer will probably plump for something more like, 'Are you completely moronic?' before repeating the point again.

Why does that work? By introducing desperation into the equation, by showing something is so important it needs to be repeated again, a *reason* is created. ('For Christ's sake, see a doctor – it's *cancer*') And where you have a reason, you have character desire.

All exposition, just like all dialogue, is driven by this desire. Indeed, bad exposition is easy to detect because the imperative that fuels all drama is absent.

Imparting information that *few* of the characters know allows the reason to be explicit. Information that *all* the characters know renders it *underlying* – in other words, it's *showing*. However, reason alone isn't always enough.

All good exposition is disguised by making it dramatic – by injecting conflict. Desire, in story structure, should always be countered by an opposite desire, and this in turn creates the conflict drama needs. The scene on the steps of Westminster Abbey at the beginning of the chapter shows exposition without conflict. If you inject contradictory goals, however, the scene automatically comes alive:

EXT. STEPS. WESTMINSTER ABBEY
Prince Regent exits Abbey.

MAN A: A fine man.

MAN B: Hardly. He's a disgrace to his mother.

MAN A: Dare you blacken the Queen's name?

MAN B: If Victoria knew her Prince Regent was a perpetual client of whores, she'd speak no more highly of him than me.

Exposition works when it's a tool a character uses to achieve their desire. If this desire is confronted with opposition, conflict is generated and exposition becomes invisible. The greater the conflict, the less visible the exposition. Exposition automatically becomes more interesting if the investigating policeman is talking to the culprit, or the doctor hates telling bad news – if the relaying of information has *impact*.

In the very first episode of *Cardiac Arrest*, Jed Mercurio (writing as John MacUre) gets a terrified junior doctor to break the news of their loved one's death to the relatives of the deceased in a scene of agonizing discomfort.

DR COLLIN *enters the relatives' room.* MRS GREY *and her friend sit by the window, eagerly awaiting news.*

DR COLLIN: Mrs Grey.

MRS GREY: You look tired, Doctor . . . why don't you have a seat?

DR COLLIN: Oh, no, please . . . er, I'm fine thanks . . . er, I wanted to, er . . . as you know, Albert wasn't a well man. He had a mesothelioma secondary . . . he had this kind of . . . this lung cancer . . . which came on because he was exposed to asbestos . . . probably, because he was exposed to . . . asbestos . . . you know, you never know for sure . . . 100 per cent yesterday . . . he wasn't a well man . . . er, we gave him injections . . . oxygen . . . nebulizers and I . . . we did everything we could for him . . . in the end, there was nothing we could do . . . actually, if there is anything you want to ask me . . . er.

MRS GREY: Well, how is Albert now? Is it very bad? Is that what you're saying?

The emotional impact renders the exposition invisible.[4] As Mercurio himself said, if you disguise exposition with 'emotional overlay', it's rendered undetectable.[5] The information about Prince Albert would take on even greater force if Man A were Albert's best friend or secret lover. Once again, good dialogue is forged in the furnace of opposition.

Apocalypse Now marries all these techniques. In the first act, Captain Willard is called before his commanding officers, who, it soon becomes apparent, are up to the same dirty tricks they are projecting onto others. In one brilliant, deft scene we learn everything we need to about all the main players in the drama – not only the crucial facts about them, but how they behave, and thus their personal standards and who they are. Note how John Milius and Francis Ford Coppola incorporate subtext, desire, conflict and the deeply personal to get across almost every fact the film needs in order to be understood.

INT. BRIEFING ROOM.

COLONEL LUCAS: Come on in . . . At ease. Want a cigarette?

WILLARD: No, thank you, sir.

LUCAS: Captain, have you ever seen this gentleman before? Met the general or myself?

WILLARD: No, sir. Not personally.

LUCAS: You have worked a lot on your own, haven't you, Captain?

WILLARD: Yes, sir, I have.

LUCAS: Your report specifies intelligence, counter-intelligence, with ComSec I Corps.

WILLARD: I'm not presently disposed to discuss these operations, sir.

LUCAS: Did you not work for the CIA in I Corps?

WILLARD: (*Uneasy*) No, sir.

LUCAS: Did you not assassinate a government tax collector in Quang Tri province, June 19th, 1968? Captain?

WILLARD: (*Realizing he's being tested*) Sir, I am unaware of any such activity or operation – nor would I be disposed to discuss such an operation if it did in fact exist, sir.

GENERAL CORMAN: (*He's passed the test*) I thought we'd have a bite of lunch while we talk. I hope you brought a good appetite with you. You have a bad hand there, are you wounded?

WILLARD: (*Lying*) A little fishing accident on R&R, sir.

CORMAN: Fishing on R&R . . . But you're feeling fit, ready for duty?

WILLARD: Yes, General. Very much so, sir.

CORMAN: Let's see what we have here . . . roast beef and . . . Usually it's not bad. Try some Jerry, pass it around. Save a little time we might we'll pass both ways. Captain, I don't know how you feel about this shrimp, but if you'll eat it, you never have to prove your courage in any other way . . . I'll take a piece here . . .

LUCAS: Captain, you heard of Colonel Walter E. Kurtz?

WILLARD: Yes, sir, I've heard the name.

LUCAS: Operations officer, 5th Special Forces.

CORMAN: Luke, would you play that tape for the captain, please. Listen carefully.

(*On tape*): October 9th, 0430 hours, sector PBK.

LUCAS: This was monitored out of Cambodia. This has been verified as Colonel Kurtz's voice.

COLONEL KURTZ: (*On tape*) I watched a snail crawl along the edge of a straight razor. That's my dream. That's my nightmare. Crawling, slithering, along the edge of a straight razor, and surviving.

(*On tape*): 11th transmission, December 30th, 0500 hours, sector KZK.

KURTZ: (*On tape*) We must kill them. We must incinerate them. Pig after pig, cow after cow, village after village, army after army. And they call me an assassin. What do you call it when the assassins accuse the assassin? They lie . . . they lie and we have to be merciful for those who lie. Those nabobs. I hate them. How I hate them . . .

CORMAN: Walt Kurtz was one of the most outstanding officers this country has ever produced. He was brilliant, he was outstanding in every way and he was a good man too. Humanitarian man, man of wit, of humor. He joined the Special Forces. And after that his ideas, methods have become unsound . . . Unsound.

LUCAS: Now he's crossed into Cambodia with his Montagnard army, who worship the man, like a god, and follow every order, however ridiculous.

CORMAN: Well, I have some other shocking news to tell you. Colonel Kurtz was about to be arrested for murder.

WILLARD: I don't follow, sir. Murdered who?

LUCAS: Kurtz had ordered executions of some Vietnamese intelligence agents. Men he believed were double agents. So he took matters into his own hands.

CORMAN: Well, you see, Willard . . . In this war, things get confused out there, power, ideals, the old morality, and practical military necessity. Out there with these natives it must be a temptation to be God. Because there's a conflict in every human heart between the rational and the irrational, between good and evil.

And good does not always triumph. Sometimes the dark side overcomes what Lincoln called the better angels of our nature. Every man has got a breaking point. You and I have. Walter Kurtz has reached his. And very obviously, he has gone insane.

WILLARD: (*Clearly unsure*) Yes, sir, very much so, sir. Obviously insane.

LUCAS: (*Uneasy*) Your mission is to proceed up to Nung River in a Navy patrol boat. Pick up Colonel Kurtz's path at Nu Mung Ba, follow it, learn what you can along the way. When you find the colonel, infiltrate his team by whatever means available and terminate the colonel's command.

WILLARD: Terminate? The colonel?

CORMAN: He's out there operating without any decent restraint. Totally beyond the pale of any acceptable human conduct. And he is still in the field commanding troops.

CIVILIAN: Terminate with extreme prejudice.

LUCAS: You understand, captain . . . that this operation does not exist, nor will it ever exist.

Every line carries each character's very clear intention. That intention may be masked, but by juxtaposing dialogue with images, by seeing Captain Willard's eyes as he denies assassinating a government tax collector, we know both that he did it and that he's proving his credentials to his superiors by denying it. We know that, because it's the Kuleshov Effect in action. Word and image combine to convey meaning beyond words – to give us subtext.

How would the scene from *Holby City* be written nowadays? Well, every writer would approach it in a different way, but the key to it will of course not lie in the dialogue at all. Much of the information about Julia's condition would be imparted previously, when it would be new to the patient, and most of the consequences would be delivered after the ultrasound. The news that Julia must have an emergency ultrasound is the only information that's really required here – that's effectively the nub of the scene – and even that can be conveyed in few if any words. Mickie, the nurse, can detect an anomaly, the patient can look worried and (subject to budget) the show can simply cut to the ultrasound being performed. Even better if Mickie tells Julia there's no need to be concerned.

Jed Mercurio, the creator of *Cardiac Arrest*, *Bodies* and *Line of Duty* said tellingly, 'Dialogue is the least important element of my writing. A lot of new writers spend an inordinate amount of time polishing dialogue to try to fix problems, when the problem is much more likely to lie in structure or character.'[6] Great dialogue, as Milius and Coppola prove, is an art, but structure remains its bedrock.

17

Subtext

On Friday, 22 November 1963, the news presenter Walter Cronkite paused on screen to pick up a message in his earpiece. 'From Dallas, Texas – a flash, apparently official . . .' his voice cracked, 'President Kennedy died at 1 p.m. Central Standard time . . .' He took off his glasses, paused, then with an almighty effort put them back on, to continue, 'Vice President Johnson has left the hospital . . .'

If you've seen it, you'll know of its impact. Certainly Kennedy's death has grown a mythic patina over the years, but there's no denying the extraordinary power of the moment Cronkite's glasses are removed, replaced, and he finds the strength to carry on. The Cronkite clip is the Kuleshov Effect in action. Presented with a phrase (the President is dead) and an action (the removal of the glasses), the audience are free to infer the truly epic nature of the news. In Cronkite we witness a man who never lost his nerve, his composure or his place being momentarily stunned beyond words. And then, because he feels it's his duty, he pulls himself together and becomes a professional once again.

Silence of the Lambs screenwriter Ted Tally put the art of writing dialogue succinctly: 'What's important is not the emotion they're playing but the emotion they're trying to conceal.'[1] Never was there a better example. Kronkite's broadcast derives its power from the emotion that lies in the subtext – from the viewer adding two and two and arriving at the answer themselves.

When Stanislavski asked his students to seek an underlying intention or objective in every line, he knew that what was said was rarely what was meant. The real meaning of dialogue was not literal – it lay beyond words. It might be in a battle for status, for control, for power, or in a desire to express love, sadness or overwhelming loss. We've already noted that every line of successful dialogue embodies an intention. However, for all kinds of reasons a character may have difficulty – or, indeed, have no desire – to make their intentions overt. Cronkite didn't feel it was his job to show emotion; his job was to do his duty, but by contrasting his words with his actions there is a subtext of overwhelming force.

Sometimes a character's desire is obvious: Michael Corleone makes no bones about his decision to murder Sollozo. But often, for any number of reasons, intention is masked, and it is from this that subtext is born.

> TREVOR: Anything you want to say?
> LITTLE MO: (*Beat*) I love you.

When Little Mo tells Trevor she loves him (*EastEnders*, 2001), it's not because it's true – the exchange occurs immediately after he has raped her on their bathroom floor. In that context her words signify an active desire for her own safety, they are used to quell the immediate threat of violence posed by her husband. She hates him but she's too scared to say it, so she tells him she loves him instead.

Subtext then emerges from the interaction between a character's façade and their actual intention or goal. Under pressure to express their true feelings, characters struggle to keep up their mask. As want collides with need, the greater truth – the gap between what characters say and do – is revealed. And that gap is the stuff of drama.

Every character comes into a scene with a desire. How they express that desire will depend on whom they're talking to, their own emotional state and where they are. As we've seen, all characters seek safety – is it safe for them to declare their intention or is there a safer way for them to achieve their goal? Much will depend on how the character wants to be perceived in each particular environment. How much of their true intention are they capable of revealing?

Safety, as we've touched on, is a subjective concept: for one character it might consist of being the highest status person in any room; for another, the lowest; for yet another it might be only if they're with their husband or wife. Wherever it's found, such security will allow overt expression; insecurity, be it with an arch-rival, a violent husband or a new girlfriend, means intention is masked and subtext occurs.

There are all kinds of reasons why characters cannot express their true feelings – ranging from their terror of doing so to their desire to manipulate others. The screenwriter's job is to convey what's underneath in a way that tells us who a character really is. Every character will attempt, for example, seduction differently.

A man walks up to a woman at a bar:

1. MAN: I'm going to take your clothes off.
2. MAN: I really like you.
3. MAN: Bit chilly for the time of year, isn't it?
4. MAN: Think you're special, don't you?

The further down the list you go, the more the intention is masked, though the underlying one – seduction – remains the same. Not only will audiences infer the true intention; they may also infer a good deal about the character. Man 4's almost naked aggression suggests a hinterland of troubles and concerns.

So masked desire is the main source of subtext. Sometimes this façade can be a conscious deception of others – as simple as that perpetrated by the gang in *The Ladykillers* or Ash, the duplicitous doctor (Ian Holm) in *Alien*. However, the façade can just as easily be an unconscious deception of the self – the result of even greater conflict and its subsequent ego defence mechanism.

The Curse of Steptoe by Brian Fillis is a fictionalized account of the massively successful BBC sitcom of the 1960s and 1970s and the effect of fame on its two stars. There's a key scene where one of them – Harry H. Corbett (Jason Isaacs) – is being interviewed on television:

INTERVIEWER: If we could turn now to *Steptoe and Son*. Your most famous creation. The rag and bone man . . .

HARRY: No! The rag and bone don't mean a thing. I mean I'm not interested in making a documentary about rag and bone men. No it's . . . er . . . when Harold . . . the domestic work is over and done within five, ten minutes. It's all politics. It's about . . . sex. It's about, er . . . general economics . . . a thousand and one things . . . the Church. Whatever you care to mention, but it's certainly not about . . . er . . . the rag and bone business. None of it . . . surprisingly enough, er, relies on . . . uh . . . double-takes, pratfalls, joey-joey grimaces, whatever you want to call it. It relies on . . . the words. And the timing. And . . . being faithful, being true to the subject matter.

The fictional Corbett, terrified of not being taken seriously, is unable to accept he just makes people laugh; he has to show his intellectual credentials.[2]

A character's façade isn't always a conscious construct – they aren't necessarily aware of the desire they're masking. The way characters lie both to others and to themselves provides an extraordinarily rich seam. Georg Simmel, the nineteenth-century sociologist, put it rather eloquently: 'All we communicate to another individual by means of words or perhaps in another fashion – even the most subjective, impulsive, intimate matters – is a selection from that psychological-real whole whose absolutely exact report . . . would drive everybody into the insane asylum.'[3] Without subtext you have a flat, linear world; everything is literal, everything spoken is meant. With subtext the writer is able to access the gap between language and thought, and in playing there, to come much closer to capturing some kind of truth.

A former BBC executive once said to me of *Casualty*, 'Oh God, please don't make it good.' The belief – particular (though not exclusive) to the soap world – that audiences aren't very bright, that they'll somehow be alienated by 'real' drama, creates a particularly toxic problem when it comes to subtext. Bad producers fear it because it requires interpretation; but that, of course, is its very point. Interpretation is the process by which the audience becomes an active participant in the drama. It doesn't alienate, it does the opposite; the minute it's deployed the writer increases their chances of hooking an audience in. As a junior script editor, I had to sit through too many meetings where every line that carried an inherent meaning was replaced with a literal one – watching as the blood was slowly drained out of a living, exciting work. Whatever a person's IQ, they can easily pick up on a nurse telling a patient that 'everything's fine' when it's not. They get it, just as they join in the game of guessing the culprit in a thriller; or shout answers at the telly when watching *Who Wants To Be a Millionaire?*

It's for the same reason that voice-over narrations almost uniformly don't work. Prolonged viewing of the American TV series *Pushing Daisies*, or even Jean-Pierre Jeunet's *A Very Long Engagement* (*Un long dimanche de fiançailles*), becomes almost impossible despite their ravishing visual beauty. In both, narrators tell you everything – there's no subtext – there's simply nothing for the audience to *do*. It's true too of Francis Ford Coppola's sumptuous *One From the Heart* – Tom Waits and Crystal Gayle appear to be beckoning you in, but instead, as their lyrics tell you everything, they push you away. Telling has replaced showing and the audience is made redundant.

It's for the very same reason that unreliable voice-overs are joyous. In *F For Fake* Orson Welles is a wonderfully devious narrator, but no one has ever quite matched one of the very first fictional liars. *Gulliver's Travels* takes the eponymous hero on a tour of human vanity and effectively dramatizes his growing disdain for the species responsible. Gulliver's increasing application of 'rationality' leads him to believe, finally, that men are so stupid the only creatures he can converse with are horses. In the interplay between the reality he describes and the way he interprets it (he ends up living in a stable, happily communing with a horse), his own madness is revealed. It is the gap between what he does and how he describes it and the growing disjunction between the two that Jonathan Swift exploits (the Kuleshov Effect again) to dramatize its horrifying birth – made more horrifying by the narrator's complete inability to recognize his own condition.

Explanation kills drama, as does the impulse to make everything everyone says immediately clear. Characters who explain their own

motives automatically sound false; partly because few but the pathological are likely to let truth shine straight through their own façade,
but also because, as Montaigne noted, 'No description is as difficult
as the description of self.' True self-knowledge is gifted to the very
few – if anything it's the endpoint of a story, not a tool to aid author-
ial exposition.

It's simply not true, as any episode of *The West Wing, Holby City* or *ER*
makes abundantly clear, that you need to understand every word of
dialogue. What you need to infer, of course, is the character's *intention*.
An audience doesn't need to know how to perform surgery. Though
they may enjoy the obscure scientific jargon a surgeon will use, they
only need to know of their goal – normally to save their patient. Secondary school pupils are taught early on that they can work out the
meaning of individual words from those that surround them, and viewers are more than able – and willing – to do the same. (If still in doubt,
read David S. Ward's masterful screenplay of *The Sting* – it doesn't
explain *anything*.) As David Simon says, the belief in television that an
audience needs to be spoon-fed can only have one outcome: every character will talk the same way. I witnessed this at first-hand on *EastEnders*
many years ago, when first of all every regional accent was banned, and
then (very briefly) every cockney one as well. It seemed the makers of
television had simply forgotten that two of the biggest hits of the previous decade – *Auf Wiedersehen, Pet* and *Minder* – revelled in a colloquial
dialect alien to all but a very small part of their audience.

King Lear tells the story of a man who, on condemning Cordelia
for speaking as she feels, learns the cost of the gap between speech
and thought. As protagonists journey towards completion, they
learn to heal the duality in their nature, between inner and outer
worlds, want and need, façade and flaw. To this list we must now
add word and deed. When Lear learns, in Edgar's words, to 'Speak
what we feel, not what we ought to say' he realizes the horrible
truth about façades, and the need to reconcile them with truth. In
doing so we realize that dialogue – and its ability to mask as much
as it reveals – is as indispensable a part of structure as character, act
division, inciting incident and story.

Act V
Home Again, Changed

18

Television and the Triumph of Structure

On 14 July 1930, shortly before 3.30 p.m., the British Prime Minister Ramsay MacDonald settled down in his armchair in 10 Downing Street to watch Britain's first television drama,[1] transmitted live from the Baird Company headquarters in Covent Garden by a fledgling BBC.[2] Sadly, MacDonald's thoughts on the adaptation of Pirandello's *The Man with the Flower in his Mouth* are lost to posterity. Fortunately however, *The Times* recorded its own impressions and, in a slightly acid review, noted, 'This afternoon . . . will prove to be a memorable one.'[3] The work itself may not have endured, but its legacy has changed entirely the way we consume stories.

British television drama is derived from the country's rich theatrical tradition. When the BBC started its regular service in 1936 its first dramatic effort was a selection of scenes from *Marigold*, a West End hit of the day transmitted live from Alexandra Palace. 'It was probably little more than a photographed version of the stage production, with the camera lying well back to preserve the picture-frame convention of the theatre,'[4] reflected Shaun Sutton, a later head of BBC Drama, and for many years it was simply accepted that that's how drama was done – it was a filmed play. Over time, cameras began to move, the basic vocabulary of television (the cross-fade, the fade-out) was introduced and the occasional use of location inserts allowed. There was the beginning of experiments with form: *Ann and Harold* has the distinction of being the first recorded example of a serial – five episodes in the life of a couple; and *Telecrime* was a series of bold ten- or twenty-minute dramas in which the audience was shown enough clues to work out the culprit of the crime themselves.[5] But the basic assumption that television was a branch of theatre, a static, sedentary medium in which visual image is subordinate to dialogue, was to continue for many more years – and in some cases to the present day.

The pivotal figure in the development of modern British TV drama was Sydney Newman. Canadian by birth, he was invited to join ABC Television, holders of the Northern and Midland weekend franchise for ITV, shortly after British commercial television began. As both a serious man and an instinctive populist, he was responsible for both *Armchair Theatre* and *The Avengers*, defining the parameters within which ITV was to operate with extraordinary success for many years to come.

In 1962 Newman accepted the invitation to become Head of BBC Drama and set about building a department that championed new writing, new forms, new ideas – but most importantly of all was unafraid to be popular. Perhaps his most important decision was to divide drama into three separate sub-departments: series, serials and plays – divisions that still define the genre to this day. Plays were soon to transform themselves into single films, and continuing drama (or soaps) was to assume much greater significance in later years, but these – and all further variations – were merely offshoots or hybrids of the elements Newman identified.

Storytelling had come a long way from a few people listening around a campfire. The desire to placate loneliness, to silence boredom, to share – all were met and fuelled first by the printed word, then by film and radio, and now by television; technology had uncorked the genie and made previously intimate local experiences universal. In less than fifty years, TV had grown from an eccentric and expensive folly to become the dominant way the world devoured narrative. It still is. The industry and its drama arm succeeded far beyond anything Ramsay MacDonald could have imagined – but how to feed such a vast appetite for product? By manipulating basic dramatic structure.

While Newman's three categories certainly still exist, series, serials and singles have been bastardized, corrupted, or – some would argue – improved to meet the insatiable demands of their audience. Some will assert too that something has been lost.

Structure and its manipulation are at the root of all genres of television drama. To understand this, we need first to be familiar with exactly what makes up the three types of storytelling Newman himself identified.

Single Films

Newman's department called these 'plays' for obvious reasons. Completely self-contained stories with beginning, middle and end, their literary antecedents were very clear. More often than not these were studio-bound pieces and until the late 1960s they were mostly transmitted live. As the medium developed, the language of film became more apparent (1965's *Up the Junction* is still striking in its contemporary feel) – though studio-shooting on videotape was only finally abandoned in the late 1980s when a cinematic vocabulary was fully adopted.

Serials (in America 'Mini-Series')

The basic form of serials can be traced back to the novels of Charles Dickens and their contemporary method of publication: one story released chapter by chapter to build to a complete whole. Indeed, the literary adaptation may well be how the serial gained its foothold in television. Versions of classic novels told in serial form have been a staple of television commissioning. The extraordinary success of the BBC's *The Forsyte Saga* in 1967 created the template and began a golden age that arguably peaked with ITV's *Brideshead Revisited* in 1981, shot entirely on location and using a film grammar (and budget) unseen elsewhere on television at that time.

Series

When Edgar Allan Poe created in C. Auguste Dupin the world's first fictional detective, he stumbled on a format that would give rise to the most successful television genre of all. Regular returning characters investigating their case of the week were originally just policemen, but as the series genre spread from the novels and short stories of Conan Doyle through comic books and onto the radio, many other types of regularly returning 'problems' did as well. 'Crime of the week' could just as easily be 'medical emergency', 'threat to national security' or even 'Alien' of the week. A medium in its infancy that began by copying radio realized very quickly that this classic series format (self-contained story of the week with regular characters that never changed) was a kind of grail. The heroes never died; there was an endless supply of story material; they were cheap to make and immensely popular – what was not to like?

Ladies and gentlemen: the story you are about to hear is true. Only the names have been changed to protect the innocent.

The opening lines of *Dragnet* resonate sixty years after their creation. Like the series itself, they linger in the public consciousness, most of us familiar with their content if not their origins. A whole generation may not know the show, but they will be more than familiar with the idea of a cop vanquishing a different rival every week. The template it created lent itself immediately to the new medium. Action, adventure, a hero who never changed and a never-ending diet of stories with happy endings – the same structure dominates the vast majority of what we still watch today. When *Dragnet* began on US radio in 1949, no one, least of all its creator Jack Webb, could have predicted its influence. Transferring to television in 1951, it quickly became a massive worldwide hit. Television watched and learned and drama series have been a core constituent of any schedule ever since: they are, by quite some length, the most dominant and significant structural form.

Western series like *Gunsmoke*, *Bonanza*, *Rawhide* and medical and police procedurals from *Dixon of Dock Green* to *Dr Finlay's Casebook* proved that not only could the one-off hits of cinema be milked endlessly (*Dixon* and *Naked City* were derived from successful films –

indeed, in the former, PC Dixon had actually been murdered) but, more importantly, that endless repetition was actually attractive to audiences who loved building long-term relationships with characters who never changed and never seemed to grow old.

Partly because of their cheapness and, I suspect, popularity, the genre is often perceived to occupy the inferior if not trashy end of the dramatic spectrum. When I first joined BBC Drama in the 1990s, it was almost impossible to find someone who wanted to work in this populist arena – everyone, it seemed, simply wanted to make their own (preferably black and white) film. Yet a roll call of some of the most famous and enduring series – *The Waltons*, *Star Trek*, *Doctor Who*, *The Sweeney*, *Kung Fu*, *Minder* and *All Creatures Great and Small* – is enough to signal a Proustian rush to all but the most hard of heart. Noël Coward remarked in *Private Lives* on the potency of 'cheap music' – the ability of the unashamedly commercial and populist to sneak under your skin and move you. So too with drama series. Many are, in truth, not very good; like all popular art they can be the victim of too much haste, budget constriction and cynicism, but it's easy to judge them too harshly. As Hitchcock found in his own time, nothing decreases critical appreciation so much as popularity. With the advent of *Spooks* and *Shameless* in Britain, and the rise of cable in the US, the genre underwent something of a renaissance. As a new generation began to realize, series at their best not only form a powerful bond with their audience; in skilled hands they are capable of great emotional depth – an art-form in their own right.

Out of singles, series and serials, then, emerged a myriad of structural variations: two-parters, three-parters, series with a serial element, serials that returned endlessly. The most ubiquitous for many years has been, of course, continuing drama or soap. Effectively a serial without end, it married the key elements of serial and series structure to produce an awesome commercial beast. Fuelled by an endless appetite for new narrative forms, however (first DVDs, then the internet, have provided a whole new lease of life), the basic structural forms of series and serials are still the genetic material of the on-going revolution. They're worth examining in more detail.

19

Series and Serial Structure

Serial Structure

Peter Moffat's *Criminal Justice* was a five-episode BBC television drama about a young student, Ben Coulter, who sleeps with a girl he's just met and wakes to discover she's been murdered. Panicking, he tries to cover his tracks, but his consequent actions, alongside a welter of forensic evidence, point clearly to his guilt. At the end of episode one he's thrown into the justice system and the story then follows his horrific experience of penal life, his fight to clear his name, and his eventual acquittal. There's a very simple structure to the first episode: the inciting incident is Ben waking to find the body beside him; the worst point is his arrest; and the last act his incarceration. But looking more widely, something else is going on too.

If the story is about a man being wrongly imprisoned and seeking release, then the end of the first episode acts as an inciting incident for the series as a whole. Episode two sees him learning the ways of a new and terrifying world; in episode three he resists his barrister's attempts to concoct a false story and demands that the truth be told (a classic midpoint); at the end of the fourth episode, his mother lets him know she thinks he is guilty (the worst kind of worst point); and in episode five the truth finally emerges. The whole story paradigm thus appears not just in each individual episode (each one has its own inciting incident, midpoint and crisis) but on a macro scale across the whole series too.

In the first series of the modern reboot of *Doctor Who*, the Doctor found himself battling an individual Dalek halfway through and then a whole army of them in the last instalment. In the penultimate episode of series one of *The Killing*, Sarah Lund's partner is brutally murdered – as is Amy in series one of *The Walking Dead*; as is Creighton in series one of David Simon's New Orleans drama *Treme*; as is Wallace in series one of *The Wire*. The fractal nature of drama asserts itself again – each series arc contains the very same structural elements as every episode, every act and every scene. A three-episode BBC adaptation of *Great Expectations* (2011) is divided into home (Magwitch and the marshes), journey (London) and return (the marshes again). Edgar Reitz's *Heimat* sets its first and last series in the fictional village of Schabbach, with a middle played out entirely in Munich; and series two of *The Walking Dead* contains a terrible gruesome truth – both literally and structurally – exactly halfway through its run.

Each episode of a serial is effectively, then, an act in the overall story. Serial structure mimics our standard act form and adjusts itself according to the scale of the story. In a six-parter, the midpoint will be in episode three; in a two-parter it will be the cliffhanger of the first episode. In Neil McKay's dramatization of the aftermath of the Fred West murders (ITV's *Appropriate Adult*), part one ends with the revelation that the seemingly innocent Rose West is as guilty as her husband. The first series of *Homeland* fits the fractal pattern to an almost comical degree. In episode seven of twelve, the protagonist (a CIA agent) and antagonist (a war hero suspected of being an enemy assassin) admit vital truths to each other and have sex, after which nothing can be the same again. The location? A cabin in the woods.

Is that conscious design? I suspect not. It's simply the primacy of the story shape reasserting itself again. The same fractal pattern can be observed in *Harry Potter* – seven books, each with their own beginning, middle and end; each with a classic quest structure and an archetypal midpoint in the fourth book when Voldemort is defeated for the first time (*The Goblet of Fire*). This obvious midpoint tips the saga from threat into open warfare, and leads directly to the death, in the penultimate tome, *The Half-Blood Prince*, of the father figure, Dumbledore. The same shapes come at us relentlessly, manipulated, rebuilt, but still somehow the same. It's possible to observe in any coherent work, whatever its duration, drama's fractal form.

Series Structure

What defines successful series? If we were to make a small but representative list of the drama series that had proved a major influence on the television landscape over the last fifty years, then one might include: *Star Trek, All Creatures Great and Small, Minder, The Sweeney, ER, Z Cars, Casualty, Hill Street Blues, The Waltons, Call the Midwife, Gunsmoke, Grey's Anatomy, Dragnet, Colombo*. It's an absurdly selective choice from a vast field, but useful for our purpose. What do they have in common?

Inevitably they all contain a self-contained story of the week; that is, after all, what makes them series. Each has a clear and renewable story engine, vital obviously for sustaining output over time. And there are very clear format rules too – in every show there are rigorously enforced points of view: *Casualty* will follow both regular characters and guests; *The Waltons* or *Hill Street Blues* will only ever meet their antagonists through the eyes of the regulars. There's almost universally a sense of status, a pecking order in which everyone knows their place; and of course empathy is absolutely vital – each have iconic and hugely lovable characters. Successful series, then, are built on the backs of certainty, of predictability and of the audience's loves – on their wish to be there too. So much perhaps is obvious – but there's more.

They're all uplifting, they all end each week happily; they all understand that audiences want to feel good and want to be entertained; they understand that if something depresses viewers it's unlikely they'll come back for more. If archetypal stories end with completion, with 'happy ever after', then series television is the perfect scaled-down product of the form. In episode one of CBS's *The Good Wife*, Alicia Florrick finds herself the innocent victim of a public sex and corruption scandal for which her husband is thrown in jail. Left with nothing but the clothes she stands up in, she has no choice but to beg for her old job as a litigator and against every conceivable obstacle (all in one forty-five-minute episode) win an impossible case. It's a master class in series TV. Somehow it retains its plausibility, it's impossible not to love the heroine and by the end it has you cheering on your feet. Story engine, lovable protagonist, self-contained story, rigorous format – all are laid out clearly and persuasively before us.

It's instructive to compare it with British television, which, though there have been significant advances since the advent of *Spooks*, has had a far more uncomfortable relationship with the series form. British drama often used to forget a central tenet – the protagonist is *us*. We might be moved by injustice in a single film (though the viewership will be small) but it's going to take a very particular kind of audience to empathize on a long-term returning basis with someone who fails. From *Beck* (1996) to *Outcasts* (2010) via *Buried* (2003) and *Paradox* (2009), British television for many years struggled to grasp this prerequisite, illustrating, I think, the unease with which serious people can approach a populist form. All the above had either deeply unempathetic characters or heroes who failed. All failed themselves too – within one series – and most were dead after one episode. It's a harsh and annoying reality, particularly for those who like to see work that subverts the norm, but only a relatively small, self-selecting group is going to tune in on a weekly basis to live by proxy the life of a failure.

Whether we feel comfortable with it or not, series television is built on an undeniable truth. While NBC's *Friday Night Lights* told the story every week of a small-town football team able to snatch victory from the jaws of defeat, ITV's bold 2012 *Titanic*, by telling the same tale four times from four different points of view, managed to give itself four unhappy endings – five if one counts the overnight ratings as well.

Isn't this all a bit trite? The *Titanic* did sink after all. Should drama reflect life rather than massage it with the glibness happiness can often bestow? Doesn't British TV have an integrity its former colony lacks? Happy endings – or the lack of them – are an important area to explore (nothing creates more friction in the corridors of television power) because, inevitably too, the secret to them lies in structure.

Writing of *The Wire*, David Simon announced grandly: 'We are bored with good and evil. We renounce the theme.'[1] Immediately casting himself as the good guy, and sticking black hats on every TV executive who'd dared to tell a story that ends 'happily ever after', Simon denounced their Manichaean worldview, while (it has to be noted) falling into the same trap himself. Is he right? 'For generations now the televised reflection of the American experience . . . has come down to us from on high. Westerns and police procedurals and legal dramas – all of it conceived in Los Angeles and New York by industry professionals, then shaped by huge corporate entities to reassure viewers that their world and their future are better and brighter than they in fact are, that the time was never more right to buy more automobiles, cell phones, dish soap and disposable diapers.'[2] Happy endings, Simon seems to suggest, are a form of prostitution.

It's absolutely undeniable that there's an economic pay-off if audiences return – simply too many dark works fail, however well made (and the irony is they often are exceptionally well made). Television demands success, and that can lead to a deep cynicism, but despite that Simon's worldview is as simplistic as the one he denounces. How would we feel if Hansel and Gretel were chained to a bed, sexually violated, then entombed in a suburban back garden just as the credits rolled? Certainly it might be more 'realistic'; and it would undeniably spell out the subtext inherent in the tale; but getting the two children home safely isn't just a product of market economics, it isn't just a question of 'selling out' – it embodies one of the essential functions of story.

No one is suggesting shows can't end in jeopardy, or even extreme distress or exhilaration. For a child, terror is a necessary part of *Doctor Who* – but only as something that can be assimilated and thus slowly understood. To end on nihilism, with Hansel and Gretel chained to a paedophile's bed, is absolutely valid, but not *just* that – the version with the happy ending is critical too. When the legendary Indian actor Amitabh Bachchan asked his father what made Indian films so interesting and exciting, he simply replied, 'You get poetic justice in three hours. You don't get poetic justice in a whole lifetime sometimes.'[3] We watch stories not just to awaken our eyes to reality but to make reality bearable as well. Truth without hope is as unbearable as hope without truth. Every healthy broadcaster should have room for *The Wire* and *The Waltons* – just as every healthy head should perhaps do too.[4]

What other criteria do successful series share? In the early 1970s, shows like *Kung Fu* and *Alias Smith and Jones* were common. In each episode the protagonists arrived in a new town to find themselves combating the evil they discovered there. Clearly derived from the tale of the 'knight errant', by the end of the decade they'd all but disappeared. The template survives to this day in novel form (Lee Child's Jack Reacher being the most successful current manifestation), but it's no longer a staple of most broadcasters, simply because it's significantly cheaper to have one key setting that lasts a whole series than a different location each week. Economic necessity has been a major factor in making the shows 'precinct-based'. While it's a shame to have lost the scale a travelling hero gives you, the imposition of one main set has, as restrictions often do, allowed writers to discover something very important: by concentrating on a character's 'home' they've found one of the most potent weapons in the series armoury – it is impossible to underrate the importance of the precinct in which the character dwells. *Battlestar Galactica* or *The Waltons* fetishize this, but it underpins almost every successful show. Take a look at the very first episode of *ER*. When Dr Greene rejects a private job offer with a six-figure salary, four holidays a year and a shower of additional benefits for a run-down inner-city Chicago public hospital, the story is telling us that this place matters, this place is *home*.

And so you realize that series aren't just successful because they're repetitive and cheap; they're not necessarily worse because their characters don't change. Instead, they tap into something much deeper – our craving for safety, security and love – a family that will stand by us and save us when the rest of the world attacks us or doesn't understand. The underlying format of all successful series is very simple – the enemy is without. Each week the precinct is invaded by a physical manifestation of the 'other' – the sick patient, the psycho killer, the lost soul – aliens in every shape and form – and every week the regulars make things better and order is restored. Every week our regular characters, our gang, our family are threatened by an external peril, which they defeat by overcoming their differences and working together. Only when Sam and Gene collaborate in *Life on Mars* can they defeat their common enemy; only when Spock, Kirk and McCoy work together can the Klingon peril be repelled. Series effectively replicate the very earliest experiences of childhood – when we felt safe, secure and, when threatened, were able, with the help of those around us, to assimilate and control the outside world. It's no accident that almost all the successful series have at their centre family structures. From *The High Chaparral* to *NYPD Blue*, all have father or mother figures (sometimes both), love interests, junior members, distant cousins; all at some level create a primal sense of true family life.

Series, finally, are also 'moral'. It's easy to underestimate the importance of dispensed justice, or what Hitchcock called 'the retribution clause'. *Hustle* may be about a bunch of conmen, but really they're avenging angels, punishing the greedy, the vain and the truly corrupt; as the characters repeatedly tell us, 'You can't con an honest man'. *Shameless* may appear to be amoral but strip it back and it's exactly the same programme (right down to the framing voice-over) as *The Waltons* – in both the family come together through love to expel the enemy. True, the enemy may have a very different guise – the police occupy a very different position on the Chatsworth Estate to those on the Blue Ridge Mountains – but the shape of the battle between protagonist and antagonist is exactly the same: a secure home is threatened, taken on a journey into the woods and shaken up, but the values of home triumph and safety is restored once again. It may sound glib, indeed it can *be* glib, but master the form and it produces extraordinarily potent work. From *The Waltons* and

Minder to *Battlestar Galactica* or *Call the Midwife* one must sometimes don a hair-shirt to stay immune to the power of the utterly archetypal.

Successful series, then, are almost entirely built on structural purity, but there is one pertinent digression from the norm. The dialectical theory we've used to explain dramatic structure so far is most commonly termed Hegelian – after the nineteenth-century philosopher's belief that a new stage is created from the synthesis of two opposites. The protagonist is *changed* – though, of course, in series the protagonist *isn't*. So while series are absolutely archetypal in seeking a happy ending, in seeking completion, they do it in a slightly different way. For series embody a more classical kind of dialectic: thesis meets antithesis and they fight it out, only for the antithesis to be refuted. In *The Waltons* or *Spooks* our heroes don't assimilate the facets of their opposite, they simply vanquish them and return to type, for the world of series is a world without change. The counter-argument must be rejected and the thesis restored. At the heart of their success, as we've seen, lies repetition, and out of repetition formats are born.

But repetition creates problems of its own; and it's striking how short the lifespans of most television series are. It's easy to conjecture that failure is down to a lack of artistic imagination, but it's more complex than that: the structural demands of series carry with them the seeds of their own destruction – a destruction born from the problems created by the very lifeblood of their success.

20

Change in Drama Series

A great part of our day in the writers' room is spent saying, 'We've done that . . .' We did towards the end start to think, 'Are there any natural disasters left? We're not really in the right climate for volcanoes and floods.'

Bob Daily, Executive Producer, *Desperate Housewives*[1]

Why does almost every series that doesn't regularly refresh its characters have a life span of only two to three years? BBC1's *Spooks* endured for ten largely because its high-stakes world allowed for the continual plausible replacement of its core cast, but with one or two notable exceptions most shows either call it quits at the top of their game (*Life on Mars*, *Fawlty Towers* or *The Office*) or die a slow, painful death from diminishing returns (*Minder*, *Only Fools and Horses* and arguably *The West Wing* too). Why do most characters in soap also seem to dissipate over time and find themselves in endlessly similar repetitive storylines, becoming paler shadows of their former selves?

The answer is simple. Characters have only one story, and all attempts to counter that are a lie. Soaps and series are lies – great and glorious ones if the lies are well told, but lies nonetheless.[2] Soaps and series are partly a product of market economics, born from a desire to attract viewers and sell to them – but equally, like sequels, they tap into an audience's desire to prolong the lives of characters they adore. As with those we love in real life, we want our fictitious friends to live forever. Authors and television executives recognize this and acknowledge too that it's much easier to attract people to the readily familiar, the tried and the tested. And so the lie is told again.

Drama demands that characters must change, but the audience by and large – 'we', let's be honest – insist they stay exactly the same. Hollywood realized this from the very beginning and set about resolving the contradiction. In the 'golden age' of the studio system they created stars who were effectively one character – a Bogart or a Dietrich – and so could appear in a series of different adventures. Then, as the studio system began to fade, sequels came to play a more important role.

Ninety-five per cent of them are a disappointment. The notable exceptions – *Terminator 2*, *Aliens*, the *Toy Storys* or *The Godfather II* – have clear structural reasons why they are as good if not better than their predecessors: either they change the protagonist's flaw or the nature and scale of the antagonist, or, in the case of *The Godfather*, continue the tragic journey all the way to spiritual death. Most sequels, though, shirk the challenge. In the conflict between milking a product and making a great work of art there tends to be only one winner. When you watch the *Lethal Weapon*, *Die Hard*, *Hangover* or *Airplane* franchises, you can almost see the template of the original stamping itself reluctantly, with a hint of self-loathing, onto the celluloid again.

Film studios have perhaps thrown too much ingenuity into fighting the irrefutable law of character mortality; legions of creatives seem preoccupied with refusing to accept that the change that gives life-blood to drama inevitably also ends in its death. The archives are littered with attempts to circumvent the demands of story structure and process it into a marketable, digestible commodity; anything is permissible to keep a product alive. Sequels (and even prequels now) have led to franchises, and when they wither, as they inevitably do, they now find themselves rebooted once again. Every generation – even every decade – is now threatened with a *Batman* 'for our times'.

But how about television? Deep down we expect film franchises to wane, but drama series are by definition a returning medium; they *must* reproduce to survive. Series characters can't get to the end of their journey or the story is over, so their creators face the same dilemma as Hollywood but massively amplified. How do they create change in a world where their characters must always stay the same?

In pure series it's not impossible. In *Dragnet* or *Starsky and Hutch* time stands still and the characters never age; each week they are reborn as before to fight a new mission once again. Stubbornly two-dimensional, they exist outside time and space, bound to their hamster wheel. It works brilliantly, but the temptation always remains for writers to introduce a serial element, to allow characters to grow.

Steven Bochco's 1981 series for NBC, *Hill Street Blues*, revolutionized US television by introducing running serial storylines in which just such growth could occur. Years later, the BBC's *Only Fools and Horses* was tempted down the same road. It was a very successful sitcom already, but when its creator John Sullivan decided to deepen it by lengthening the episodes and introducing birth, marriage and death – that is, corporeality – it became a broadcasting phenomenon. He gave it mortality, which made it real, but because life can't exist without its opposite, it sowed the seeds of its future demise. It was the same with *Hill Street*. In both, the characters exhausted themselves, the storyliners reached for ever more implausible things for their stars to do and they ground to an undignified halt. Faced with the challenge of volume *Desperate Housewives* found itself, like many, grasping for sensation. The annual 'disaster' episode became a ritual and over eight seasons a tornado, a fire, a plane crash and a riot all hit Wisteria Lane. As one of its stars, Eva Longoria, said, 'How many more affairs can you have? And how many more deaths?'[3]

Most of us have been frustrated by long-running shows where ingénue characters never seem to learn from their experiences, or equally annoyed when they do learn and stop being the character we first fell in love with. Outside of single stories or worlds unaffected by time, change is a very difficult conceit to manage. If it's not done well, it leads to immediate and fairly grotesque implausibility from which follow all the hideous clichés that soap in particular *can* be blamed for. But it can be done.

The basic tools in a show-runner's armoury are to make change small, two-dimensional or temporary, but the most potent weapon in the box is selective amnesia. Nothing is as useful in long-running drama as the fine art of forgetting.

Many years ago in *EastEnders*, Michelle Fowler's baby Vicki was snatched from her pram outside a supermarket. The child was missing for a month and Michelle was forced amongst other things to make a nationwide TV appeal, admit she was a failure as a mother and partially (though not correctly) accept that she was responsible. To the relief of all, Vicki was discovered safe and sound and Michelle slowly began to rebuild her life. So far so good. In real life, however, the chances of any full psychological recovery would be minimal – the level of trauma, of guilt and of public notoriety would leave a lifetime's scars. Michelle entirely forgot about it, and after six weeks it was never to be mentioned again.

In cop shows a regular character will often learn a valuable lesson – they will just forget it again by the following week. When we made *Life on Mars*,[4] John Simm (who played Sam Tyler) used to get frustrated that his character never seemed to learn anything, just as Gene never learned anything about him. John had almost entirely worked in single films and so was unused to the idea that character change was impossible. Every week in *Life on Mars* Sam learned to be a little bit more instinctive and Gene a little more rational; but the next week they went back to how they were to learn the same lesson again. John was completely right logically, but without the amnesia the character journeys would be over and the dynamic of the series destroyed. Sam and Gene couldn't, until the very end, get on.

At the end of the second series everybody felt we'd pushed it far enough. There were a number of key serial arcs running that made total forgetfulness almost impossible to believe; the more times the restart button was pressed the less believable the universe threatened to become. In an entirely self-contained world (*Father Brown/Kojak*) this doesn't matter; anywhere else it does. But why forget? Why not build on a character's rich heritage? There is an exchange from Sammy to her boyfriend in Channel 4's long-running soap *Brookside* which should perhaps be hung on every show-runner's wall. Trying to recall a forgotten event, she prodded him: 'You remember, it was when you were in a wheelchair, and I was an alcoholic.'

'Jumping the shark' became a glorious metaphor for the moment any show runs out of creative steam. It was inspired by an episode of the 1970s sitcom *Happy Days* in which its star, the Fonz, paid a trip to Florida to water-ski-jump over said fish. So absurd in its conception, so far from the original DNA of the series, the episode was to give its name to a website (www.jumptheshark.com) dedicated to marking the moment of creative death that occurs when a plot is generated from pure sensation or absurdity. *Brookside* contained perhaps the very best British example of this, too, when the middle-class Liverpool housing estate found itself harbouring a flesh-eating killer virus. With seventy-four unnatural deaths in twenty-one years, the series itself succumbed not long after.

As American series in particular are contracted for seven or eight seasons, you can see where the sometimes desperate search for story material leads. Outside of natural disasters show-runners seek story by fiddling with plot dynamics or resolving long-standing sexual (or other) tensions. As *Moonlighting* and *Frasier* both attest, such tinkering rarely works. When Maddie and David and Niles and Daphne became couples and 'will they?/won't they?' became 'they have', viewers had nothing to root for. The story engine that drove each show was turned off as the characters' goals were achieved, the questions were answered and their quests complete.

And yet all characters in drama naturally seek completion. As Macbeth says after his plan to kill both Banquo and his son goes awry:

> . . . I had else been perfect;
> Whole as the marble, founded as the rock,
> As broad and general as the casing air.

Every great story in drama forces the protagonist to confront their needs and flaws and if a character does overcome them they're complete – but dead. The golden rule in series is that the needs/flaws should either be overcome fleetingly, or possibly never, but certainly not until the final episode – which is why the relationships between Donna and Josh in *The West Wing* and Rachel and Ross in *Friends* worked so well. Nice as it was to see an old friend, *Only Fools and Horses* really should have ended when Del Boy and Rodney became millionaires.

In recent times the sovereignty of shark-jumping has been threatened by 'Nuking the fridge' – coined from the spectacularly implausible way Indiana Jones escapes an atomic explosion in *Kingdom of the Crystal Skull*. All series that outstay their welcome tend to 'jump the shark', but they 'nuke the fridge' because structurally they don't have any choice. Unless they have a plausible story engine, a regular throughput of new and different characters, or stay stubbornly in two dimensions (thus removing themselves from the ravages of time), they will almost always die, spiritually if not physically, after an average of around three seasons. There's a striking pattern to it: year one is initial enthusiasm, year two consolidation, year three is 'what on earth do we do now'?

21

Home Again

Out of our quarrel with others we make rhetoric; out of the quarrel with ourselves we make poetry.

W. B. Yeats

Jimmy McGovern was an angry young schoolteacher when he started working on *Brookside* thirty years ago; he was also the most exciting new writer on British television. He wrote about working-class life with a rawness and intensity that stopped you mid-step – no one, you felt, had ever written with such anger, such humour; no one had trumpeted quite so eloquently the socialist ideals they believed in. The show was a bastion of old Labour values, largely conveyed through the figures of Bobby Grant, a shop steward, and his supportive wife Sheila. It was strong, powerful, radical stuff, the more so because it was anomalous to most of television at the time. BBC 1's *Play for Today* was on its last legs (it died in 1984) and Alan Bleasdale's 1982 lament for labour, *Boys from the Blackstuff*, felt like a reading of the last rites for the radical consensus. In the shadow of their passing, however, *Brookside* emerged, crying defiantly, 'We're not dead yet'. It was ground-breaking in terms of its passion and the locality of its voice, indeed it redefined the soap genre – but it was also one-dimensional. No one disagreed with Bobby. It teetered on propaganda. And then something extraordinary happened.

McGovern became a truly great writer when he not only introduced the Corkhills, a family of strike-breakers with an errant policeman son, but, far more significantly, gave them 'equal rights'.[1]

He loved them as much as his left-wing heroes, and insisted that we love them just the same. Almost overnight (and this was long before the virus came along), it transformed *Brookside* from a very good soap to the best drama on TV.

So what happened? Essentially McGovern got bored with preaching to the choir. 'Making a paedophile sympathetic', he discovered, 'is a fantastic challenge for a writer.'[2] It was a lesson that was to serve him well. In 1999 he was to supervise the making of a film about the Liverpool docks strike. Leading a workshop full of sacked union members, he asked them to write a speech from a scab's point of view. They refused, unable to accept such an idea was valid, so McGovern took the task on himself. A Channel 4 documentary (*Writing the Wrongs*)[3] recorded the moment he read the speech to them; four angry minutes culminate in the conclusion that because the strikers finally accepted a pay-off, they had sold out their principles while the strike-breakers had resolutely stuck by theirs. It's a remarkable scene and remains the most powerful moment of the whole project. He was to do the same thing in his film *Priest*, where one character gives a chilling defence of incest, justifying it as God's work.

McGovern believed neither of the two arguments, but he'd mastered a very important principle: that whatever you believe should be tested to destruction. He rejected the simplistic formulas of agitprop, realizing that without proper, powerful opposition, storytelling is trite. Because all storytelling is an argument – argument is at the heart of its being.

The Importance of Theme

'It is not necessary to press the analogy,' says Thomas Baldwin of Terence, 'but it will be noticed that Terence's plays do in a general way follow the process of an oration for a lawsuit . . . [T]here is a close analogy with the kind of oration Cicero and contemporary rhetoricians thought best suited to a court of law.'[4] In the spirit of argument, I must disagree – one *must* press the analogy; it reveals something profoundly important about the storyteller's art.

A theory is posited, an argument explored and a conclusion reached. That, in a nutshell, is what theme is. It's often confused with subject matter, but while the two things can be similar they are not always the same thing. The subject matter of *Crash* is race, but its theme is 'Is isolation an obstacle to empathy?'

Subject matter, then, is a static given. Theme, on the other hand, is an active exploration of an idea, it's a premise to be explored, it's a question. The subject matter of *Die Hard* is terrorists taking over a skyscraper, but (because both John McClane and Al the cop only find peace by admitting their deepest flaws) the theme is 'Can we only become strong by facing our weakness?'

Fourteen minutes into the first episode of *Mad Men*,[5] the show announces what it's about. Responding to psychiatric theory, the (very) secretly gay Sal says incredulously, while flicking through *Playboy*, 'So we're supposed to believe that people are living one way while secretly thinking the exact opposite? That's ridiculous.' In *Crash*, Det. Graham Waters' opening lines posit a different theme – the idea that 'we crash into each other just to feel something'. Both, of course, are theses, and both will be explored or challenged in their second act with conclusions drawn in the third. Once again, we stumble on the underlying structural principle of thesis, antithesis and synthesis. For the theme *is* the drama. All dramas are arguments about the nature of the world.

Stories work exactly like essays, like lawsuits and, indeed, like perception itself: they posit an idea, explore it, then come to a conclusion that, if the drama is convincing, is proved true. *When Harry Met Sally* postulates one simple notion: 'Men and women can't be friends because the sex part always gets in the way.' Act one poses a question – 'Can men and women just be friends?'; act two explores it through antithesis – men and women try being friends – and act three comes to a conclusion through synthesis – men and women can't be friends unless they are in love. Look at the relationship between a screenplay's inciting incident and its worst point – it is here that you will find the theme played out. Harry and Sally try to be friends, and at the crisis they find themselves in total misery. Macbeth kills a king and at the end of Act IV finds himself (though he is incapable of perceiving it) in a similar situation. As we've already noted, the inciting incident asks the question 'What are the consequences of *this*?' and the worst point provides the answer – but it is the *writer's* answer. In *Macbeth*, Shakespeare argues that regicide will lead to damnation, but another writer more forgiving of insurrection – a Bertholt Brecht or an Edward Bond perhaps – might have a very different take on the murder of a king. The relationship between inciting incident and crisis is thus the theme in action. Theme is a writer's *interpretation* of life.

As anyone who's observed the judicial process will tell you, the stronger both sides argue, the more riveting the trial. If a writer is going to make an argument about life, then they really should test it to destruction. The Corkhill family in *Brookside* were classic antagonists and, as Hitchcock said, a film is only as good as its villain; drama can only really work when it fulfils its structural duty to validate both sides. A story is only as good as its counter-argument: when a protagonist journeys into the woods, the woods have to be as frightening, as dark and foreboding as home is welcoming. Writers must love them as they love their heroes.

The novelist Arnold Bennett noted the importance of seeing both sides. The 'essential characteristic of the really great novelist', he said, is 'a Christ-like, all-embracing compassion'.[6] One of the reasons for the endurance of Shakespeare's work – and for the infinite variety of its interpretations – is that his plays encompass this. All his major characters have a valid if not passionate point of view; in some, *Julius Caesar* for example, protagonist and antagonist are like finely balanced scales.[7] It's even more the case with Chekhov – who memorably wrote to his brother of *Ivanov*, 'I did not portray a single villain or a single angel . . . did not blame nor exculpate anyone.'[8] In his very greatest plays it's almost impossible to distinguish protagonist from antagonist – all are effectively both.[9] Both of course are still required; drama is *about* opposition; simply promulgating one position negates the dialectic. As Andrew Stanton says, 'You often hear the term "You should have something to say in a story" but that doesn't always mean a message. It means truth, some value that you yourself as a story-teller believe in, and then through the course of the story are able to debate that truth. Try to prove it wrong. Test it to its limits.'[10]

The lack of a suitably heavyweight antagonist can cause grave damage to a show. In *The Wire* everyone was both protagonist and antagonist to someone else; every battle was balanced and you didn't know who would win – the writers showed Bennett's compassion in spades. When *Treme*, however, fell to inventing cardboard British journalists and naïve tourists to find something to rail against, you knew it was on less safe ground – fatally flawed by its desire to be loved by the people of New Orleans. Drama destroys itself when it falls prey to the very sin it should be attacking – when it wants its characters to be right, it *needs* them to be at war with themselves. Be wary of works where the protagonist is merely an author's mouth-piece. Ricky Gervais and Stephen Merchant's *Cemetery Junction* shares a similar premise to *American Graffiti*, yet there's no nuance – all the heroes are genii waiting to be discovered and every antagonist is moronic. It's simply too easy for the characters to up sticks and leave their small provincial town – unlike in Modesto, there's nothing to keep them there. There's no drama – for without a worthwhile antagonist there can be no valid theme, and without theme, no story.

Lajos Egri postulated the need for every drama to have 'a well-formulated premise'.[11] He was absolutely right in essence, but he ignored something more important: themes *emerge*. Many writers sit down with a conscious theme in mind – but many more don't, yet somehow produce them anyway. They arise organically, for they are the product of the writer's argument with reality. When one writes dialectically themes emerge, as both are built on the same foundation: thesis/antithesis/synthesis. It's an important point, partly because it further confirms that structure is a product of the unconscious and partly, too, because it leads us much closer to understanding just how and why we tell stories.

Before we pursue that, however, we must take a step back, because we need to call something else in evidence.

'All Television is Storytelling'[12]

Addressing the Royal Television Society in 1997, the legendary journalist Alistair Cooke uttered a singular truth (and, if you listen to *Letter from America*, disclosed much of the secret of its success). 'Broadcasting', he said, 'is the control of suspense. No matter what you're talking about. Gardening, economics, murder – you're telling a story. Every sentence should lead to the next sentence. If you say a dull sentence people have the right to turn off.'[13]

In the early years of the new millennium TV executives finally learned this brilliant lesson – that all narrative demands a dramatic arc and that television in particular lends itself exceptionally well to its shape. They realized that by following the rules of dramatic structure but applying it to real people, they could provide on a weekly basis the visceral thrill that traditional TV drama could only deliver sporadically. In discovering that drama could be manufactured at a quarter of the old price (actors for free!), *and* that dramatic peaks could occur not just at the end of a series but every week, they found themselves a whole new grail.

Supernanny, Faking It, Wife Swap, The Apprentice, Secret Millionaire and *Grand Designs* – all giants of the reality genre. All have very clear first and last acts – a call to action and a final judgement – but between them too, within the constraints of reality they're derived from, the same structure as Shakespeare, as Terence and as Horace. In all you can see the pattern – initial enthusiasm, goals achieved, things falling apart, catastrophe faced and victory snatched from the jaws of defeat. The king of them all, *The X Factor*, works by following a very clear – if elongated – act structure; in fact all reality television is built on classic Shakespearean shape, so much so that when it breaks the rules of the archetype – as Simon Cowell's *Red or Black?* did by featuring almost entirely passive protagonists – it suffers the fate of any drama that does the same. *Wife Swap* tells an instructive tale too.

No longer made in Britain, *Wife Swap*'s eventual failure can be laid at the same shark-jumping door as series television. Audiences initially tuned in to enjoy the brutality of the conflict (it's hard not to be prurient occasionally), but the programme was at its most effective and rewarding when the protagonists *changed* – when the repressed and emotionally crippled father learned to play with his children. Perhaps because it's harder to manufacture real change from reality, but perhaps, too, because the programme-makers prioritized argument and sensation over growth and maturity, viewers eventually tired of the carnage and the show was cancelled (it is harder still to sustain prurience for long). When the show worked, it embodied archetypal change; it became uncomfortable to watch when the protagonists strayed and refused to learn anything at all.

What it forgot was our old staple: drama demands transformation. In recent years there have been few more powerful and moving stories than the 2004 episode of Channel 4's *Faking It*. A working-class punk from Leeds was challenged to conduct the Royal Philharmonic Orchestra; he changed; the middle-class family who took him in changed; his girlfriend left him at the last minute; yet against all odds he produced a performance of Rossini's *The Italian Girl in Algiers* that blew the roof off the Albert Hall. However cynical the construction (and in this case it didn't look cynical), change and emotional growth fitted perfectly into the archetype, making for an extraordinary dramatic experience. It was as if it had been written by Richard Curtis, with a force and power most television drama can only dream of.

So reality TV stole the clothes of television drama and appropriated its archetypal form. But is there really a truly archetypal form? It is, as we've already seen, an argument that infuriates some writers. Tony Jordan – who incidentally produces perfect structures – rails against it.[14] Arguments against it, however, are – mostly – based on a false assumption. Great work doesn't have to slavishly follow the shape, and we must be wary of any insistence that one size fits all.

Subverting the Norm

The tension between creativity and commerce, tradition and its subversion radiates across all forms of art. Alex Ross's monumental history of twentieth-century music, *The Rest is Noise*, gleefully illustrates the fundamentalism that overtook classical music after the Second World War – a world where any hint of tonality was labelled fascist and John Cage could announce that 'Beethoven was wrong'. In every artistic medium there is always an iconoclast who will insist, like the composer Pierre Boulez, 'it is not enough to deface the *Mona Lisa* because that does not kill the *Mona Lisa*. All the art of the past must be destroyed.' Out of that urge, great work can be made. It may be un-archetypal, and inevitably more difficult, but then – as *The Wire* proves so well – some work should be.

Nevertheless, such work doesn't invalidate the story archetype – it confirms it. All stories share – at some level – similar characteristics, even if, as they become more explicitly avant-garde, they are a reaction *to* the story archetype. In Francis Spufford's *Red Plenty*, itself a bastardized version of the archetypal story form, one of the characters listens to another play the solo from Miles Davis's 'Blue in Green':

> He lifted the horn and began to blow high, exact phrases. There was nothing to anchor them into the rest of a song, and you could tell, anyway, that they were carefully refusing expectation, declining sweetly to close or to resolve, to fall in with the hints of structure they themselves were constantly giving.

Marcel Duchamp famously drew a moustache on the *Mona Lisa*. As he well knew, his work could not exist without the painting itself, and however much one might wish it the painting can never be destroyed. So it is with stories. They may choose not to follow conventional form, but even when they don't they are, like jazz, a commentary on and a reaction to it. *The White Ribbon*, Michael Haneke's study of pre-First World War German village life, studiously refuses to embrace dramatic convention. It's a profoundly disquieting film: much of its power is drawn from refusing to follow the archetypal shape the audience demand. Questions deliberately remain unanswered, meaning is deliberately elusive, and in frustrating our desire for narrative closure it fights the shape we want it to be.

King Lear is largely an archetypally structured work, except in the fourth act where Shakespeare departs from strict convention to essay what the artistic director of Shakespeare's Globe, Dominic Dromgoole, describes as 'a jazz riff on structure'. Does that diminish the play? Not at all, it merely underlines the sense of madness that is its underlying theme.

Samuel Johnson attacked John Donne's poetry for its 'heterogeneous ideas yoked by violence together'. He felt the disparity of imagery and its brutal juxtaposition didn't fit the form Donne had chosen to write in. Donne's metaphysical conceits and his rejection of metre (for which Ben Jonson said he 'deserved hanging') were of course his strengths; it was the interplay of form and content that was the foundation stone of his genius. John Coltrane's 'My Favourite Things' is a potent piece of music, but it becomes truly great only when one is aware of the *Sound of Music* original. The film *No Country for Old Men* derives its power from an event that you know structurally *shouldn't* happen, but less extreme examples – the dropping of an act, the subtle shift of midpoint to later or earlier, what musicians would call *rubato* (the borrowing of beats from a different bar) – add to the extraordinary richness and variety of story.

Towards the end of Michelangelo Antonioni's *L'eclisse*, Monica Vitti exits a close-up from screen right to screen left. In terms of film grammar, she should be in the next shot, entering from the right – but she simply isn't there.[15] It's her last scene, yet she's robbed of the traditional grammatical ending a leading lady would expect. There's no wide shot, there's no crane-up; instead, six minutes of empty streets follow her departure. The scene's startling, dramatic power comes from its betrayal of our expectation. Her absence makes no sense, but of course metaphorically (as an 'eclipse') it speaks volumes. Cinema, from Italian neo-realism to the work of Bergman, Tarkovsky and Dreyer, periodically reacts against the archetype and in so doing produces extraordinary work,[16] but the work still gains its power, like the cubism of Braque and Picasso, from its relationship to traditional form.

It would be absurd to suggest that every narrative is identical to *Thelma & Louise*; it would be absurd to say all works of narrative are symmetrical – clearly they're not. When we talk of 'perfect structure', however, this is what is unconsciously meant: perfect balance, perfect opposition, all square, all proportionate. Of course 'perfect' is a word freighted with connotations and 'perfect' doesn't always mean good. There is much that is perfect that is awful, much imperfect that is transcendent. Stories *aspire* to one shape as water seeks a level, but missing needn't be a mark of failure.

Richard Ford's novel *Canada* (2012) is a useful example. It tells the story of a young boy whose unremarkable parents commit a bank robbery that goes remarkably wrong. Abandoned as they're taken into custody, the young narrator finds himself in the Canada of the title (spiritually and literally), living with a stranger who himself is hunted down by two others for a violent crime he committed half a lifetime ago. Told in three parts, it follows the 'perfect' archetype while at the same time liberating itself seamlessly. In a classic ('perfect') film structure there would be three acts, and the entire story would be about the robbery and the son's coming to terms with his parents' act – probably with the victims of the original crime taking the role of antagonist and seeking revenge in the last third of the story. But that's not what happens. Instead, it's told in two large parts, the third effectively a postscript. The separate events are seemingly random and disparate, but even so it's impossible not to detect the X-ray of archetypal structure within. There's a very clear inciting incident – the parents' decision to commit the crime; a very clear midpoint – their capture and the narrator's exile to Canada; a crisis and climax – the bloody shoot-out at the end with the stranger's enemies. And the protagonist? He seems a passive observer, but of course he's not – he's narrating the book – *that's* the pursuit of his desire. The bank robbery and the new father figure who's committed a completely different crime – in one sense they're totally different stories, but they are also, of course, the same. The hero is brought face to face with the consequences of crime, but the baton one antagonist carries is passed to another to complete the arc (just as the baton of protagonist is passed on in *Pulp Fiction* and exactly halfway through *Psycho* too). Like every other narrative *Canada* is built on the same bedrock: a protagonist is thrown into the woods to find his way home. The fictional narrator of *Canada*, looking back on his life, discovers the key – both to the novel itself and, I think, to story structure too:

> When I think of those times – beginning with anticipating school in Great Falls, to our parents' robbery, to my sister's departure, to crossing into Canada, and the Americans' death, stretching on to Winnipeg and to where I am today – it is all of a piece, like a musical score with movements, or a puzzle, wherein I am seeking to restore and maintain my life in a whole and acceptable state, regardless of the frontiers I've crossed. I know it's only me who makes these connections. But not to try to make them is to commit yourself to the waves that toss you and dash you against the rocks of despair. There is much to learn from the game of chess, whose individual engagements are all part of one long engagement seeking a condition not of adversity or conflict or defeat or even victory, but of the harmony underlying all.[17]

Ford's narrator cites the great Victorian art critic who struggled to outline a theory of beauty:

> Ruskin wrote that composition is the arrangement of unequal things. Which means it's for the composer to determine what's equal to what, and what matters more and what can be set to the side of life's hurtling passage onward.

There are endless riffs on story shape – sometimes subtle, sometimes brutal explorations and excavations of an original tune. Often you may have to search long and hard to find it, but the tune – even in its absence – will be there. In music, poetry, film – arguably all art – digression merely confirms the archetype's importance. A minor chord is linked to its root; it is the relationship between the two that yields the story. Javed Akhtar, the co-writer of *Sholay*, the most successful Indian movie of all time, made a shrewd observation:

> You must have seen children playing with a string and a pebble. They tie a string and the pebble and they start swinging it over their head. And slowly they keep loosening the string, and it makes bigger and bigger circles. Now this pebble is the revolt from the tradition, it wants to move away . . . The string is the tradition, the continuity. It's holding it. But if you break the string the pebble will fall. If you remove the pebble the string cannot go that far. This tension of tradition and revolt against the tradition . . . are in a way contradictory, but as a matter of fact [are] a synthesis. You will always find a synthesis of tradition and revolt from tradition together in any good art.[18]

However radical the work, it is radical in relation to the primal shape.[19] And the shape seems undeniable. When Peter Morgan dramatized the story of David Frost's interviews with President Nixon he made a number of significant changes: he made Frost down on his uppers (he wasn't); and he introduced the last-minute discovery of some crucial evidence (it wasn't last-minute – it had been in their possession for eight months). The 'worst point' – the drunken phone call between Nixon and Frost – never happened and the final climactic interview in which Nixon confessed all in fact occurred on days 8 and 9, not the final twelfth day, of taping. All legitimate changes but all changes imposed to give the film a classic story design.[20]

Frost/Nixon has an almost identical structure to Morgan's other factually based works: *The Deal*, *The Queen*, *Longford* and *The Damned United*. And if you look at other writers who use source material, you'll find, at some level, they are doing exactly the same thing.

'It is only through fiction that facts can be made instructive or even intelligible,' said George Bernard Shaw. '[The] artist-poet-philosopher rescues them from the unintelligible chaos of their actual occurrence and arranges them in works of art.'[21] The facts change to fit the shape, hoping to capture a greater truth than the randomness of reality can provide.

Three-dimensional, two-dimensional, temporary flaw, sleight-of-hand, single protagonist, multi-protagonist – whatever the story they all share or aspire to the same pattern. Our hunger for that shape is absolute and insatiable. Audiences, contrary to David Hare's assertion, are really not 'tired of genre', as any examination of the relative box office returns of *Transformers: Dark of the Moon* and *Paris by Night* will attest. We will gobble up anything that feeds us that pattern. To most of us stories are not a luxury, they appeal directly to an innate desire. We hunger for the journey into the woods in however bastardized a form, but the less it's bastardized, the keener we seem to accept it.

David Hare doesn't present his work in classic three-act shape (*Plenty* is twelve scenes; *Fanshen* two acts), any more than Frank Cottrell Boyce consciously mimics the classic Shakespearean pattern. Rightly they rail against writing-by-numbers and they continually approach their art in unique and challenging ways. But because their work isn't presented in the traditional three-act structure it doesn't mean it doesn't *inhabit* it, for seeking act structure is a distraction. In the end it's neither about three acts nor about five; both are just tools that have allowed us to uncover story shape. *The Godfather* isn't written in five acts, any more than *Thelma & Louise*. Hare and Cottrell Boyce write in reference to a pattern; all their work very clearly follows a basic structural form, and though they approach it with a passion to be different – to be unique – they cannot help but follow the underlying shape themselves.

But why? And why is it *that* shape? The two questions are mutually dependent, and by broaching one we will uncover the answer to the other, while at the same time discovering just why stories are so important to us all.

22

Why?

If even iconoclasts find themselves writing to a predetermined shape, then what does that tell us? Not that they're fraudulent, though inevitably all art movements contain their share of those who mistake style for revolt. Rather, it suggests that there has to be a reason that lies beyond more imitation. Why do stories manifestly recur in a similar pattern? From the evidence gathered, both here and elsewhere, there are a number of theories we must consider.

The Societal Reason

'The mythological hero is the champion not of things become but of things becoming,' wrote Joseph Campbell.[1] If it is indeed possible for stories to carry in their DNA a blueprint for survival then it's possible to see the roadmap of change as a template for that wider purpose. Societies survive by adaptation, rejecting orthodoxy and embracing change – in exactly the same pattern reflected by the archetype. Why shouldn't storytelling be a codification of this process, one in which, through empathy, individuals are invited to take part? As Campbell sees it, the mythological hero must slay the dragon of 'the status quo: Holdfast, the keeper of the past'. As for myth, so perhaps for all tales told.

There can be no doubt that storytelling is at some level about learning; the protagonist discovers something and we do too. Seen in this way, the story archetype can easily be interpreted as a map that encourages us to rid ourselves of societal and psychological repression and in the process give birth to a new self, embrace the unknown, learn from it and prosper.

The Rehearsal Reason

Stories allow us to understand and navigate a strange and alien world. By rehearsing situations, problems, conflicts and emotions in fictional form we grow more adept at understanding, coping with and resolving them in real life too.

The neurologist Susan Greenfield[2] argues that the brain is a muscle – it grows and becomes more proficient through use – and that stories develop the connections between cells. The more we listen to stories, the more we tell, the more we write, she argues, the more our brains develop branches that will then enable us to process and act on the challenges of real life.

The Healing Reason

It's possible to feed any flaw into the archetype and resolve it during the course of a story, so clearly at some level stories offer a model for overcoming faults – a paradigm, if you like, for healing. As a story engine this can be incredibly useful; indeed, long-running series survive by taking momentary flaws such as jealousy or annoyance with an individual (or even, in one memorable episode of *EastEnders*, annoyance over a lost hairbrush) and feeding them into the story machine for resolution.

Whether the story paradigm is 'designed' with this in mind is debatable; it seems more likely to be (like the societal explanation) a corruption of a purer purpose – certainly we've illustrated how at one level it appears to still neurotic conflict. However, even if it's merely a by-product of something more profound, the fact that you can theoretically import any problem into the story machine and resolve it is both useful – and rather pleasing.

The Information Retrieval Reason

How much information must a fifty-year-old hold in their head? Even the worst educated will carry a lifetime's worth of opinions, knowledge and experience. How do they store it? And, more importantly, how is that information retrieved? In *The Black Swan: The Impact of the Highly Improbable*, Nassim Nicholas Taleb writes: 'The more orderly, less random, patterned and *narratized* a series of words or symbols, the easier it is to store that series in one's mind or jot it down in a book so your grandchildren can read it some day.' We squirrel away random, chaotic information, and then tend to retrieve it as stories. Like a computer folder fronting a mass of overwhelming code, so stories link our knowledge into a narrative that, like a good operating system, is vivid, clear and easy to navigate.

The Panacea Reason

A survivor of the Holocaust went to see *Schindler's List*. Asked afterwards for his thoughts, he replied, 'It was OK, but do you know what was wrong? They escaped.' It's a poignant criticism, but it helps illustrate another reason we tell some tales, why we have happy endings – they give hope. Such an addition is an extreme form of making order out of chaos – of extracting sense from senselessness. It makes reality palatable and digestible – it gives it meaning. Without such hope the real world can be unbearable.

The Procreation Reason

The sheer volume of stories that end in sexual union and/or its symbolic manifestation in marriage suggest that at one level stories provide a template for healthy procreation. From the earliest folk tales to the rom-coms of today the same message proliferates: only on achieving balance and harmony as an individual will one be rewarded with sexual congress.

It's a pattern that occurs in almost every tale that ends 'happily ever after'; it's the one Darcy follows in *Pride and Prejudice* just as William Thacker does in *Notting Hill*. The pattern may be ruthlessly processed in James Bond, or corrupted in films like *Star Wars*, where – as we've noted – the archetype is desexualized, the love interest becomes the sister and the reward, public approbation, but the underlying story source is still apparent. (Not that it's without antecedents – it's instructive to compare Star Wars with Rider Haggard's *King Solomon's Mines*, another desexualized romp through the archetype from an earlier century, and a massive hit in its time. 'Boy's Own', indeed.)

From *E.T.* to *When Harry Met Sally* and *Notting Hill*; from *Star Wars* to *Aladdin* and *A Few Good Men* – the same story skeleton in which boys learn to become men is readily apparent. Nor is it confined to the male sex. From *The Taming of the Shrew* via *Sense and Sensibility* and *Jane Eyre* to almost every chick-lit novel, the same process is visible: girls slough off their juvenile flaws and grow into fully realized women.

The Psychological Reason

Clearly not all stories are about reaching sexual maturity. Hal in *Henry IV* becomes complete, but his inner psychological conflict is nothing to do with procreation – it's about becoming a soldier, and finally a king.

Arguably, the procreational pattern one finds in so many stories exists because of, and as part of, a larger and more encompassing reason. In order to achieve fulfilment – be it sexual or otherwise – stories tell us we have to be psychologically balanced, and psychological balance, as laid out in Jungian terms, presents a model that both fits and seems to make sense. It's possible to argue that all stories are manifestations of these inner psychological wars. Certainly the conflict between ego-driven desire and the deeper flaw-ridden id or need is at the heart of the archetype, and it is this that suggests Jung may offer us one of the best explanations for story.[3]

Jung believed in individuation. 'Happiness' is achieved by integrating the experiences, aspects and contradictions of an immature personality into a greater whole. To Jung, mental health lay in balancing the contradictory elements within, whether male and female (anima/animus) or through what he called 'quaternity' – an individual integrating wisdom from a mentor, femininity from a love interest and missing flaws from an antagonist.[4] *The Wizard of Oz* is a literal playing out of this inner psychological pattern. A troubled Dorothy projects her inner worries into a dream world where she discovers the missing parts of herself and her anxieties are resolved. According to the same logic, the ugly sisters in *Cinderella* are really external symbols of the protagonist's inner lack of self-esteem. By exorcizing, assimilating and thus neutering her antagonists, the story rids her of her own sense of inferiority and makes her whole. Conversely, as one would expect from a dark inversion, every time Michael Corleone kills he's really just destroying the better parts of himself. Fredo's death in *The Godfather II* is, of course, the death of his own conscience, the cold-blooded murder of his own empathy and vulnerability.

'Detectives', A. A. Gill argues, are 'the collective superegos, and the crimes they solve are reflections of our own fears and desires.'[5] If we accept this, then logically there's no reason we shouldn't accept that *all* stories are a manifestation of inner psychological conflict and all external antagonists are really projections of the inner divisions of the mind. You can see how this might be true simply by looking at the structure of three-dimensional tales: at the midpoint the ego-driven conscious *want* is abandoned for the more nourishing recognition of *need* – the story thus becoming a tale of how the protagonist masters the sudden rise to consciousness of that which is buried within.

It's a pattern apparent in numerous myths, but Darren Aronofsky's film *Black Swan* is a rather brilliant and contemporary visualization of the process: Nina and her dark shadow entwine in a dance of death and completion. When a queue of ballet experts lined up to dismiss the film as unrealistic,[6] one couldn't help but feel they were rather missing the point – it's not about ballet. It's a film that understands the importance of darkness and just why fairy tales hover on the edges of cruelty; it's about how 'baddies' are the products of inner conflict – the demons and darkness that exist deep within us all. 'All of us are potential villains,' the legendary Disney animators Frank Thomas and Ollie Johnston once remarked.[7] 'If we are pushed far enough, pressured beyond our breaking point, our self-preservation system takes over and we are capable of terrible villainy.' We can deny and bury those feelings (that's what our ego defence mechanisms do), but true mental health relies on acknowledging and incorporating them. Beast gains Beauty by learning the ruthlessness and sadism from Gaston he needs to overcome him, just as Hauptmann Wiesler (in *The Lives of Others*) assimilates empathy from his antagonist to redeem his own soul. Nina, too, murders the black swan so she can dance her role. All learn from their dark shadows. All, like children, grow safer and healthier from playing in the dirt.

The assimilation of darkness, then, is crucial to growth. Nowhere is this Jungian undercurrent clearer than in the myth of Persephone, the sexually innocent girl kidnapped by Hades and dragged to the male-dominated Underworld, only to be rescued by Zeus (Hades' 'good' half-brother). She returns home, but not before being forced to swallow the pomegranate seeds that ensure she will travel back again for a portion of the year. The symbolism is rich: male is fused with female; balance is achieved. We integrate the 'other' to be immunized by it, just as neurosis is cured by assimilating its root cause. Stories act as a map for us, a pathway to greater individuation and consequent mental health.

This explains, too, why politically correct drama feels as anaemic and unmoving as agitprop and why those who wish to censor story-telling may well be doing more damage than the very works they fear. Censorship removes psychological truth and replaces it with denial, with wish-fulfilment – propaganda. A generation of children may never know there were originally guns in *E.T.* (Spielberg felt the need to remove them from his twentieth-anniversary reissue, though he wisely reinstated them for the thirtieth) nor that *Dennis the Menace* once had a pea-shooter that he used to shoot at weedy Walter; indeed, Walter in his 2009 cartoon manifestation (*Dennis & Gnasher*) has had a makeover and is manlier too. It makes for neither better drama nor better psychology. Pretending that the world isn't cruel, as Bruno Bettelheim argues in *The Uses of Enchantment: The Meaning and Importance of Fairy Tales*, may be far more damaging for children than showing that it is.

These, then, are the most common arguments for telling stories, but there are others too, especially if one trawls the studies of comparative mythology and religion.[8] The search for an under-lying pattern in our most sacred texts, prompted by the desire to trace them back to a single source, became a particularly popular nineteenth-century pastime – a classic Enlightenment sport. Many theories were developed; myths were seen as everything from the corruption of abstract thought by language[9] to an externalization of the rhythms of nature through life, death and rebirth.[10]

They're all interesting theories. They all have weight. But which if any are true? Can any of them explain classic story shape? For that has to be the litmus test. If the shape is not rooted in content, the argument that supports it can have no validity at all.

Certainly the Jungian paradigm fits with striking uniformity our overarching structural pattern, and in terms of its foundation on opposites it also makes complete sense. It's a persuasive match, but we must be wary. If 90 per cent of prisoners drink tea, we can't conclude that tea is responsible for 90 per cent of all crime. Correlation does not imply causation – if something fits, we can't conclude that it's right.

Persephone's journey offers an instructive lesson. If pomegranate seeds are a symbol of male fertility then the psychological subtext is readily apparent – but then so is the procreational one, and it isn't too much of a stretch to accommodate healing, rehearsal, retrieval and societal interpretations, too, into the tale. In addition, the story's most common, most literal interpretation – as a creation myth for the seasons – is readily apparent. Which leaves us in something of a quandary. If we can find multiple reasons that fit – is it even possible to find one definitive answer?

Why Do We Tell Stories?

Anyone who pronounces with certainty one concrete reason for storytelling faces obloquy. Just as once we insisted the heavens circled the earth, so those who declare that the Jungian premise for storytelling is the only truth risk a similar fate. To state boldly one theory is to risk becoming like Casaubon of *Middlemarch*.

Each theory of storytelling has its value, but the most convincing explanation is the one that accommodates all the others. That won't make it right, but it will edge us closer to possible cause. If Jungian theory tends to hold the most water (and it absolutely underpins both Joseph Campbell and the work of his many acolytes), we must remember that the mental health Jung himself advocated is predicated on the ability, as Scott Fitzgerald said, to make sense of the disparate while retaining the ability to function. Mental health, finally, is about the ability to impose order.

The role of order

For all its flaws existentialism pinpointed an essential truth: in a godless universe, the abject horror of meaningless existence is too much for any individual to bear. The idea that we are here and then we die, that all circumstances are random and all achievements are finally futile, is too overwhelming to contemplate. Staring into the abyss, we find we are incapable of *not* ordering the world. We simply cannot conceive of the random or arbitrary; in order to stay sane we must impose some kind of pattern. The Bible's role as the cornerstone of Western culture only enforces this, its sheer ubiquity and influence underlining the fact that God is a story we tell to assuage the terror within ourselves.

Laurence Sterne's eponymous hero of *Tristram Shandy* plans to write his life-story but in nearly 600 pages cannot get past the day of his birth. Shandy discovers the universe is un-orderable and chaotic. Ironically, and unbeknown to the hero, the very act of writing imposes order (Shandy's task gives it a classic 'quest' structure) on the world. Shandy cannot help it – and nor can we, for we *are* Sterne's eighteenth-century hero and the quest for order lies as much within us as within him. For some, the tendency can be extreme, for others less so. At one end of the spectrum lie Asperger's and autism, at the other (along the trajectory from trainspotting) we find ourselves cataloguing – well, *everything*, from arranging our books in an alphabetical progression to aligning our bathroom towels. We are obsessed with the need to confer shape. The astounding success of iTunes clearly has far less to do with a love of music than its ability to impose order on a random selection of songs; if we are asked to generate a list of arbitrary numbers, then, over time, a pattern will emerge; even anarchists are unable to resist the urge to codify it as a system.

Jackson Pollock didn't plan to paint fractals, but in his alcoholic madness he found a way of reigning in chaos just as Edgar Allan Poe created the world's first fictional detective to silence the terrors within. It is perhaps no accident that C. Auguste Dupin was the perfect purveyor of reason, a man capable of making sense out of any kind of chaos. 'Instead of bathing insanely in hideous crime, [this] new protagonist crisply hunts it down,' said the contemporary critic Joseph Wood Krutch. Poe himself was notoriously unstable and Krutch noted pithily that Poe probably 'invented the detective story that he might not go mad'. In seeking to tame his own demons, Poe found a way to tame ours as well. 'Humankind cannot bear very much reality,' said T. S. Eliot – unless we subject the sprawling chaos of the universe to some kind of classification it is impossible to stay sane.[11]

All of our storytelling theories have one thing in common, all revolve around one central idea: the incomplete is made complete; sense is made. It sounds simplistic to say that ordering is at the root of storytelling, but ordering is absolutely about how we navigate the gap between our inner selves and the outer world. Indeed, the 'home' we have talked about throughout this book *is* our inner self and our journey into the woods is a journey to everything beyond. Our attempt to make sense of things encompasses the psychological process: how do we bring inner and outer into balance, how does subjective meet objective, how do we square want and need? How do we fit in?

Whether psychological, sexual or societal, each of our story definitions is built around the same principle: order is made out of chaos; sense is conferred on an overwhelming world. An inciting incident blows a seemingly ordered reality into a thousand fragments, then a detective arrives to hunt down the culprits and restore things to their rightful place.

We've already seen that the three-act structure is a product of this process. It's the corral within which we marshal reality, a structure that comes as easily to us as breathing. Ordering *is* an act of perception, and it is this action that gives us narrative, rhetoric, drama. As the cognitive scientist Steven Pinker puts it, 'It is no coincidence that [the] standard definition of plot is identical to the definition of intelligence . . . Characters in a fictitious world do exactly what our intelligence allows us to do in the real world.'[12] Our intelligence behaves like a detective. It's sent on a mission, assimilates the available evidence, finds the truth that's out there and brings it to heel. All narrative is at some level detective fiction. The narrative shape – the dramatic arc – is merely an externalization of this process. All stories aren't just quests, they're detections.

Storytelling, then, is the *dramatization* of the process of knowledge assimilation. The protagonist in drama mimics both the author's and reader's desire – all are detectives in pursuit of a truth. In every archetypal story a protagonist learns – in exactly the same way we do. We are both brought face to face with the consequences of not learning – we will remain unenlightened[13] – and thus, if we continue to read or watch, we choose to learn too. The assimilation of knowledge is in the very cells of drama – a character's flaw is merely knowledge not yet learned. In seeking to rectify that flaw the story progresses, with the character's gradual learning imitating the process of perception.

Drama, therefore, mimics the way the brain assimilates knowledge, which is why it's identical to both legal argument and the basic essay structure we are taught at school. It is why theme is essential and why it arises unbidden from any work. Consciously or unconsciously, all drama is an argument with reality in which a conclusion is drawn and reality tamed. We are all detectives, seeking our case to be closed.

But this doesn't just apply to drama.

What is poetry but an act of moulding the disparate into sense ('Shall I compare thee to a summer's day?')? You see exactly the same process – and the same structure – in all narrative, fiction and non-fiction alike. There are differences between the forms: drama is told in acts because it's designed for one sitting, but biography, poetry and the novel all share the same underlying structural uniformity (as indeed does music – the pop song with its middle eight and the sonata structure of exposition, development and recapitulation both bear an uncanny similarity to act form). In drama you will have an act, in a book you will have chapters; in books you will have paragraphs, in drama scenes. Sentences and notes, phrases and beats – all are units specific to each form and, when joined together in a specific manner, render reality into story. In both prose and plays, if each point does not follow and build from the last, order is lost and the reader becomes lost too – in chaos once again.

So it's not strictly true that reality TV appropriated the clothes of drama. Drama may have come before reality TV simply because the economic and technological climate favoured it first, but both are separate manifestations of the narrative process. Dramatic structure isn't the forefather of other forms of storytelling; rather, its study, as I suggested at the beginning, provides us with the best key to understanding the narrative process. For narrative is in almost everything we see and everything we do – we render *all* experience into story.

Take any factual book, any treatise, any piece of journalism and you will see a strikingly familiar pattern, one in which the author will actively pursue a specific goal (the point they are trying to make), positing a theory, exploring it and coming to a conclusion. The writer becomes the protagonist. What all these different forms of narrative are doing is behaving like detectives, enclosing phenomena into linked chains of cause and effect. Their structure is identical to dramatic structure.

Drama, then, is our argument with reality *shown*. Thinking is sequential, and ideas, as Susan Greenfield has said, are a series of facts linked by the idea that 'this happens because of this'. As one point is proved, we link it to the next, striving for meaning, and in so doing story is born.

The chain of cause and effect

Daniel Kahneman begins his investigation of the tricks played by the conscious and unconscious mind by juxtaposing two words: 'Bananas Vomit'. He notes how the mind immediately imposes 'a temporal sequence and a causal connection between the words . . . forming a sketchy scenario in which bananas caused the sickness'.[14] Faced with disparity, we immediately apply what Kahneman calls 'the rules of associative coherence'. This is of course a process we've already observed – it's the Kuleshov Effect.

In the second ever episode of *The West Wing*, President Bartlet finds that shortly after he's told a joke about Texans his polling in Texas is down. His staff are convinced he needs to apologize for the joke, only to find Bartlet ruminating on the episode's Latin title: 'Post hoc ergo propter hoc' ('after this, therefore because of this'). His polling may be down in Texas, he explains, but that doesn't mean it's *because* of the joke. The idea that because something occurs *after* something else, the former has *caused* the latter is not only a common logical fallacy, it is of course the wellspring of narrative too. Narrative *is* cause and effect, linked into a chain; 'Post hoc ergo propter hoc' *is* storytelling.

Both Kahneman in *Thinking, Fast and Slow* and Nassim Nicholas Taleb in *The Black Swan* write at some length about our tendency to fall into what Taleb calls 'the narrative fallacy', the 'post hoc' trap. This report appeared on a BBC local news item some years ago:

- Police are today investigating a house fire.
- A woman and three children are being kept in hospital.
- It's understood she was involved in a custody battle.

'What happened?' we immediately want to ask, and we find our answer by linking the three statements together in the most simplistic manner possible. Most will conclude the husband was behind the fire (just as the bananas caused the sickness), but, of course, there's nothing in those sentences to suggest that at all.

This endless urge to link cause and effect is of course a gift for filmmakers. In J. Blakeson's 2009 film *The Disappearance of Alice Creed*, two ex-cons kidnap a millionaire's daughter and hold her to ransom, except of course the real target is not Alice's parents but one of the kidnappers and nothing, not even the film's title, is what it seems. Blakeson takes complete advantage of our desire to impose sequential reasoning and, by the clever ordering of events, forces us to assume the opposite of what is actually occurring. He understands, as Agatha Christie did before him, that juxtaposition is all that's required to tell an audience a great big lie, the reveal of which gives us the plot twists so beloved of the genre. But the desire to impose narrative on sequential events, one which thriller writers can so deftly exploit has, as we can now see, an importance far beyond editing.

As both Kahneman and Taleb warn, we can't help but impose story on everything. It's why in 1970s Britain six innocent Irishmen leaving Birmingham on a train were found guilty of planting an IRA bomb that had just caused devastation in the city; it's why Margaret Thatcher was photographed bestriding a tank. Associative coherence affects us all. If you've worked in TV you'll know that anyone involved with a hit drama immediately becomes more employable – not just the cast, but the production company – everyone. If that show's on your CV, you can effectively double your salary, because employers fall for a narrative fallacy. In reality, either 90 per cent of those who worked on any show will be interchangeable, or the magic will have come only from that one particular combination of people with that particular script. But we ignore that – we see their name, we see their CV and we automatically infer their part in its success. The wisest advice I ever received after soaking up one too many plaudits for *Shameless* was painful but true: 'It might just have been a success *despite* you.'

Our inability to cope with randomness, our terror of a world out of control, throws us into this total reliance on narrative – this happens because of *this*; you must vote for this person because of *this*; if you drive *this* car you'll get the girl – and it's almost impossible to confound this desire. Aaron Sorkin's *Moneyball* tells the true-life story of Billy Beane, the manager of Oakland Athletics baseball team, who pioneered a non-narrative approach to team selection, and in so doing produced a squad capable of beating those with three times their income at their disposal. Rejecting the traditional and universal approach of subjective evaluation and replacing it with the objective analysis of statistics, more 'workmanlike' players were selected instead of 'stars' and the appeal of the 'David Beckham' narrative (the instinctive belief that good-looking players are somehow better) was rejected. Despite huge scepticism by outsiders, the team went on to win an American league record of twenty consecutive games.

The film lionizes the rejection of narrative but, in a notable irony, places Brad Pitt at its centre. Neatly contradicting its own thesis, the film, despite itself, becomes a classic American manifesto for one man's fight against all odds. *Moneyball* is testament to the fact that we just cannot stop rendering reality into story.

At school I was part of a generation of English children who were taught that Captain Scott was a great British hero – all the more so for dying on his way to the South Pole. In 1979 a completely new version of the story appeared, portraying Scott as an incompetent buffoon. In 2011, a third version emerged in which he wasn't really racing for the Pole at all – he was more interested in science than in vainglory.[15] Which one was true? Probably all of them. Facts are observed and in linking them together suppositions are made and a narrative is drawn. What should be remembered is that the story an author tells is, like an obstacle skirted by an antagonist, as revealing about the writer and the period they are writing in as it is about those they wish to portray.[16] Each generation co-opts seemingly objective information into alternative versions of reality. We can never know the truth about Scott. We weren't there, and even if we were, Scott's truth, and Captain Oates' truth – and Amundsen's – would each be different. The journalist and political commentator Polly Toynbee, dismissing the lofty claims others were making for her own trade, described her job as a quest for knowledge in which, 'we précis a muddled reality into a narrative of right and wrong'.[17] It's a great observation, but it's not just true of journalism, it's true of life.

So why, if stories bring the world to heel, do so many theorists believe they have their origins in myth, and therefore can be explained by Jungian thought? Why, from Christopher Vogler to Christopher Booker, do they find story's foundation stone here?

The role of mythology

Cast out of an inheritance rightly his, the virtuous Irish Prince Conn-eda is confronted with an appalling choice: in order to continue his quest and gain entrance to the Fortress of the Fairies he must kill and flay his horse. The prince hesitates, but it is the horse itself that persuades him he must perform the brutal act. After much agony he murders his trusty steed and gains access to the kingdom. The dead horse is miraculously reborn as another handsome prince and order, as in all good fables, is restored.

This ancient pagan myth[18] is retold by the Indologist Heinrich Zimmer in *The King and the Corpse* (1948),[19] one of the earliest published studies of comparative mythology. It tells the story of a man who:

> though faultless in the virtues of youth . . . is still ignorant of the possibilities of evil which are present everywhere in his realm and in the world . . . He knows nothing of the sinister other half, nothing of the ruthless, destructive powers that counterbalance virtue – the selfish, disruptive, fiendish violences of ambition and aggression. These, under his benign rule, would have emerged to wreck the harmony of the realm . . .
>
> Conn-eda, that is to say, has everything to learn. Before he can cope with the multiplicity of life's forces, he must be introduced to the universal law of coexisting opposites. He has to realize that completeness consists in opposites co-operating through conflict, and that harmony is essentially a resolution of irreducible tensions. [He must] . . . confront and integrate the reality most contrary and antagonistic to his own character. He must come to grips with the forces of evil, hence the necessity to follow the hidden road of the dolorous quest. His myth, his wonder tale, is an allegory of the agony of self-completion through the mastery and assimilation of conflicting opposites. The process is described in the typical symbolic terms of encounters, perils, feats, and trials.

It should be no surprise that Joseph Campbell was a student of Zimmer's – indeed, he edited his writings posthumously. In his own work, *The Hero with a Thousand Faces,* Campbell notes the endlessly recurring motif of the hero passing through pairs of opposites (he cites Jason, but it is perhaps even more potent in Homer's *Odyssey*) and he says:

The hero, whether god or goddess, man or woman, the figure in a myth or the dreamer of a dream, discovers and assimilates his opposite (his own unsuspected self) either by swallowing it or by being swallowed. One by one the resistances are broken. He must put aside his pride, his virtue, beauty, and life, and bow or submit to the absolutely intolerable. Then he finds that he and his opposite are not of differing species, but one flesh.

Like Zimmer before him, Campbell believed he had discerned this unifying pattern in all the great myths of civilization. However, in their belief that myth and its Jungian foundations was the cornerstone of all story, both writers, ironically, were falling prey to a narrative fallacy themselves. When Campbell writes of Prometheus stealing fire, Jason seeking the Golden Fleece and Aeneas descending into the Underworld, he detects only one pattern: 'The standard path of the mythological adventure of the hero is a magnification of the formula represented in the rites of passage: *separation – initiation – return:* which might be named the nuclear unit of the monomyth.'

The 'journey there; journey back' structure he detects in myth is, as we have seen, present in all stories. Certainly myths are the primal embodiment of basic story structure but myth didn't give birth to structure, structure gave birth to myth. Why?

Newton's third law of motion declaims: 'To every action there is always an equal and opposite reaction.'[20] So it is in scene structure, which is why the strength of any antagonist is so important. That doesn't just make the drama better; it has a far more important structural function too. Kat from *EastEnders* wants to stop her daughter going to Spain because she's going with Uncle Harry, whom she knows to be a paedophile. Kat knows this because Uncle Harry raped her when she was a child and Zoe was the result, so she can't stop her child going without revealing she's her mother. When we join them in the Indian restaurant, the characters are playing a truth game; each revealing a secret. It's at this point Zoe announces her travel plans and Kat's lies are juxtaposed with Zoe's honesty. In order for her to stop Zoe travelling, she must borrow and assimilate her antagonist's qualities – she must assimilate Zoe's honesty and tell her the truth.

ZOE: You ain't my mother!
KAT: Yes I am!

We know this moment as a subversion of expectation (you can hear the drums), and we know too that in stories protagonists take on the qualities of their adversaries in order to achieve their goal (we see that in the tale of Prince Conn-eda). Here we see exactly the same process occur at a cellular level as well.

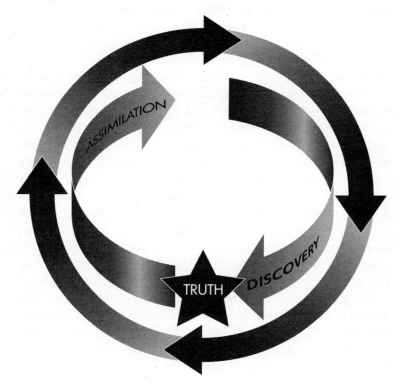

And so what Campbell refers to as 'the nuclear unit of the mono-myth' is really just a scene. It's two constituents weighed against each other; it's the building block of every story. A character goes on a journey to encounter their opposite; thesis meets antithesis, and both assimilate the other's qualities to start the process once again (see diagram opposite).

Hamlet remains the best example. At heart it's a classic detective story, the first half built around the question 'Did Claudius murder the king?' and the second around the reaction to the truth discovered halfway through – 'He did'. Every story, indeed every scene, is a product of this shape. A character goes on a journey to meet their opposite, and then assimilates that opposite into themselves. Opposites are where we must focus our attention.

The role of opposites

At the beginning of the fourth century BC the Greeks developed a form of reasoning known as Socratic dialogue. Two characters were presented dramatically – one often Socrates himself – and the truth sought through a series of questions and answers. You can detect the process very clearly underpinning Sophocles' *Antigone*, but in it one can also see the birth of democracy, of a the judicial system,[21] a free press and the interviewing technique of a whole school of British TV journalists from Sir Robin Day to Jeremy Paxman.

Georg Hegel adapted and expanded this idea. Truth, he argued, could only be found through a journey of continual opposition; an idea is posited, challenged and a new idea is born.[22] This too is then challenged and the process repeated until a totality, built from fractals, is found. So it is with story.

David Simon noted an extraordinary duality when pitching *The Wire* to HBO: 'Suddenly, the police bureaucracy is amoral, dysfunctional; and criminality, in the form of the drug culture, is just as suddenly a bureaucracy.'[23] It was this observation that was to form the basis of his masterpiece. Andrew Stanton and his co-writer Bob

Peterson called it two plus two; the Greeks, *peripeteia* and *anagnorisis*. Kuleshov saw it in the juxtaposition of images; Duchamp exploited it with his urinal. Shakespeare embodied it in Othello and Iago; Jane Austen felt it with Elizabeth and Darcy; and when Zoe yelled at her sister 'You ain't my mother!', Kat replied, 'Yes I am!'

In 2011, Frankenstein and his monster were played to great acclaim by alternating actors on the London stage, but it's not a new idea. In 1973 John Barton pulled off a similar trick at the RSC, interchanging the casting of Bolingbroke and Richard II, of which the *Guardian* wrote: 'suddenly they became a mirror image'.[24] Structurally, of course, they always were – as are Beatrice and Benedick, Katharina and Petruchio, Romeo and Juliet, Antony and Cleopatra, Prospero and Caliban, Macbeth and Lady Macbeth, Lear and Cordelia, Falstaff and Henry, Hotspur and Hal, the Greeks and Trojans of *Troilus and Cressida*, the Antipholuses and Dromios of *The Comedy of Errors* and the gentry and mechanicals of *A Midsummer Night's Dream*. All of Shakespeare is built on it, because all archetypal drama is built on it. From Antigone and Creon via *A Passage to India*'s Adela and Aziz to the founding families of *EastEnders* – the Fowlers and the Watts – the confrontation between opposites lies at story's very heart.

Let us return once again to our 'graphical' interpretation of character. We have seen in a very simplistic fashion how internal change delineates a protagonist, and we've charted the progress of a character in *Legally Blonde* and *Macbeth*. But the roadmap of change is also built on the same pattern: Thelma and Louise act in continual opposition, the dialectic between them effecting constant change until they both swap roles. This is even better illustrated in Shakespeare's *Richard II*: Bolingbroke and the king travel on an identical journey to Thelma and Louise in their twentieth-century quest. At the beginning, Richard is a king with the shadow of the death of Gloucester hanging over him, while Bolingbroke stands before him condemned. Four acts later, Bolingbroke is king, Richard is captive and the new king is impugned of a death in exactly the same manner as his predecessor. The dance of opposites (without a hint of Jungian growth) not only illustrates this – it gives us the perfect structure.

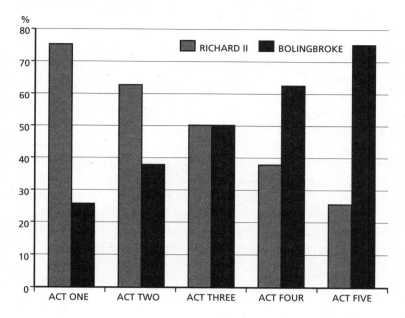

The graph charts the fortunes of protagonist and antagonist – and you can see very clearly (if absurdly schematically) how those opposites fare in every act. The midpoint of course is deeply significant. In act 3 scene 2, Richard II gives up the ghost and his divine kingship to Bolingbroke in all but name. It's strikingly similar to *The Godfather*. When Michael Corleone points his gun at Sollozzo and McCluskey, he is facing the absolute opposite of everything he previously believed in. Staring into the woods he pulls the trigger, the opposites become one and a new character is born.[25]

Frank Cottrell Boyce said of the three-act structure, it's 'a useless model. It's static.'[26] The only sensible riposte is, well yes, if it *is* static, it's useless. It is for this reason that protagonists *have* to be active and why stories wither the minute they become inert. Without desire – unless Michael pulls the trigger – there is nothing to catalyse the scene. Only activity can bridge the two opposites and cause fusion to occur. Without this energy the cell cannot produce – it effectively malfunctions. In writing factually – as I am now – it is my *intent* to synthesize opposites and build into a coherent whole, just as a reader will attempt to synthesize a picture of a VW Beetle with the word 'lemon'. In drama, we watch as the protagonist does the very same thing. Their desire is an energy passing through the cell, converting it to meaning.[27] Each moment of synthesis keeps the torch alive – and the flame is passed on. Meaning is born from opposites bridged.

Given our knowledge of chemistry, physics and biology, perhaps we shouldn't be surprised; 'Purists', Nye Bevan once said, 'are barren.' Our world is made from moments of fusion, from planetary creation to procreation. Michelangelo captured it on the ceiling of the Sistine Chapel. He was painting God giving life to Adam, but what we really see is two perfectly balanced opposites coming together – and through the fusing of that relationship, from fingertip to fingertip, *life*.

The genesis of story shape

Any reason we proffer for how and why we tell stories, must in the end explain the ubiquity of the narrative arc. A scene has a beginning, middle and end and encompasses change. Put these scenes together and they grow into acts; put the acts together and you have a story.

But watch what happens when you link scenes together. Take one scene, add another and a new middle is created, add a third and the first and last parts echo each other. Every time a new link is added, the overall shape adjusts to mimic the structure of the original 'cell'. What was once a crisis now becomes an act break, then a midpoint or an inciting incident, and so on indefinitely as the chain lengthens. The replication of the singular building block gives shape to form as the story expands, from scene to act, from act to story, from story to trilogy (and *The Oresteia* would be a really good example) and beyond.

Scenes work when they are juxtapositions of opposites – each opposite carrying a new reality or 'truth'. Does that truth have to be an opposite? Of course not. Disparate is fine, but opposites work best. As the story grows, does it have to be symmetrical? Of course not, but symmetry just fits; like water seeking the easiest course, perception – and thus storytelling – seeks the most pleasing and digestible pattern. So the midpoint – the moment that carries the central 'truth' – goes at the centre, and the protagonist who lacks those qualities starts from an opposite point. After they reach that midpoint, the qualities learned must be assimilated, and the easiest way of showing that is to *compare* them with the old character – and from that a parallel shape evolves from simple structural beats.

As the story unfolds and opposites are bridged, the audience infers causality and the story comes alive. Each scene emerges from the fusion of material in the previous one – each dying like an exploding sun to create the raw material for the scene that follows. And as they build, a new shape emerges. Narrative mimics intelligence; perception mimics detection. Making sense, assimilating opposites; ordering the world. And the emerging shape is of course very familiar, and it explains both why there is an archetype and story structure in its entirety.

What is it?

It's a fractal enlargement of a single scene.

That's what story structure is – single units of perception, endlessly seeking to mimic each other as they build into one giant version of their constituent parts.

In every individual scene a character is confronted by their opposite; an inner being is confronted by an external mystery. That mystery is tamed, the lessons assimilated and the character, changed, moves on. Nina slowly incorporates the characteristics of the black swan, changing and growing, scene by scene, until the antagonist is assimilated. Each scene builds from the endpoint of the last – new state encounters opposite and incorporates it, ready to encounter an opposite again. Characters don't just go into the woods in every story, they go into the woods in every scene. It's really no more complicated than that. Archetypal stories are fractal enlargements of the basic unit of perception. For story structure and scene structure are the same thing.

And that's why a nine-year-old can tell a perfectly structured story.

Joseph Campbell's monomyth is, similarly, nothing more than a macrocosm of scene structure – a simple journey of milliseconds to assimilate and order that which lies without.[28] Once that is recognized, the realization follows that the 'Hero's Journey' isn't just a construct. What Campbell first articulated and Vogler popularized is nothing more than a product of physics,[29] a chain of cause and effect with beginning, middle and end, seeking symmetry. In any given act structure a character has to change and grow according to a pattern – a pattern decreed by dramatic structure that itself is a product of the unconscious mind. A character will thus travel to and from the midpoint, tending to take (though they don't of course have to) the easiest possible route. So the hero's journey is really nothing more than the quickest way between points decreed by structure. The 'roadmap of change' is simply a logical beat-by-beat progression from A to B via a symmetrical arc. It's a natural shape. It occurs (and writers follow it) unconsciously, which is why it appears in both *Beowulf* and *Jaws*. It's not really mystical at all, but nor is it sinister. It's not to be feared.[30] It's a natural by-product of how we order the world.

Universal stories

So there isn't so much one single story, as one single story shape. But if that's true, how do we explain the continual recurrence of literary motifs? Why do some themes – and myths – recur again and again? Surely there must be some universal stories?

Stories strive for meaning, for resonance – why else would we share them? And when they achieve meaning, they are repeated and become embedded in our collective consciousness. Stories about mothers, fathers, burgeoning sexuality and the passing of life from one generation to the next will always resonate and for that reason those stories will tend to survive because they tap into our universal desires, feelings and symbols – effectively Jung's definition of the collective unconscious. Jung believed that as a race we share universal symbols we can all relate to. Clearly we do, but that isn't *why* we create stories. Such an assumption is again a narrative fallacy – it merely explains why so many stories cluster around potent themes. Story structure, built as it is on opposites, is the perfect host for Jungian thought, which is why it colonizes it again and again – but we must not mistake symptom for cause. We tell countless stories about all kinds of things – but only a handful stick – only a few last the course.

Stories that *do* last, then, are the ultimate result of the free market. If the content of a story has something to offer, it will endure. Few remember Nahum Tate's 1681 version of *King Lear*, probably because he gave it an implausibly happy ending. Like much that is briefly fashionable, it didn't survive because it had nothing meaningful to say. A greater test of worth must be whether a work lasts for more than a generation. Shakespeare's *King Lear* has been with us over four hundred years; like so many Greek myths it touches something deep within. Stories endure if they contain content that resonates, and not just truths; fantasies (like *Cinderella*) also have the capability to last. A free market keeps both things we know to be true, and things we *want* to believe, alive.

'What's Hecuba to him or he to Hecuba that he should weep for her?'

Hamlet's question of the Player is really a question about empathy. Four days after the attack on the Twin Towers in September 2001, the *Guardian* published a response in the form of an essay by the novelist Ian McEwan.[31]

> This is the nature of empathy, to think oneself into the minds of others . . . If the hijackers had been able to imagine themselves into the thoughts and feelings of the passengers, they would have been

unable to proceed. It is hard to be cruel once you permit yourself to enter the mind of your victim. Imagining what it is like to be some-one other than yourself is at the core of our humanity. It is the essence of compassion, and it is the beginning of morality.

Empathy appears to be more than just a theory. Professor Christian Keysers of the Netherlands Institute for Neuroscience has con-ducted extensive research into the way we watch – and react to – stories.[32] A whole generation remembers how they flinched when they witnessed the fisherman's decapitated head fall out of the boat in *Jaws*, or squirmed in the snake pit in *Raiders of the Lost Ark*. Keysers' analysis suggests that when empathy occurs we really do become one, physiologically, with the protagonist. Think of how your body reacts to the juxtaposition of 'Bananas Vomit'; think how you feel when you watch *Saw* or the laser beam creep up the inside of James Bond's leg in *Goldfinger*. As his heart accelerates, ours beats faster too. Watching someone being hit activates exactly the same areas of the brain as *being* hit – the physiological reactions, though fortunately not the pain, are identical. Stories thus literally place us all 'on the same wavelength'. This is the 'pity and fear' Aristotle talks of us experiencing in *The Poetics*.[33] We live what our protago-nists live.

As engaged observers we experience in our own heads what the object of our gaze is going through, and thus begin to understand. This not only explains just why showing is far more powerful than telling; it means there is a neural basis to empathy. Both emotion-ally and scientifically McEwan is right: stories have the power to make us connect; stories make us human. And that is why what I've referred to as the 'true archetype' – the story engine that substitutes want for need as a tale progresses – exists. Stories in which protago-nists just want are by their very nature rejections of the outer world; we are the protagonist and the stories exist to tell us we are correct. Bond appeals because he is us and we are therefore right, just as series television too exists to reassure us that life is OK. The world would be not only duller, but significantly bleaker without such tales; but they're not, finally, ever going to offer the same reward as those in which a protagonist can connect with that beyond themselves. That's why in non-genre narratives, characters *learn*. Only then can we transcend our own egos; only then can connection be really made.

'The greatest benefit we owe to the artist . . .', wrote George Eliot,[34] 'is the extension of our sympathies. Appeals founded on generalizations and statistics require a sympathy ready-made, a moral sentiment already in activity; but a picture of human life such as a great artist can give, surprises even the trivial and the selfish into that attention to what is apart from themselves, which may be called the raw material of moral sentiment.' 'Art', she says, is our way of 'extending our contact with our fellow-men beyond the bounds of our personal lot'. Stories make us one, and it is the process by which that occurs which gives us structure.

Gyorgy Lukács, the Hungarian philosopher and literary critic, wrote, 'The essence of art is form; it is to defeat oppositions, to conquer opposing forces, to create coherence from every centrifugal force, from all things that have been deeply and eternally alien to one another before and outside this form. The creation of form is the last judgment over things, a last judgment that redeems all that could be redeemed, that enforces salvation on all things with divine force.'[35]

Our absolute necessity to impose order is where narrative structure begins. Sylvia Plath spoke of her creative process:[36] 'I think my poems immediately come out of the sensuous and emotional experiences I have, but I must say I cannot sympathize with these cries from the heart that are informed by nothing except a needle or a knife, or whatever it is. I believe that one should be able to control and manipulate experiences, even the most terrifying, like madness, being tortured, this sort of experience, and one should be able to manipulate these experiences with an informed and an intelligent mind.' Out of feeling comes structure, and out of structure communication.

*

We might close as we began, with an observation from Robert Hughes: 'The basic project of art is always to make the world whole and comprehensible, to restore it to us in all its glory and its occasional nastiness, not through argument but through feeling, and then to close the gap between you and everything that is not you, and in this way pass from feeling to meaning.'[37]

Storytelling, then, is born from our need to order everything outside ourselves. A story is like a magnet dragged through randomness, pulling the chaos of things into some kind of shape and – if we're very lucky – some kind of sense. Every tale is an attempt to lasso a terrifying reality, tame it and bring it to heel.

Into the Woods

Every generation interprets the world according to the facts available. In medieval times people supposed that the Earth was supported on the shoulders of Atlas, just as later they would believe it was the centre of the solar system, that planetary orbits were circular, that the universe was made from crystal spheres or that cigarettes were good for you.

All have been presented as facts in their time – the cold, hard results of scientific reasoning. And yet all, of course, are products of the 'narrative fallacy' – this happens because of *this* – and all have been proved wrong. Science isn't fact, it's a model, constructed not only out of the knowledge available to us in any particular time but also from what people *wish* to see. If you're looking for proof of God's existence, you're more likely to concentrate on and select the facts that support it. Our history is littered with the corpses of those who from known facts have deduced wrongful – and occasionally disastrous – conclusions.

So it is with story theory. Many have studied narrative, many books on story structure have been written. All contain truths peculiar to the knowledge available to their authors. From Propp to Nabokov, Vogler to McKee – all have proposed models that seek to codify the story process. But they're not 'facts' – and neither is the model proposed in this book. They are models that often – though clearly not always – fit most of the current empirical evidence. Like science, the models are metaphors for something finally unknowable. Jung's work, finally, is a metaphor. So why not, in the end, embrace the metaphor? Stories could be the product of our capacity for order, our desire to resolve neurosis, models for living or for procreation; stories could be – and indeed probably are – all of these things. What kind of metaphor might actually embrace them all?

In the 2010 movie *Winter's Bone* a girl searches for her lost father in the heart of the Ozark forest, but the wolves and ogres that lie there are now the ravaged dealers and addicts of crystal meth. It's still a fairy tale – just a fairy tale set now. We cannot help but tell the same tale. 'The journey into the wood is part of the journey of the psyche from birth through death to rebirth.' The journey Hilary Mantel describes is a metaphor for the act of perception and growth. Once upon a time God was the story we told to make sense of our terror in the light of existence. Storytelling has that same fundamentally religious function – it fuses the disparate, gives us shape, and in doing so instils in us quiet.

It could be that brings us closer to God, to a sexual partner, to appropriate behaviour, or to better mental health. In the end, we simply can't know. But the journey into the woods, the finding of the missing part, its retrieval and the making of something whole, is integral. That something can be us, a puzzle, a mystery or any number of corruptions. As in scenes, so in story, a ridiculously simple process defines them all: two opposites are assimilated and a conflict is stilled. That is why we crave stories like a drug – for it is only through story that we are able to bring our inner selves into line with the external world. In that process some kind of sense is made, and if we're lucky, some kind of truth discovered.

Stories appear to be both as simple – and complex – as that.

Appendices

Appendix I. Act Structure of Raiders of the Lost Ark

ACT 1

It's 1936, and archaeologist Indiana Jones is in the Peruvian jungle seeking a golden idol hidden inside a booby-trapped temple. He finds the idol, exits the temple only to be confronted by arch rival archaeologist René Belloq, who steals the idol from him and leaves him for dead. Indy escapes in a waiting seaplane.

ACT 2

Back in the USA, Indy is teaching archaeology when army intelligence agents arrive to inform him that the Nazis are searching for his mentor, Abner Ravenwood. He is believed to be in possession of the head piece of the Staff of Ra, an ancient Egyptian artefact that can reveal the whereabouts of the lost Ark of the Covenant. Knowing that its retrieval would give the Nazis almost immeasurable power, Indy is tasked with finding it himself.

ACT 3

Indy seeks Ravenwood in Nepal, only to find him dead and the headpiece in possession of his obstreperous daughter – and Indy's former girlfriend – Marion. Marion is refusing to sell it to Indy when her tavern is invaded by Nazi agents, who burn it to the ground. During the struggle, evil Major Toht burns his hand on the headpiece, leaving an imprint. Marion and Indy escape with the headpiece, and Marion declares that from now on they will seek the lost Ark together.

ACT 4

They find themselves in Cairo, where they learn that Indy's nemesis, René Belloq, is aiding a Nazi dig for the 'Well of Souls', the last resting place of the Ark. Using the burn imprint on Major Toht's hand, the Nazis have created a replica headpiece which, they believe, has revealed its location. The Nazis have miscalculated, however, and it is Indy, using the real headpiece, who finds the true location of the Ark (MIDPOINT).

Indy and Marion are surprised by the Nazis, who have followed them and now take the Ark. They are imprisoned in the Well of Souls, but manage to escape.

ACT 5

Indy and Marion follow the Ark to an airstrip where the Nazis are planning to load it onto a plane. Killing a giant mechanic, they pursue the Ark as the Nazis attempt to remove it in a convoy of trucks. Indy is shot in the arm, but manages to rescue the Ark before it can be taken back to Germany.

ACT 6

On board a tramp steamer heading for England, Belloq intercepts them once again, this time in a submarine. The Ark is stolen and Marion kidnapped. Indy dives into the sea, stowing away on their U-boat.

ACT 7

Tracking them to an isolated island, Indy is captured when, after threatening to blow up the Ark, Beloq calls his bluff. Tied to a post with Marion, he is forced to watch the Nazis open the Ark. Indy, aware of the danger of staring the contents in the face, instructs

Marion to cover her eyes. Demonic creatures emerge, killing the Nazis and the Ark is restored to Indy.

Coda

The Ark is hidden away in a giant government warehouse, sealed in a wooden crate marked 'top secret'. Countless other crates surround it.

Appendix II.
Hamlet – *The Structural Form*

Very few works fit with total accuracy the five-act template Horace prescribed, largely because very few people write following such a precise template to begin with. What's uncanny, though, is how works written in different centuries, in different mediums, bear such striking similarity. All our physical bodies are different but it's still possible to discern the same skeletal frame at the heart of each one, and so it is with stories. Space precludes a litany of examples, but *Hamlet*, arguably the greatest dramatic work in the English language, can serve as a useful metaphor for them all.

The five-act structure of the play is immediately apparent, each act containing a major turning point launching a new desire. The 'roadmap of change', too, is fascinating. There are moments that don't quite fit (Ophelia's death comes, as we would now expect, at the end of Act IV but Hamlet has already, after seeing Fortinbras' army, decided to act) but the overarching shape is very clear. It seems slightly absurd to draw structural parallels between *Hamlet* and *Thelma & Louise*, but they are there, serving to illustrate the uniformity and universality of the storytelling shape.

Hamlet – *A Brief Synopsis*

ACT 1

Hamlet, Prince of Denmark, sees the ghost of his father, the king, who tells him that his brother Claudius has murdered him. He demands Hamlet avenge his death.

ACT 2

Hamlet, unsure whether the ghost is real or a product of his fevered imagination, is paralysed into inaction. Encouraged by the revelation that Claudius has sent his old friends Rosencrantz and Guildenstern to spy on him, he resolves to prove Claudius's guilt by using a troupe of travelling players to pique his guilt. 'The play's the thing/', he resolves, 'Wherein I'll catch the conscience of the king.'

ACT 3

Receiving advice from Hamlet, the players stage their enactment and in Act III, scene 2 (of four scenes – an almost entirely symmetrical structure), Claudius's guilt is confirmed by his reaction to the play. Hamlet is giddy with his success and confronts Gertrude in her chamber, kills Polonius, the king's adviser who first raised doubts about the prince's disposition. Hamlet hides Polonius's body.

ACT 4

Claudius resolves to send Hamlet to England, planning secretly to murder him mid-passage. On his way into exile he sees Fortinbras' army marching to capture 'a little patch of ground/That hath in it no profit but the name'. Fascinated that someone is willing to die for something so insignificant, Hamlet resolves to seek vengeance. Meanwhile Polonius's daughter Ophelia goes mad at the news of the death of her father. Her brother Laertes returns from abroad and, enraged at the news of the murder, is persuaded by Claudius to kill Hamlet. Claudius constructs a plot that will keep all blame from his shoulders. Laertes concurs, when news comes of the tragic suicide of Ophelia.

ACT 5

Hamlet, escaped from exile, finds himself at the site of Ophelia's grave: 'Alas, poor Yorick . . .' Here Laertes confronts him and the details of the fencing match are fixed. Laertes anoints his blade with poison and Claudius laces the wine. The fight takes place, Hamlet mortally wounds Laertes, but not before receiving a fatal scratch himself. Gertrude drinks the wine; Laertes reveals Claudius's plot; and Hamlet finally kills the man who murdered his father before dying himself. Fortinbras arrives and is anointed successor. Declaring Hamlet a hero, order is restored.

The Roadmap of Change – Applied to Hamlet

ACT 1

No knowledge	Hamlet knows nothing of the ghost
Growing knowledge	Hamlet learns of the ghost
Awakening	Hamlet sees ghost who demands revenge

ACT 2

Doubt	Ponders suicide: 'I have of late . . . lost all my mirth'
Overcoming reluctance	Learns Rosencrantz and Guildenstern are spies

Acceptance

Resolves to entrap Claudius using the players
('the play's the thing . . .')

ACT 3

Experimenting with knowledge

Trains the players with new enthusiasm

BIG CHANGE (midpoint) KNOWLEDGE

Entraps Claudius and Gertrude and proves their guilt

Experimenting post-knowledge
> Damns Gertrude, kills Polonius, banished to England

ACT 4

Doubt   Departs for England
Growing reluctance We learn of Claudius's plan to murder him
Regression   Sees Fortinbras' army. Reaffirms his
                      commitment to revenge. Death of Ophelia

ACT 5

Reawakening   'Alas, poor Yorick', Laertes confronts
                      Hamlet
Re-acceptance   The sword fight. Hamlet kills Claudius.
                      All are slain
Total mastery   Dies, knowing his story will be passed on,
                      his body borne off in honour.

Appendix III. Being John Malkovich – The Structural Form

It's fascinating that a work that's as iconoclastic (and brilliant) in so many ways should also clearly conform to classic structural shape, but *Being John Malkovich*, Charlie Kaufman's riff on the process of empathy, is almost totally archetypal in its structure.

One hundred and eight minutes long, with act durations almost entirely symmetrically balanced, the 'into the woods' pattern is very clear: a journey into another place to find the missing part of oneself is the subtext, if not surtext, of the film. While it elides 'beats' and steals them from one act to pass to another (the discovery of the portal comes in what would classically be defined as act two), you can still see how effortlessly the film fits into the archetypal mould.

ACT 1

Craig Schwartz is a failure in life, a failure in his marriage, but an unacknowledged but brilliant puppeteer. He finds himself a job as a filing clerk through the mysterious Dr Lester, where he is immediately drawn to the dazzling beauty of a co-worker, Maxine – the very opposite of his rather dowdy wife. He becomes fixated, creating a puppet version of her to simulate sex.

ACT 2

After he declares his love one day, Maxine spurns him the next, only for Craig to discover a small door behind a filing cabinet. Entering it, he finds himself inside the head of John Malkovich, seeing and experiencing things as the famous actor does. He learns he's able to stay there for fifteen minutes before being ejected just beyond the New Jersey Turnpike. Craig reveals the portal to Maxine, who suggests they let others use it at $200 a turn. He tells his wife Lotte too, and she visits the portal herself. She becomes obsessed with the experience; it changes her life.

ACT 3

Maxine and Craig embark on their plan to sell tours of Malkovich's head. Meanwhile, drunk on her experience, Lotte announces she's transsexual. She meets Maxine for the first time and becomes infatuated. It's not reciprocated directly but fortunately for Lotte, Maxine is attracted to John Malkovich, so a plan is constructed whereby Lotte, inside John's head, can have sex with Maxine – and exactly halfway through the film (at fifty-four minutes in) intercourse takes place.

A furious and jealous Craig – the only one not gaining from the experience – kidnaps Lotte, locks her up in a cage and enters the head of Malkovich himself. He then proceeds to fulfil his carnal desires with Maxine. Malkovich starts to get suspicious, as Craig becomes puppet-master inside his head. The actor breaks into Dr Lester's building, discovers the scam and enters the portal into his own head. Confronting Craig at the New Jersey Turnpike, he demands that the portal be closed.

ACT 4

Lotte escapes from her cage to tell Maxine what has happened, but Maxine, ironically, has found the experience of having sex with Craig, as John, rather exciting . . .

Lotte goes to see Dr Lester, who recites a long monologue explaining the existence of the portal – and how it can provide the secret of eternal youth. He and his gang of elderly conspirators need to occupy Malkovich's head on his forty-fourth birthday to ensure they live on. Meanwhile Craig grows in confidence and, realizing his puppet skills are the perfect gift, decides to inhabit Malkovich full-time and turn him into a world-famous puppeteer, with Maxine by his side . . .

Lester offers Lotte a full-time place in Malkovich. She says there's something they should know (WORST POINT for Craig).

ACT 5

Craig, as John Malkovich, launches his puppet career to huge success. He marries Maxine, who discovers she's pregnant, but their relationship starts to deteriorate. Meanwhile, Dr Lester's gang, tipped off by Lotte, have kidnapped Maxine and are using her as a hostage in order to force Craig to leave Malkovich. In the big showdown, Maxine and Lotte find themselves falling through his head together and Lotte learns that she (as Malkovich) and not Craig (as Malkovich) is the mother/father of Maxine's child.

Craig, in a moment of remorse, leaves Malkovich; the old people enter, and Lotte ends up with Maxine. Jealous, Craig attempts to re-enter the portal, only to find himself in a terrible new place . . . the portal has shifted . . .

We cut to seven years later where we meet Maxine and Lotte's child, Emily. Seeing through her eyes, we realize that Craig is now imprisoned inside her – and will be there for the next forty years.

The Roadmap of Change – Applied to Being John Malkovich

The theme of *Being John Malkovich* is announced by Maxine fifty-one minutes into the film. At dinner with a fixated Lotte and Craig, she ponders:

> I think the world is divided into those who go after what they want and then those who don't . . . Right? The passionate ones, the ones who go after what they want, they may not get what they want . . .

but at least they remain vital, you know . . . so when they lie on their death beds they have fewer regrets. Right?

When we meet Craig at the beginning he has nothing, but on discovering both Maxine and the portal a new world is tantalizingly dangled in front of him – one where, if he grabs what he wants, the world promises to be his. In essence he goes on a journey to escape his old self – but with terrible consequences . . .

The worst point here is where Craig isn't aware of the forces ranged against him. While it could be interpreted as a regression (after all he's only ever wanted to be a puppeteer), it's also a common riff on tragic structure – the worst point is inverted to become the classic highpoint of the protagonist's ambition.

ACT 1

No knowledge	Craig knows nothing about anything outside his own world
Growing knowledge	Craig gets the job and starts to become aware
Awakening	Discovers the portal to a whole new world

ACT 2

Doubt	Enters but is unsure what he's found
Overcoming reluctance	Tells Lotte, who insists on trying portal herself
Acceptance	Craig goes into business with Maxine

ACT 3

Experimenting with knowledge	Lotte convinces Maxine to have sex with her inside Malkovich
BIG CHANGE (midpoint)	They have sex – Craig's fury erupts
KNOWLEDGE	

Experimenting post-knowledge	Craig kidnaps Lotte, climbs inside Malkovich and has sex with Maxine himself

ACT 4

Doubt	Craig starts to doubt the monster he's become
Growing reluctance	But it's only fraudulent. He starts to overwhelm JM
Regression	He hatches the plan that will be his downfall

ACT 5

Reawakening	As Maxine and Lotte fight inside JM, Craig doubts . . .
Re-acceptance	before recommitting to his path of domination
Total mastery	He achieves total domination of another person (just not the one he expected).

Appendix IV.
My Zinc Bed – *The Structural Form*

David Hare's study of addiction is entirely built around the reconciliation of opposites: passion and repression, feeling and intensity, living and surviving. With a line reaching as far back as Sophocles' *Antigone*, the juxtaposition of two polarized views and their eventual assimilation is not just the form of the play, it's very much its content too. In its study of a reformed alcoholic and his employment by a bon viveur (each fighting over a love interest), it's uncannily archetypal. Indeed, Hare's play touches on the central dialectic inherent in all story structure – it's even quoted by one of the characters. 'Jung says that when we love another person what we are really doing is trying to compensate for a lack in ourselves. But Jung also says that the search to complete yourself with another person can never succeed.'

My Zinc Bed is not just a work about feeling and repression of feeling – living and addiction; it's a work that may serve as a metaphor for story structure as well. As Victor provocatively makes a margarita in front of Paul, he describes it as 'cold as hell in the mouth, then hot as hell as it goes down. Contradiction, at the very heart of life. Wouldn't you say?' It's the very theme of the work . . .

Of course it's not written in five acts, but two – each containing six scenes. In order to illustrate the underlying shape and its fidelity to structural norms, however, I've taken the liberty of presenting it in five acts (with the original divisions marked alongside) to show that, whatever the constructs we place on narrative, the skeleton remains identical.

Observe how Paul goes from repression towards passion, then

finds understanding somewhere in between, and thus an ambiguous kind of healing.

My Zinc Bed – *A Brief Synopsis*

ACT 1

Paul Peplow, a recovering alcohol and poet, turns up at the house of internet millionaire Victor Quinn. After conducting a fairly disastrous interview, and against both Paul's expectations and ours, Victor offers Paul a job as a copywriter (*end of scene 3*).

ACT 2

Paul meets Elsa, Victor's wife, herself a recovering cocaine addict, and at the end of a passionate argument over whether Alcoholics Anonymous is a cult – whether it saved Paul or created an excuse for the breakdown for his previous relationship – against both their expectations they end up kissing (*end of scene 4*).

ACT 3

Paul fully enters Victor's world and starts to live again, feeling fear, terror and excitement as he becomes more embroiled in Victor and Elsa's universe. Victor is Paul's opposite, not scared of drink, happy to believe that there's no such thing as the 'one drink' maxim, and provocatively mixing margaritas to imbibe in front of Paul. Paul himself becomes intoxicated by the danger and (*at the end of scene 6*) he takes his first drink – indeed, demands it – associating the drink with love.

(END OF PART ONE–MIDPOINT)

Victor goes away and a drunken Paul turns up at the house. He tells Elsa that if he knew he had her he'd renounce drink for ever (*at end of scene 8*). He pours his bottle of whisky into a flowerpot.

ACT 4

Paul becomes suspicious that Victor knows about the affair. Summer is ending, Victor and Elsa have rowed – he's accused her of drinking too much. His business is in trouble too. Paul tells us he's back in AA, and that he's quitting the job with Victor and leaving (*halfway through scene 9*).

ACT 5

Elsa begs him not to go and says that she loves him. But he tells her that loving her is just replacing one kind of addiction with another. The sky darkens as Victor enters. It is hinted that he knows about the affair, and despite Elsa's pleading Paul resolves to move on. We learn that Victor dies drunk in a car crash. Paul tells us he's still going to AA meetings, but, having rediscovered his confidence, his judgement, and perhaps the ability to love again, there's a (suitably ambiguous) suggestion that he has learned to live again too.

The Roadmap of Change – Applied to My Zinc Bed

ACT 1

No knowledge	Paul enters Victor's house
Growing knowledge	Paul starts to learn about Victor
Awakening	Paul takes the job offered by Victor

ACT 2

Doubt	Talking about old self
Overcoming reluctance	Starting to see flaws in old self
Acceptance	Kisses Elsa for the first time

ACT 3

Experimenting with knowledge	Admits being scared/growing more attracted to Elsa
BIG CHANGE (midpoint) **KNOWLEDGE**	Paul drinks – symbolically set up as a declaration of love. Feels the force of 'life'
Experimenting post-knowledge	Overwhelming excitement of life/drunk. Renounces alcohol for Elsa

ACT 4

Doubt	Retreats from affair as Victor becomes suspicious
Growing reluctance	Sees the dark side of Victor and Elsa's dependency
Regression	Announces he's in meetings and leaving

ACT 5

Reawakening	Counters Elsa's pleas – loving her is just another addiction
Re-acceptance	Hands in notice to Victor – no longer dependent
Total mastery	Paul leaves.

Appendix V.
The Godfather – *The Structural Form*

The Godfather runs like the print in a stick of rock through this book – so perfect is its structural form. The classic example of a modern tragedy (a hero spiritually if not physically dead), it follows to the letter the change paradigm as it appears in tragic form: it's an archetypal dark inversion. Again, whether it was written in five acts is to all intents academic; the template serves to reveal with unnerving clarity the underlying 'into the woods' shape.

The Godfather – *A Brief Synopsis*

ACT 1

Michael Corleone attends his sister Connie's wedding to Carlo with his fiancé Kay. Explaining the family business he remarks, 'That's my family Kay. Not me.' While Christmas shopping in New York, he learns that his father, Don Corleone, has been shot.

ACT 2

Michael's older brother Sonny takes charge while Michael returns to the family to look after his father. Visiting him in hospital, he thwarts a second assassination attempt, and realizes that he finds the experience not terrifying but exhilarating. McCluskey breaks Michael's jaw, frustrated by his lack of success.

ACT 3

Michael conceives the plan to murder the corrupt police captain McCluskey and Sollozzo, the corrupt drug baron he knows is behind the attack on his father.

Michael executes them both (*midpoint*) and flees to Sicily, where he falls in love and gets married, before his wife is murdered by those seeking revenge. Back in New York, Sonny is murdered too. Don Corleone forswears vengeance, recognizing Don Barzini's power, and seeking from him reassurance that Michael will be safe if he returns home.

ACT 4

Michael returns to New York and to Kay, promising her he will make the family legitimate within five years. Pressure grows on the family from the other New York families, and his plans to expand and move to Nevada are ridiculed by Moe Greene, the casino entrepreneur who derides the Corleones as dinosaurs. Things deteriorate further as younger brother Fredo falls under Greene's spell.

Don Corleone dies peacefully in his garden, but not before warning Michael that there is a traitor in their midst, who will reveal himself by offering to broker a deal.

ACT 5

At his father's funeral, the family stalwart Tessio approaches Michael offering to broker a deal with Don Barzini. On the day of the christening of Connie's son, Michael acts, murdering Tessio, Barzini, Greene, the other New York Dons and of course Carlo too – who he knows was behind Sonny's death. Kay asks Michael if he was responsible for widowing Connie; he looks her in the eye and denies it.

The Roadmap of Change – *Applied to* The Godfather

ACT 1

No knowledge	Michael stands outside the family firm
Growing knowledge	Hears of assassination attempt on his father
Awakening	Rushes to the family side

ACT 2

Doubt	Allows Sonny to take charge
Overcoming reluctance	Formulates own revenge plan
Acceptance	Plan is accepted by others

ACT 3

Experimenting with knowledge	The plan is put into operation
BIG CHANGE (midpoint) KNOWLEDGE	Michael kills Sollozzo and McCluskey
Experimenting post-knowledge	Michael flees to Sicily. Wife is killed

ACT 4

Doubt	Returns to NY; promises to go legit.
Growing reluctance	Pressure builds from other families and Greene
Regression	Father dies after warning of traitor in midst

ACT 5

Reawakening	Learns Tessio is the traitor
Re-acceptance	Kills everyone
Total mastery	Head of the family. Lies to Kay.

Appendix VI.
First and Last Act Parallels:
Some Further Examples

In *The King's Speech*:

ACT 1

1) Makes dreadful speech
2) Refuses to talk to anyone
3) Rejects Logue

ACT 5

1) Seeks out Logue
2) Insists he has a voice
3) Makes brilliant speech.

In *The Fabulous Baker Boys*:

ACT 1

1) 'Will I see you again?' 'No'
2) Cool façade – loathes being with brother
3) Meets Suzy – wants to pursue her

ACT 5

1) Meets Monica – turns her down
2) Throws façade aside and embraces brother
3) 'Will I see you again?' 'Maybe?'

Appendix VII. A Lightning Guide to Screenwriting Gurus

If you ever doubted that snake-oil salesmen traversed the screen-writing frontier, then you could do worse than type 'screenplay structure' into your internet search engine.

There are an awful lot of screenwriting gurus – some are entertaining, some less so. The hallmarks of the worst are grotesque over-complication, bizarre terminology, blind certainty and in a number of cases ceaseless demands for money in return for 'truth'. Like so many promising truth in exchange for currency, their main achievement is to give the serious study of structure a bad name.

What's fascinating, however, is that if you follow their instructions you may very well learn to write a good script – because fundamentally all gurus are trying to articulate the same thing. Indeed, there is no greater proof of an archetype than the realization that all these separate theories – indeed my own too – are really identical.

The chart overleaf, in abbreviated form, is a simple illustration of the underlying similarity of just some of the key names. I have included Vladimir Propp and Joseph Campbell in the table, neither of whom would have seen themselves as 'gurus' but whose inclusion underlines the argument for a unifying structure. All their models *fit*, though some more readily than others. It's grossly simplistic, and for more detail all should be read, but it serves I hope to illustrate the main point – all are grasping to capture the true shape of story.

	ONE	TWO	THREE	FOUR	FIVE
TERENCE/ FREYTAG	Set-up and call to action	Things go well — Initial objectives achieved	Things start to go wrong as forces of antagonism gather strength	Things go really badly wrong precipitating final confrontation with antagonist	Overcoming flaw — Matte resolv for goo or
	Inciting incident	*Turning point*	*Midpoint*	*Turning point/worst point*	
VLADIMIR PROPP	Villainy or lack	Departure	Struggle / Victory — *Midpoint* — Liquidation	Return / Pursuit / Unrecognized Arrival	Difficult Task — Marriag
JOSEPH CAMPBELL	Innocent / Call to world of adventure / Childhood separation	Refusal of call / Supernatural aid	Crossing threshold / Atonement With father — *Midpoint* / Apotheosis	Refusal of the return / Magic flight	Rescue / Freedom to live / Master of two world
MAUREEN MURDOCK*	Separation from feminine / Identification with masculine	Road of trials / 2-headed dragon / Slaying the ogre	Illusory boon / Initiation and descent to goddess — *Midpoint* / Yearning to connect with feminine	Wild woman / Healing	Integrating the feminine / Beyond duality

	ONE	TWO	THREE
SYD FIELD	Set up	Confrontation — *Pinch Point* — *Pinch Point*	Climax and resolution

	ONE	TWO	THREE	FOUR	FIVE
VOGLER	Ordinary world — Call to adventure	Reluctance or refusal of call — Encouragement by mentor	Crossing 1st threshold — Supreme ordeal — Reward / *Midpoint* / Tests allies enemies	Pursuit on the road back — 3rd threshold / Death	Resurrection — Return wit eli
BLAKE SNYDER	Opening image — Set-up / Theme stated — Catalyst / *Inciting incident*	Debate — B-Story / Break into Act Two	Fun and games — *Midpoint* — Bad guys close in	All is lost — Dark Night of the Soul	Break into last act / Finale / Fin imag
JOHN TRUBY	Need/ Desire — 1st reversal	Plan — 1st Counter-attack	Drive — Seeming defeats — 2nd reversal	Audience revelation by ally — 3rd reversal	Battle — Moral decison — New equili rium

	ONE	TWO	THREE	FOUR	FIVE	SIX	SEVEN	EIGHT
FRANK DANIEL†	Status quo	The external want made explicit	Exploring the new world	1st big test overcome	Forces gathering	Hitting the wall	Desperate action	Success and aftermath

LINDA ARONSON	Normality Disturbance Protagonist Plan Surprise Obstacle Complications Sub-stories More complications and Obstacles Climax Resolutio

CHRISTOPHER BOOKER	Call to action	Dream	Frustration	Nightmare	Matters resolved

MICHAEL HAUGE	1.Set-up	2. New situation	3. Progress	4. Complications & higher stakes	5. Final push	6. Aftermath

* Maureen Murdock, *The Heroine's Journey : Women's Quest for Wholesomeness* (1990).

† Frank Daniel was a screenwriting teacher who developed the 'eight-sequence structure' (see Paul Joseph Gulino, *Screenwriting: The Sequence Approach* (2...

Notes

Introduction

1. See endless internet forum chatter: <theweek.com/.../top-4-avatar-pocahontas-mash-up-vide...-United States> is one of many sites drawing comparisons.
2. The son of a writer for *Casualty*, from an email to the author in 2007.
3. The only one who comes close is Lajos Egri in *The Art of Dramatic Writing* (first published in 1942 as *How to Write a Play*) and even that is more poetry than 'truth'.
4. In his 1912 book on stagecraft, *Play-Making: A Manual of Craftsmanship*, William Archer articulated the dilemma of the would-be theorist very well:

   > There is thus a fine opening for pedantry on the one side, and quackery on the other, to rush in. The pedant, in this context, is he who constructs a set of rules from metaphysical or psychological first principles, and professes to bring down a dramatic decalogue from the Sinai of some lecture-room in the University of Weissnichtwo. The quack, on the other hand, is he who generalizes from the worst practices of the most vulgar theatrical journeymen, and has no higher ambition than to interpret the oracles of the box-office. If he succeeded in so doing, his function would not be wholly despicable; but as he is generally devoid of insight, and as, moreover, the oracles of the box-office vary from season to season, if not from month to month, his lucubrations are about as valuable as those of Zadkiel or Old Moore.

5. Guillermo del Toro speaking at the International Screenwriters' festival; reported in *Time Out*, 12 July 2006.
6. In December 2010, BBC Radio 4's *Front Row* brought three of Britain's most successful writers together to discuss the art of screenwriting. While there was much that was illuminating, the conversations at times

began to resemble a parody of Monty Python's 'Four Yorkshiremen' sketch as they rushed to be the first to denounce structure and craft.

7. David Hare, writing in *Ten Bad Dates with De Niro: A Book of Alternative Movie Lists*, edited by Richard T. Kelly (2007).

8. Transcript of Charlie Kaufman master-class at BFI 52nd London Film Festival, 2008.

9. That the study of structure has been belittled is hardly surprising. If you read the average screenwriting tome, the gurus have only got themselves to blame. Any system that propagates absolute certainty without analytical rigour, any system that refuses to be questioned, any system that has a guru at its head, can have no basis in empirical fact. When someone can write with a straight face of an inciting incident: 'Put it where it belongs: page 12 . . . Page 12 – Catalyst. Do it . . .' (*Save the Cat! The Last Book on Screenwriting That You'll Ever Need* by Blake Snyder) you know you're in an upside-down world. The endless unnecessary complications (*The Anatomy of Story: 22 Steps to Becoming a Master Storyteller* by John Truby), the temptation to give simple basic tenets such as 'theme' whole new, more complex and entirely unnecessary terminologies (*Story* by Robert McKee), and the language that might be better found on the rear of a 1960s Grateful Dead album sleeve (*The Writer's Journey* by Christopher Vogler) are not a help, they are reminiscent of the classic marketing techniques of a cult. It's a shame. Much of what these people have to say has worth, but they do themselves no favours. They present themselves as a religion, demanding a blind faith. No science would accept such theorizing without working its way back to principal cause – I don't see why the study of structure should either.

10. Aaron Sorkin, interviewed by *On Writing* magazine, February 2003, vol. 18.

11. Friedrich Engels, *Anti-Dühring* (1878).

12. From *The Shock of the New* (1980) by Robert Hughes.

1 *What is a Story?*

1. Frank Cottrell Boyce, 'How to Write a Movie', *Guardian*, 30 June 2008.

2. David Edgar, 'In Defence of Evil', *Observer*, 30 April 2000. He continues:

When, understandably but sadly, the parents of Mary Bell's victims wrote in the *Sun* that 'Mary Bell is not worthy of consideration as a feeling human being', they were letting the rest of us off the hook. The notion that there is a thing called evil which separates the wicked off from the rest of us is a comforting illusion. The uncomfortable truth is that to understand does involve recognition and even empathy. It does require seeing the world through the eyes of the wicked person, and thus finding those impulses and resentments and fears within ourselves that could – we painfully have to admit – drive us to commit dreadful acts under different circumstances.

As Peter Brook writes in *The Empty Space*, 'In the theatre the slate is wiped clean all the time.' Drama is a test-bed on which we can test and confront our darkest impulses under laboratory conditions; where we can experience the desires without having to confront the consequences. Drama enables us to peer into the soul, not of the person who has driven his father out onto the heath, but the person who has wanted to.

But that's only the first shock. The second is that we enjoy the view. Indeed, the pleasure is the thing that allows us to confront these unbearable aspects of ourselves.

3. Paul Schrader says of *Taxi Driver*, 'You can make [the audience] empathize with someone they do not feel is worthy of empathy. And then you're in a very interesting place' (from Mark Cousins, *The Story of Film*, More4, 2011).

4. See Robert McKee, *Story: Substance, Structure, Style and the Principles of Screenwriting* (1999).

5. Quoted in *Hitchcock* by François Truffaut (1985).

6. It's all very postmodern – the Joker is actually quoting the film *Jerry Maguire* (1996).

7. Aaron Sorkin, interviewed by *On Writing* magazine, February 2003, vol. 18.

8. Stanislavski articulated it to actors, that is – others got to proclaim its wider implications. At the end of the nineteenth century, the French drama critic Ferdinand Brunetière declaimed, 'Drama is a representation of the will of man in conflict with the mysterious powers or natural forces which limit and belittle us; it is one of us thrown living

upon the stage, there to struggle against fatality, against social law, against one of his fellow-mortals, against himself, if need be, against the ambitions, the interests, the prejudices, the folly, the malevolence of those who surround him.' See *Études Critiques*, Vol. VII (1880–98).

9. To be more accurate, this was a character of Chekhov's, Nikolai Stepanovich, who narrates his own tale in 'A Dreary Story' (1889).

10. Alfred Hitchcock, in a lecture at Columbia University in 1939; quoted from *The Dark Side of Genius* by Donald Spoto (1999).

11. There have been periodic attempts to give Bond more depth – *On Her Majesty's Secret Service*, *Casino Royale* and *Skyfall*. The latter two are effectively creation myths, which allow the possibility of change, and the former is a love story which gives scope for three dimensions too. Bond can only change so much, however, before he stops being Bond (see Chapter 20 for the problems inherent in change), so it will be interesting to see where the producers feel they can take him next.

12. As far as I can ascertain, the term was first coined by Thomas Baldwin in 1945. It is used once by Syd Field, but undoubtedly gained modern currency through the work of Robert McKee. In screenwriting circles now it's almost universally adopted, probably because it describes its function extremely well.

13. There is a long history of the attempts to articulate what inciting incidents actually are. Schlegel's *Lectures on Dramatic Art and Literature* (1808) defined them as the first act of free will in a tragic landscape. Gustav Freytag was again central to its codification. In his *Technique of the Drama* of 1863 (in which his pyramid was first articulated), he wrote: 'Between the [five parts of a drama] stand three important scenic effects, through which the parts are separated as well as bound together. Of these dramatic moments or crises one, which indicates the beginning of the stirring action, stands between the introduction and the rise. It is called the exciting moment or force.' (It's only fair to say that Freytag's paragraph neatly encapsulates the premise of this book.)

In 1892, in his own *Technique of the Drama*, Professor William Thompson Price announced, 'It is when issue is joined that the action really begins . . . The moment the hero of the play or his following, or the opposing force, announces a purpose, the mechanism is set in motion . . . It must occur in every first act, and is usually not distant from the conclusion of it.' Six years later, in *The Drama; Its Law and Its Technique* (1898), Elisabeth Woodbridge Morris declared, 'The action proper of a play begins with what is called the "exciting force", that is, the force which is to change things from their condition of balance or repose, and precipitate the dramatic conflict.' In 1902, Bliss Perry noted in his *A Study of Prose Fiction* the position of what we now call the inciting incident: 'Then comes, commonly in the middle or towards the end of the first act of the play, and not far from the beginning of a well-constructed tale, what is called the "exciting" (or "inciting") force or "moment".' William Archer, in his book *Play-Making* (1912), concurred: 'What Freytag calls the *erregende Moment* ought by all means to fall within the first act. What is the *erregende Moment*? One is inclined to render it "the firing of the fuse". In legal parlance, it might be interpreted as the joining of issue. It means the point at which the drama, hitherto latent, plainly declares itself. It means the germination of the crisis, the appearance on the horizon of the cloud no bigger than a man's hand.'

For most of the above, I am extremely grateful to James D. Bruner, who in 1908 published a brilliant paper on this subject entitled 'The Exciting Force in the Drama'. Not only did he summarize the existing scholarship up to that time (pre-Archer), he then resolved the contradictions that were apparent (see my own Chapter 8). Realizing there was some confusion between event and action, he concluded: 'The solution of the difficulty that I propose to offer is as follows. In the first place, the exciting cause of the dramatic action should be clearly and rigidly separated from the exciting commencement of this action. The first I would call the exciting or inciting case, and the second the exciting or initial force or moment. For example, in the *Antigone* of Sophocles, the exciting cause is Creon's edict that whoever buries the body of Polyneices shall be punished with death; the exciting force is Antigone's resolve to bury her brother.' The paper appears in *Modern Language Notes* (January 1908).

14. In *Casino Royale* Bond doesn't get the girl. Although technically the Terminator does achieve his goal in *Terminator 2*, he does it without killing anyone – the true lesson he needed to learn.

15. Interestingly this moment in *Aliens* was removed from the first release of the film. It was then reintroduced in the director's cut (1992).

16. Pamela Douglas, *Writing the TV Drama Series* (2005).

17. In *Story*, Robert McKee calls this the crisis point, but I think he's wrong.

18. Lajos Egri insists all scenes are obligatory, which is a good, if slightly pedantic point. His argument was with John Howard Lawson, who claimed, in *Theory and Technique of Playwriting* (1936), that it's 'the immediate goal toward which the play is driving' – an equally fair observation. Francisque Sarcey is actually arguing that there can be more than one obligatory scene (indeed, one is prescribed every time a play asks a question). But there is one overriding, structural obligatory scene inspired by the inciting incident – to all intents and purposes it's the showdown between protagonist and antagonist and thus, I would argue, the entire last act.

19. *Skyfall* offers a particularly postmodern twist to the formula – Bond saves the world and gets . . . a secretary. I can't help thinking that's not really what feminism was fighting for.

20. I am grateful to Christopher Booker for the *Star Wars* insight.

21. Jan Kott, *Shakespeare our Contemporary* (1962).

22. It's always possible to find a story that doesn't seem to fit this pattern, and it's commonly said of Chekhov's *Three Sisters* that the central characters don't actually do anything much, apart from dream of Moscow. Chekhov's genius, however, was to show pictorial stills that are the *result* of desire; one looks beyond the boredom and ennui the characters exhibit to find the structure of burning desire underlying it – from Natasha's takeover to Masha's disastrous adultery with Vershinin; the staples of dramatic construction are all present and correct, just buried beneath the illusion of 'plotlessness'. Chekhov dramatizes not the processes of dramatic desire, but their ever-changing results in time, from which our minds work back to first cause.

23. I am grateful to Christopher Booker for the terminology – from *The Seven Basic Plots* (2004) – though the description of how it works is my own.

24. This of course depends on how 'hamartia' is translated in *The Poetics*. Some say 'flaw', but the 1996 Penguin edition comes down firmly on

the side of 'error'. This obviously fits more comfortably with our own definition.

25. <http://www.filmmakermagazine.com/news/2011/12/tragedy-in-slow-motion-amcs-breaking-bad/>

26. Many (e.g. David Edgar in *How Plays Work*) have noted the similarity between Ibsen's play and *Jaws*, but while the latter displays a classic hero's journey, any way you read *An Enemy of the People* – either as one man's path to enlightenment, or with a darker hue – both are profoundly different in tone from Spielberg's film. The latter's hero is reintegrated; Ibsen's Dr Stockmann ends up at war with his community. That kind of darkness simply never happens in a Spielberg film.

27. Another variation is the journey to darkness and back again, which you can find in both *Hitchcock* (the film) and in *One Day* (film and book). Even in these, though, it's possible to trace a more straightforward linear journey underlying the superficial descent, from selfishness to selflessness.

2 *Three-Act Structure*

1. Story told to author by Alan Plater in 2007.

2. The act break effectively works as a midpoint (see later in the book for clarification), raising the stakes significantly.

3. *The Poetics* make no specific mention of act structure beyond Aristotle's belief that stories should have a beginning, middle and end, linked by a causal chain of events – as good a definition of traditional three-act structure as any.

4. From Marc Norman, *What Happens Next? – A History of American Screenwriting* (2008).

5. From David Mamet, *Three Uses of the Knife* (1998).

6. I don't claim this as an original thought. Mamet states it most eloquently; Blake Snyder mentions it in passing in *Save the Cat! The Last Book on Screenwriting That You'll Ever Need* and Lajos Egri builds his whole theory of drama around dialectics in his *Art of Dramatic Writing* (1946). None, however, dig into it in significant detail or explore its full implications, structural or otherwise.

3 Five-Act Structure

1. In *Play-Making* (1912) William Archer argues:

   Alexandrian precept, handed on by Horace, gave to the five-act division a purely arbitrary sanction, which induced playwrights to mask the natural rhythm of their themes beneath this artificial one. But in truth the three-act division ought no more to be elevated into an absolute rule than the five-act division. We have seen that a play consists, or ought to consist, of a great crisis, worked out through a series of minor crises. An act, then, ought to consist either of a minor crisis, carried to its temporary solution, or of a well-marked group of such crises; and there can be no rule as to the number of such crises which ought to present themselves in the development of a given theme. On the modern stage, five acts may be regarded as the maximum, simply by reason of the time limit imposed by social custom on a performance. But one frequently sees a melodrama divided into 'five acts and eight tableaux', or even more; which practically means that the play is in eight, or nine, or ten acts, but that there will be only the four conventional interacts in the course of the evening. The playwright should not let himself be constrained by custom to force his theme into the arbitrary mould of a stated number of acts. Three acts is a good number, four acts is a good number, there is no positive objection to five acts. Should he find himself hankering after more acts, he will do well to consider whether he be not, at one point or another, failing in the art of condensation and trespassing on the domain of the novelist.

   Archer was convinced (most scholars now think wrongly) that Shakespeare ruthlessly followed a five-act template (see note 7 below).

2. Rafael Behr, *Guardian*, and blog, 1 March 2007.
3. Thomas W. Baldwin, *Shakspere's Five-Act Structure* (1947).
4. Baldwin in turn credits the fourth-century Roman grammarian Donatus, who was the first to notice that plays could be divided into three

parts, (protasis, epitasis and catastasis) – and his earlier Roman counterpart Varro, who has some claim to being the founder of the study of liberal arts.

5. Thomas W. Baldwin, *Shakspere's Five-Act Structure* (1947).
6. As was Sophocles' *Oedipus* – though with an added epilogue.
7. In his book, *Act Division in Elizabethan and Jacobean Plays 1583–1616*, (1958), Wilfred T. Jewkes reviewed 236 plays written between 1583 and 1616 and found that about half were divided into five acts. Jewkes argues that many of these divisions are arbitrary or added by publishers – as is the case with many of the plays in the Shakespeare First Folio. By 1616, it was considered normal for act divisions to be used in plays.

To give you some idea of the nature of the quarrel, in Quarto 1 of *Romeo and Juliet* one of the two printers used ornaments extensively where act divisions might be marked. Some argue, however, that these were solely employed to use up the allocated paper that came from using a smaller font. W. W. Greg reviewed 102 plays printed between 1591 and 1610. He concluded that about 19% were divided into acts ('Act-Divisions in Shakespeare', *Review of English Studies* 4, April 1928).

In his textual analysis of *Richard II* in the Arden Shakespeare (Third Series, 2002), Charles R. Forker writes:

'Whether the Folio divisions – particularly the numbering of scenes – represent Shakespeare's original conception or simply reflect Jacobean editorial or theatrical convention is a nice question. It is possible, of course, that the Folio's separation into five acts evinces little more than the increasing respect for classical tradition that fully established itself, in the popular theatres at least, only in the seventeenth century; although it may hint in addition at a shift towards structural breaks in post-Elizabethan theatrical practice. On the evidence of other quartos as close to holograph origin as Richard II, it seems unlikely that the formal marking of acts and scenes ever appeared in Shakespeare's drafts; but such a conclusion, of course, by no means rules out a conscious five-movement principle of structure on the dramatist's part.

8. The précis is by American scholar Frank Deis. (http://www.tci.rutgers. edu/~deis/fiveact.html) Freytag's work is complex and sometimes difficult to follow in translation. Deis's is the best single distillation I have found.

9. The novelist Hilary Mantel said of this scene in *Julius Caesar* ('Friends, Romans, countrymen': Act III, scene 2), 'Everything I have done is somehow wrapped into that scene. I have been concerned with revolution, with persuasion, with rhetoric, with the point where a crowd turns into a mob; in a larger sense, with the moment when one thing turns into another, whether a ghost into a solid person or a riot into a revolution. Everything, it seems to me, is in this scene' (*Guardian*, 15 August 2012). Her words of course describe not just her own writing but fairly precisely the function of a midpoint too.

10. Christopher Vogler argues that midpoints are 'a moment of death' but bases his argument simply on the fact that that is where Janet Leigh dies in *Psycho*, and that it is also where E.T. dies too (he doesn't). Both examples seem specious to me. For a fuller dissection of Vogler's theories, see Chapter 4 – and further notes below.

11. Booker's work (*The Seven Basic Plots*) is a frustrating tome. In his rush to impose a unifying pattern, he ignores the crucial importance of elements that don't seem to fit (in particular the midpoint). However, he does make many valid – and some brilliant – observations.

12. Booker observes that his 'pattern' matches the act structure of *Macbeth*, though he doesn't explicitly pursue the direct relationship of his shape to act structure as a whole.

13. In 1912 William Archer wrote the following in *Play-Making*. I quote it in full as it articulates well the universal shape:

> It used to be the fashion in mid-Victorian melodramas to give each act a more or less alluring title of its own. I am far from recommending the revival of this practice; but it might be no bad plan for a beginner, in sketching out a play, to have in his mind, or in his private notes, a descriptive head-line for each act, thereby assuring himself that each had a character of its own, and at the same time contributed its due share to the advancement of the whole design. Let us apply this prin-

ciple to a Shakespearean play – for example, to *Macbeth*. The act headings might run somewhat as follows –

ACT I. – TEMPTATION.
ACT II. – MURDER AND USURPATION.
ACT III. – THE FRENZY OF CRIME AND THE HAUNTING OF REMORSE.
ACT IV. – GATHERING RETRIBUTION.
ACT V. – RETRIBUTION CONSUMMATED.

Can it be doubted that Shakespeare had in his mind the rhythm marked by this act-division? I do not mean, of course, that these phrases, or anything like them, were present to his consciousness, but merely that he 'thought in acts', and mentally assigned to each act its definite share in the development of the crisis.

Turning now to Ibsen, let us draw up an act-scheme for the simplest and most straightforward of his plays, *An Enemy of the People*. It might run as follows: –

ACT I. – THE INCURABLE OPTIMIST. – Dr Stockmann announces his discovery of the insanitary condition of the Baths.
ACT II. – THE COMPACT MAJORITY. – Dr Stockmann finds that he will have to fight vested interests before the evils he has discovered can be remedied, but is assured that the Compact Majority is at his back.
ACT III. – THE TURN OF FORTUNE. – The Doctor falls from the pinnacle of his optimistic confidence, and learns that he will have the Compact Majority, not *at*, but *on*, his back,
ACT IV. – THE COMPACT MAJORITY ON THE WARPATH. – The crowd, finding that its immediate interests are identical with those of the privileged few, joins with the bureaucracy in shouting down the truth, and organizing a conspiracy of silence.
ACT V. – OPTIMISM DISILLUSIONED BUT INDOMIT-ABLE. – Dr Stockmann, gagged and thrown back into poverty, is tempted to take flight, but determines to remain in his native place and fight for its moral, if not for its physical, sanitation.

> Each of these acts is a little drama in itself, while each leads forward
> to the next, and marks a distinct phase in the development of the crisis.

Archer conveys the five-act pattern very clearly, though not, of course, articulating the underlying shape.

14. Syd Field talks of 'pinch points' – two moments in the traditional second act that refocus a protagonist's goal. These are, of course, act breaks. Without knowing it, Field is advocating the use of five acts.

15. It's fascinating to see how over the years scholars have attempted to articulate the underlying five-act shape. A. C. Bradley (the English literary scholar and Professor of Poetry at Oxford University from 1901 to 1906) dominated Shakespearean criticism for much of the twentieth century. One of the few academics to acknowledge Freytag and take structural form seriously, he wrote:

> In all the tragedies, though more clearly in some than in others, one side is distinctly felt to be on the whole advancing up to a certain point in the conflict, and then to be on the whole declining before the reaction of the other. There is therefore felt to be a critical point in the action, which proves also to be a turning point. It is critical sometimes in the sense that, until it is reached, the conflict is not, so to speak, clenched; one of the two sets of forces might subside, or reconciliation might somehow be effected; while, as soon as it is reached, we feel this can no longer be. It is critical also because the advancing force has apparently asserted itself victoriously, gaining, if not all it could wish, still a very substantial advantage; whereas really it is on the point of turning downward toward its fall. This Crisis, as a rule, comes somewhere near the middle of the play; and where it is well marked it has the effect, as to construction, of dividing the play into five parts instead of three; these parts showing (1) a situation not yet one of conflict, (2) the rise and development of the conflict, in which A or B advances on the whole till it reaches (3) the Crisis, on which follows (4) the decline of A or B towards (5) the Catastrophe. And it will be seen that the fourth and fifth parts repeat, though

with a reversal of direction as regards A or B, the movement of the second and third, working towards the catastrophe as the second and third worked towards the crisis. (From *Shakespearean Tragedy: Lectures on Hamlet, Othello, King Lear, Macbeth*, 2nd edn, 1905)

By 'crisis', Bradley of course means what we would refer to as the midpoint. He's right, however: the midpoint is an obstacle that presents the protagonist with the kernel of their dilemma and thus a massive, life-saving choice. Bradley made some mistakes – interestingly he thought the climax of the rising action in *Romeo and Juliet* was the marriage at the end of Act II (it is of course Romeo slaying Tybalt and his consequent banishment from Verona, inevitably in Act III) – but his description of act structure is impressively accurate.

16. Transcript of Charlie Kaufman master-class at the BFI 52nd London Film Festival, 2008.

17. John Russell Taylor on Eugène Scribe in *The Rise and Fall of the Well-Made Play* (1967): 'His prime originality lay in his realization that the most reliable formula for holding an audience's attention was a well-told story . . . [W]hat he set out to do was not to tame and discipline Romantic extravagance, but to devise a mould into which any sort of material, however extravagant and seemingly uncontrollable, could be poured.'

18. This is Scribe's full formula – it's not hard to detect the Shakespearean pattern:

ACT I: Mainly expository and lighthearted. Toward the end of the act, the antagonists are engaged and the conflict is initiated.

ACTS II & III: The action oscillates in an atmosphere of mounting tension from good fortune to bad, etc.

ACT IV: *The Act of the Ball.* The stage is generally filled with people and there is an outburst of some kind – a scandal, a quarrel, a challenge. At this point, things usually look pretty bad for the hero. The climax is in this act.

> ACT V: Everything is worked out logically so that in the final scene, the cast assembles and reconciliations take place, and there is an equitable distribution of prizes in accordance with poetic justice and reinforcing the morals of the day. Everyone leaves the theatre *bien content*.

The above definition is taken from an essay/blog by Wayne Turney about Scribe. It's not clear whether the definition is original to Scribe, but it's an accurate description of the general shape of his work.

19. As recorded by Archibald Henderson in his book *Bernard Shaw: Playboy and Prophet* (1932). Henderson further notes, 'As a matter of fact Shaw was full of the great dramatists, knew nothing about Scribe, and cared less.' This quote is also reported in the fascinating essay by Stephen S. Stanton, 'Shaw's Debt to Scribe', *PMLA*, Vol. 76, No. 5 (December 1961). Henderson's assertion appears to be false – Stanton argues persuasively for the similarity between Shaw's and Scribe's work.
20. William and Charles Archer (eds), Introduction to *The Works of Henrik Ibsen,* Vol. 1 (1911).
21. See Stanton, 'Shaw's Debt to Scribe'.
22. A very good description of Shaw's *Pygmalion* in fact. The last act has always felt deeply undramatic to me, however, whereas the last act of *The Doll's House* is a tour de force.
23. See *The Quintessence of Ibsenism* by George Bernard Shaw (1891).
24. See Taylor, *The Rise and Fall of the Well-Made Play*.

4 The Importance of Change

1. The image every TV director in fact or fiction always looks for is the close-up of the human face as it registers change. It's as true of *The Apprentice* as of *The Street*; but for the best examples sport is hard to beat. The moment an athlete realizes they've won or lost is gold to television executives – and there are few more beautiful and moving examples than the British rower Katherine Copeland computing her

unexpected success in the London Olympics of 2012. Watch carefully as, just after passing the finish line in the women's lightweight double sculls, the magnitude of her achievement sinks in. You can read her lips as she says incredulously to her partner Sophie Hosking, 'We're going to be on a stamp!'

2. From Vince Gilligan's *Breaking Bad*, episode one, series one.

3. It's important to stress that some stages can and should be left out. At the end of the second act of *Richard II* there is no commitment or acknowledgement by Richard that he must change; instead, Shakespeare focuses on his allies slipping away. These actions by others will be the direct cause of Richard's change in personality – the change, if you like, happens in his absence. Likewise in *Henry IV, Part I*, you don't see the moment Hal accepts his destiny, but in his strange and haunting response to Falstaff's mock request not to be banished, he replies 'I do, I will'. The next time we see him, Hal has gone to seek the king. The commitment to making himself anew has begun.

4. Those familiar with the work of Christopher Vogler will know he sketches a superficial outline of the first part of what I've termed the 'roadmap of change'. Though he fails to acknowledge its tripartite shape and essential symmetry and misses completely its full significance, my analysis is indebted to his initial work, as is my terminology. Credit should go also to Lajos Egri, who finds a similar pattern of character transition in *The Doll's House*, *Romeo and Juliet* and *Tartuffe*, but doesn't fully explore its implications, nor acknowledge the role of prevarication.

5. George Lucas said, 'It came to me that there really was no modern use of mythology . . . The Western was possibly the last generically American fairy tale, telling us about our values. And once the Western disappeared, nothing has ever taken its place. In literature we were going off into science fiction . . . so that's when I started doing more strenuous research on fairy tales, folklore and mythology.' Quoted by James B. Grossman of Princeton University, in his essay 'The Hero with Two Faces'.

6. From Joseph Campbell's authorized biography by Stephen and Robin Larsen, *Joseph Campbell: A Fire in the Mind* (2002), interview with George Lucas. Lucas discusses the influence at some length.

7. The memo was entitled 'A Practical Guide to *The Hero with a Thousand Faces*' (1985). The original can be found in full here: <http://www.thewritersjourney.com/hero's_journey.htm#Memo>.

8. Joseph Campbell, *The Hero with a Thousand Faces*. The term 'monomyth' is taken from James Joyce's *Finnegans Wake*.

9. Once again I am indebted to Vogler's initial insights, though he continually fails to capture the significance of his own discoveries and ignores both the symmetrical and tripartite nature of structure. However, this shouldn't detract from the work's significance – certainly this book couldn't have been written without it.

10. Vogler makes a great deal of character flaw at the beginning of his book, and indeed suggests a change paradigm, but he never follows this – very smart – observation through to its logical conclusion.

11. The mythic language can be off-putting too. Its mix of the archaic and New Age and its absence of intellectual rigour drapes it with an unfortunate cloak of shamanism. In addition, it's not that easy to apply – as Vogler's own attempts illustrate (see note 12 below). What's important to remember, though, is that it's a metaphor. Strip away the Tolkienisms and what you're left with is a very simple shape: the archetypal story boiled down to the search for a cure, its discovery and its implementation. If nothing else, its true importance lies in underlining Campbell's own revelation. Vogler's examples seem curiously lame – it is simply not enough to label someone a 'threshold guardian' just because they're standing in front of a door. Stuart Voytilla (who wrote *Myth and the Movies*, a whole book attempting to show how it's used) is full of even more embarrassing examples and Vogler does himself no favours by endorsing it.

12. It seems to me that Vogler gets this terribly wrong. In his analysis of *The Wizard of Oz* he completely confuses midpoint and crisis – the former is, of course, the meeting with the Wizard, where the protagonists find their courage for the first time. Vogler places it at the defeat of the Wicked Witch. He makes the similar mistake of confusing midpoint and crisis with *E.T.* too. The fact that it doesn't matter, that if you follow the paradigm it will still work, tells you everything about the smoke and mirrors of guru-dom.

5 How We Tell Stories

1. From David Lodge, *The Art of Fiction* (1992).
2. Interview with Mondrian in 1919, taken from Tate Modern catalogue, Van Doesburg exhibition, 2010.
3. *Spooks*, series three, episode ten, written by Ben Richards (Kudos Film and Television production for BBC 1).
4. From *Goldfinger* to *Skyfall*, the midpoint of many Bond films is the discovery of the villain's lair. Dark caves abound . . .
5. Umberto Eco, in his essay 'Narrative Structures in Fleming' from *The Role of the Reader: Explorations in the Semiotics of Texts* (1979), notes Bond's fairy-tale ancestry (the damsel rescued from the clutches of the dragon) and the fact that all Fleming's works are built on Manichaean opposites. In addition he notes a formula:

> A. M moves and gives task to Bond;
> B. Villain moves and appears to Bond (perhaps in vicarious forms);
> C. Bond moves and gives a first check to Villain or Villain gives first check to Bond;
> D. Woman moves and shows herself to Bond;
> E. Bond takes woman (possesses her or begins her seduction);
> F. Villain captures Bond (with or without Woman, or at different moments);
> G. Villain tortures Bond (with or without Woman);
> H. Bond beats Villain (kills him or kills his representative or helps at their killing);
> I. Bond, convalescing, enjoys woman, whom he then loses.

It's not hard to discern the 'into the woods' shape (with capture by villain at its centre and woman as prize) in Eco's scheme. In fact the woman is usually an addendum to the prize – the real narrative goal being, for example, either to find what the baddy is up to (*Goldfinger*), to stop it or to steal the Lektor decoding machine (*From Russia with Love*). Women are, of course, intrinsically linked to the goal – a kind of *bonus* prize. Eco notes at the end that Bond loses the woman. In most of the films (with the exception of the three-dimensional ones in the canon – *On Her Majesty's Secret Service, Casino Royale* and *Skyfall*), he doesn't really want her, just the sex she can provide. Bond's über-goal, as the film of *Casino Royale* underlines, is total, ruthless self-sufficiency.

6. If you decode Vladimir Propp's brilliant but complex *Morphology of the Folk Tale* (1928) – a key study of early storytelling – you will find exactly the same shape, although it has to be disinterred from a proposed thirty-one key stages, most of which are to do with genre rather than structure. Simplified, the underlying pattern becomes very clear:

> VILLAINY OR LACK: something causes harm to a family member; or something is missing in family or community that becomes desirable
> DEPARTURE: hero leaves home to find or seek
> STRUGGLE: hero finds villain and they engage
> VICTORY: hero beats them
> LIQUIDATION: the 'lack' is eliminated
> RETURN: hero returns
> PURSUIT: hero is chased
> UNRECOGNIZED ARRIVAL: hero loses identity
> DIFFICULT TASK: final trial
> MARRIAGE: identity revealed and final union.

7. Hilary Mantel, 'Wicked parents in fairytales', Introduction to free booklet on fairy tales, *Guardian*, 10 October 2009.

8. William Goldman, *Adventures in the Screen Trade: A Personal View of Hollywood and Screenwriting* (1983).

6 Fractals

1. Try looking at Polycleitus' *Doryphoros* or *Spear-Bearer*: note the tension between movement and stasis, the way the right arm and leg mirror each other; how it achieves balance while appearing off-centre.

2. Interview with Jimmy McGovern on Channel 4's *Right to Reply*, 1985, and conversation with author.

3. Again, Lajos Egri first made a similar observation, though without acknowledging the role of the midpoint or symmetrical structure.

7 Acts

1. Robert McKee purloins a term from Hegel to describe this: 'the negation of the negation'. As a double negative is a positive (and that's how Hegel meant it), it's hard to understand what McKee is getting at. I have yet to meet a writer who knows quite what he means.

8 The Inciting Incident

1. Syd Field calls this Plot Point 1. It's exactly the same thing. Field also notes the tripartite nature of acts, but fails to explore the implications of his observation.
2. In *Story*, Robert McKee claims the inciting incident in *Ordinary People* is the moment when Conrad's neurotic mother smashes up the boy's breakfast of French toast. However, a clear tripartite structure reveals the throwing away of the French toast is in fact only the first turning point. It is the later flashback to the boating accident itself that actually causes Conrad to call the psychiatrist. McKee argues that Conrad's father is in fact the main protagonist of the film. Even if true (and he's so passive it's a hard argument to sustain), it's not the French toast that propels him into a different world.
3. 'Commitment' to change is actually a much better way of looking at the endpoint of act two than Booker's 'initial objective achieved'. In pursuing their initial objective, a character has to change to achieve it – they *commit* to stepping outside of their ordinary world. They *accept* their need to change.
4. It's a popular but often misunderstood technique. Christopher Vogler argues that every first act contains a refusal of the call – citing *Star Wars* as an example. While it's true that it can, it is much more common – and perhaps interesting – to delay acceptance until the end

of the Shakespearean second act. Sometimes they're quite hard to detect. Deferred calls are often accompanied by first act 'elisions'. The dictum of 'come in late, get out early' applies just as equally to acts as scenes, and it's very common to miss out the mini-climax of the first act and play out instead a longer deferred response to the call, culminating in the climax of act two.

5. In *The Hero with a Thousand Faces*, Joseph Campbell cites the moment where the princess drops her ball in the water in *The Frog King*, saying: 'This is one of the ways in which the adventure can begin. A blunder – apparently the merest chance – reveals an unsuspected world, and the individual is drawn into a relationship with forces that are not rightly understood.'

9 Scenes

1. Dustin Hoffman actually portrays Jack Crabb from the age of seventeen in *Little Big Man* – but it's still the longest age span to be covered by a single actor on film.

2. William Goldman in *Adventures in the Screen Trade* (1983).

3. E. M. Forster, *Aspects of the Novel* (1927).

4. From an interview with David Sexton, 'Clash of the Titans', *Evening Standard*, 31 March 2010.

5. Conversation with author, 2006.

10 Putting It All Together

1. It's fascinating (though not scientific) to see just how many midpoints do occur in caves, forests or their proxy equivalents.

2. From Gustav Freytag's *Technique of the Drama* (authorized translation of the sixth German edition by Elias J. MacEwan, 1900).

3. To name but a few recent examples I've seen or read: MOVIES: *The Bourne Ultimatum*, *The Last Crusade*, *Apocalypse Now*, *Romeo and Juliet*, *The Winter's Tale*, *Coriolanus*, *Star Wars*, *Tinker Tailor Soldier Spy*, *Four*

Weddings and a Funeral, Pulp Fiction, Drive, The Ides of March, Raise the Red Lantern, The Guard, Attack the Block; Les Miserables; Amour BOOKS: *Rebecca, The Hare with Amber Eyes, The Human Stain, Freedom* (Franzen), *Karoo*; PLAYS: *Flare Path, Hamlet, Henry IV, Part I* – in every genre the examples are almost overwhelming. Note they span fiction and non-fiction too.

As you might expect, the mini crisis points in every act often contain moments of death too – act one of both *The Godfather* and *Thelma & Louise* and act two of *Macbeth* are classic examples. Is there some quasi-spiritual reason for this? Certainly the death and rebirth argument is persuasive, and it's clearly the moment when thesis is superseded by antithesis, but it's worth remembering too that every crisis point is merely a dilemma in which the protagonist has to decide whether to stay the same or change. If dramatic turning points are built around bringing a protagonist face to face with the consequences of *not* changing, then those consequences, story structure dictates, should be as bad as possible. The preponderance of physical death at crisis points may simply be the consequence of this.

11 *Showing and Telling*

1. From an interview with Mike Skinner (aka The Streets), in *The South Bank Show* on ITV, 21 September 2008.
2. Andrew Stanton, lecture, 'Understanding Story: or My Journey of Pain' (2006).
3. The actor was Ivan Mozzhukhin. Kuleshov's colleague Vsevolod Pudovkin later wrote how the audience 'raved about the acting of the artist. They pointed out the heavy pensiveness of his mood over the forgotten soup, were touched and moved by the deep sorrow with which he looked on the dead woman, and admired the light, happy smile with which he surveyed the girl at play. But we knew that in all three cases the face was exactly the same.' Pudovkin, 'Naturshchik vmesto aktera', in *Sobranie sochinenii*, vol. I (1974). Pudovkin was to perfect the technique in his own work as a director, of which the most notable example is probably *Mother*.

There are some discrepancies concerning the exact nature of the experiment (whether there were two shots or three, what the objects were and whether it was specifically shot or assembled from pre-existing footage). Kuleshov himself wrote, 'I alternated the same shot of Mozzhukhin with various other shots . . . and these shots acquired a different meaning. The discovery stunned me – so convinced was I of the enormous power of montage.' *Kuleshov on Film: Writings of Lev Kuleshov* (1974).

4. Stanton, 'Understanding Story: or My Journey of Pain'.

5. John Peel, *Observer*, 17 July 1988.

6. Michael Billington in the *Guardian*, for example – here's just one example: <http://www.guardian.co.uk/culture/2010/dec/15/michael-billington-shakespeare-tv>, or Dominic Dromgoole in his book *Will and Me: How Shakespeare Took Over My Life* (2006). Ironically, from the late 1970s, with the growth of the radical fringe and the development of writers such as Edward Bond, Howard Brenton and David Hare, theatre became much more filmic. The latter's stage collaboration *Brassneck* is a movie in all but name.

7. Adaptations, in which I would include the BBC's 2012 Shakespeare *Hollow Crown* season, are of course a different matter. But the sheer amount of work the directors had to do in making the plays (*Richard II, Henry IV, Parts I* and *II* and *Henry V*) suitable for television – cutting, reordering, opening out, eliding, etc. – only underlines the point. They were very good, but they weren't theatre. Shakespeare is a particularly moot issue. His language is so visual that it works almost like radio dialogue. 'Think, when we talk of horses,' invites the Chorus of *Henry V*, 'that you see them/Printing their proud hoofs' the receiving earth;/ For 'tis your thoughts that now must deck our kings,/Carry them here and there.' Polanski's *Macbeth* or Luhrmann's *Romeo + Juliet* may be fine films, but for me the power of Shakespeare's work is felt most profoundly on an empty stage.

8. My own take. 'Genius' is so vastly overused a word it has become bankrupt terminology. Duchamp's *Fountain* was an insightful, ironic and mischievous work – perfect for its time. Unfortunately it opened the floodgates to an awful lot of nonsense.

9. E. M. Forster, *Aspects of the Novel* (1927).

10. Interview with Nick Hornby, *The Believer* magazine, August 2007.

11. Pressed to define the difference between soap and drama, I would argue that bad soap (and I have a vested interest in saying that not all soap is bad) commits this sin.

12. Aristotle, *The Poetics* (translated by Malcolm Heath; 1996).

12 *Character and Characterization*

1. *Steve Jobs: The Exclusive Biography* by Walter Isaacson (2011).

2. When *Observer* journalist Euan Ferguson wrote of *The Killing*, 'The Danish drama had the nation talking like no new crime thriller has for years', he was in reality talking about an audience of 300,000 in a population of 56 million. Such are the lengths we go to to convince ourselves that we are arbiters of the consensus – at the very centre of a fashionable club.

3. Though an individual's definition of safety is inevitably specific to them. In *EastEnders*, David Wicks only found it in danger: every choice he made was to make himself feel *alive*. In his book *The Megahit Movies* (2001), Richard Michaels Stefanik notes just how many successful movies have at their heart the search for security embodied in Maslow's pyramid.

4. See *The Social Network* DVD extra: 'Trent Reznor, Atticus Ross and David Fincher on the Score'.

5. I am grateful to Tony Jordan for first alerting me to this fascinating paradox.

6. During the long (thirty-five drafts!) development of *Life on Mars* I wrote to Jane Featherstone, MD of Kudos Film and TV, in my capacity as Head of Drama at Channel 4:

> I'm not really getting any sense of the other characters. I still think we should team Tom up with a complete Reaganesque 70s copper, and embody the whole idea of the show right in a buddy pairing. It will save us a lot of work – I'm assuming this would be Geoff . . . We have the perfect formula here for 48 Hours buddy movie – two guys with completely different takes on the same subject – let's exploit it. (Email, 23 June 2003)

I claim no great foresight, and we'd certainly talked around the subject already. What we all knew was that the show wasn't quite working – and there was something about the buddy idea that just *felt* right (Tom and Geoff, of course, soon became Sam and Gene). None of us were aware of the theory of opposites, but writers don't need to be. The more I explore structure, the more I believe it to be instinctive. Great writers *feel* it; at some level we all understand the need for opposites.

7. Ricky Gervais, *The Word* magazine, June 2011.
8. You can see a similar trope in *Modern Family*.

13 *Character and Structural Design*

1. I am grateful to Laurie Hutzler and her work on 'character mapping' for her insights here. Though her theories seem excessively complex, her articulation of different 'trouble traits' is I think valuable.

For the launch of *Breaking Bad*'s fifth and final season, *Entertainment Weekly* (20 July 2012) interviewed its star, Bryan Cranston. Cranston played Walter White, the mild-mannered chemistry teacher turned crystal-meth manufacturer. Journalist Dan Snierson wrote:

This season, the show presents the most soul-rotted, megalomaniac Walter yet, one who can never seem to earn enough money and respect to fill the hole inside him. 'Just as in the early years Walter White was mostly good with some corruption seeping into his being, now it's flipped,' says Cranston. 'It's a lot more corruption with some goodness attached to it . . . I like the complexity of·the man . . .We are multifaceted people and we have the capability of feeling different things. I would love to see him do something heroic and save someone or something . . .' Like a school bus of children? 'Let's call it a school bus of children. And then I have those children work for me in my meth lab,' he continues with dark delight. 'They should be grateful. I just saved their lives. "You're not going home until you finish!"' Gilligan [Vince, the show's creator] sees that possibility and raises it: 'Maybe they work together to make the meth grape-flavored. You know, for the kids.'

2. Egri differs here, believing one side should win, which seems to negate the idea of 'synthesis'.

14 Character Individuation

1. *The Ego and the Mechanisms of Defence* by Anna Freud (1937; revised edition, 1968).

2. George E. Vaillant's categorization from *Adaptation to Life* (1977). Like most things in psychoanalysis, there are many disagreements and variations, but it serves as useful shorthand here.

3. I must acknowledge the insights of William Indick here, whose *Psychology for Screenwriters* (2004) proffers some fascinating hypotheses and was incredibly useful in helping me get to grips with the basics. One or two of the film examples are his – they're simply the best examples.

4. Sidney Lumet wrote in *Making Movies* (1995):

> In the early days of television, when the 'kitchen sink' school of realism held sway, we always reached a point where we 'explained' the character. Around two-thirds of the way through, someone articulated the psychological truth that made the character the person he was. [Paddy] Chayefsky and I used to call this the 'rubber-ducky' school of drama: 'Someone once took his rubber ducky away from him, and that's why he's a deranged killer.' That was the fashion then, and with many producers and studios it still is.
>
> I always try to eliminate the rubber-ducky explanations. A character should be clear from his present actions. And his behaviour as the picture goes on should reveal the psychological motivations. If the writer has to state the reasons, something's wrong in the way the character has been written.

5. In *Screenplay* (1979), Syd Field refers to the 'Circle of Being', notes its dramatic value, but doesn't explore either its origination or its real purpose.

6. Interview with Simon Stephens in the *Observer*, 30 August 2009.

7. From David Mamet, *Bambi vs. Godzilla: On the Nature, Purpose, and Practice of the Movie Business* (2007).

8. E. M. Forster, *Aspects of the Novel* (1927).

9. In *Skyfall* (2012) the producer has attempted to flesh out some of Bond's back-story. It's subjective obviously, but I stand with Mamet on this – I don't want to know.

10. Interview with David Fincher in the *Guardian*, 2 February 2011.

11. This is what I believe Aristotle meant by 'Katharsis' or, in the Penguin 1996 translation of *The Poetics*, 'purification'. We live our fears and terrors through empathy with others; we exorcize our own demons through empathy.

15 Dialogue and Characterization

1. David Hare, BAFTA/BFI Lecture, September 2010.

2. The most commonly cited date is 1918, though there seems to be no definitive account.

3. From Joss Whedon's 'Top 10 Writing Tips', initially published in Channel 4's talent magazine by Catherine Bray.

16 Exposition

1. Opening lines from British TV series, 1990s.

2. A term of Robert McKee's from *Story*. A surprising, but nonetheless good example is Ibsen's *Hedda Gabler* in which Miss Tesman and the servant Bertha lay out the action. As William Archer noted in *Play-Making* (1912), it came 'as near as Ibsen ever did to the conventional exposition of the French stage, conducted by a footman and a parlour-maid engaged in dusting the furniture'. Archer notes too the fascinating development of Ibsen's expositional technique from *The Pillars of Society*, via *A Doll's House* to *The Wild Duck*. The first begins with a 'sewing-bee' gossiping about the characters; the second employs the method of a confidant; while in the third the essential facts are conveyed in a

full- blooded, fully fledged argument. The three stages chart the whole history of expositional development – from novice to master.

3. I have a vested interest obviously as from 2005 to 2012 I was in charge of *Holby City*. I would argue that it's very different now and, particularly in the last few years, has become a far more intelligent show.

4. In fact, at this point in the episode, the audience already knows the patient is dead and Dr Collin's information is technically repetition. Another cardinal sin of the novice writer, repetition works here *because* of the emotional overlay – the repeat exposition is ironically being used to show Collin's emotional state, removing the need to explain that he's nervous and daunted. The point remains valid – information rendered through emotion fuses it to characterization, eliminating any sense of the writer's presence. I am grateful to Jed Mercurio for his incredibly helpful explanations and illustrations.

5. Email exchange between Jed Mercurio and author, July 2006.

6. Email exchange between Jed Mercurio and author, July 2006.

17 Subtext

1. Ted Tally in *Screenwriters' Masterclass*, edited by Kevin Conroy Scott (2005).

2. The lines are actually taken verbatim from a real interview Harry H. Corbett did for a BBC series with Clive Goodwin: *Acting in the Sixties*, later published in book form in 1970. Brian Fillis's skill was to weave the words into a context that gave them even further meaning.

3. From 'The Secret and the Secret Society', Part IV of *The Sociology of Georg Simmel*, translated by Kurt H. Wolff (1950).

18 Television and the Triumph of Structure

1. The very first television drama is said to have been *The Queen's Messenger*. Written by the Irish playwright J. Harley Manners, it was transmitted on W2XB (owned by General Electric) in Schenectady,

New York State, in September 1928. The *New York Herald Tribune* described the scene:

> The Director Mortimer Stewart stood between the two television cam-
> eras that focused upon Miss Isetta Jewell, the heroine, and Maurice
> Randall, the hero. In front of Stewart was a television receiver in which
> he could at all times see the images that went out over the transmitter;
> and by means of a small control box he was able to control the output
> of pictures, cutting in one or another of the cameras and fading the
> image out and in. Whether it was successfully received at any point,
> other than the operation installation of the General Electric Laboratory,
> could not immediately be ascertained. It was the general opinion among
> those that watched the experiment that the day of radio moving pictures
> was still a long, long way in the future. Whether the present system can
> be brought to commercial practicability and public usefulness remains a
> question.

The *New York Times* was more prescient:

> The curtains of time and space, which have been drawn back pretty far
> in the past few years, were pushed asunder still further this afternoon,
> giving a glimpse of future marvels, in a demonstration of the latest
> thing in radio television at the General Electric Company research
> laboratory.

It concluded:

> Great as has been the success of talking movies, they may easily be out-
> done by radio-television if the technical difficulties are overcome.

2. Asa Briggs, *The History of Broadcasting in the United Kingdom*, Volume Two: *The Golden Age of Wireless* (1995).
3. 'The First Play by Television – BBC and Baird Experiment', *The Times*, 15 July 1930.
4. Shaun Sutton, 'Dramatis Personae', *The Times*, 2 November 1972.
5. Tise Vahimagi, *British Television: An Illustrated Guide* (1994).

19 Series and Serial Structure

1. From David Simon's Introduction to *The Wire: Truth Be Told* by Rafael Alvarez (2004 edition).
2. Ibid.
3. From Mark Cousins' TV series, *The Story of Film*, More4, 2011.
4. As an interesting adjunct I would add this: David Simon's view has currency, especially for the simple reason that the more difficult and demanding the work the more it tends to gain critical kudos. When I was Head of Drama at Channel 4, we learned quickly that if we killed our protagonists it gave us more chance of winning awards. We discovered, too, that the chances were increased further if they died by their own hand. *Boy A*, *Secret Life* and *Red Riding* were all in this fine tradition, gleefully parodied as 'Gritty Bafta' on YouTube <http://www.youtube.com/watch?v=-HXaj2IYYn8>. This isn't to negate their worth, merely to suggest it's probably not worth entering a comedy. Once the makers are dead, of course, it's a different matter – Hitchcock, once derided for his tawdry showmanship, became a genius after his death.

   Series television in this country, however successful it might have been (and Ted Childs' reign at ITV in the last quarter of the last century – which gave us *The Sweeney, Minder, Inspector Morse, Peak Practice, Soldier Soldier* and more – was just extraordinary), wasn't really taken seriously until American cable gave us *The Sopranos* and *Six Feet Under*. Childs' work (though it's perhaps unfair to single him out) was the equivalent of anything more 'serious' television has produced, and it's very sad, I think, that the single most successful producer in British television drama has never been acknowledged while far lesser talents are lauded.

20 Change in Drama Series

1. Interview with Bob Daily from *Entertainment Weekly*, 30 March 2012.
2. That's not as pejorative as it sounds. Much of drama is a lie. John le Carré described *Spooks* as 'crap' because it didn't portray the world of

Intelligence he knew, which is a bit like criticizing a cat for not being a dog – it didn't set out to tell the truth, it set out to entertain. Drama lies all the time.

3. Interview with Eve Longoria from *Entertainment Weekly*, 30 March 2012.

4. I was the original commissioning editor at Channel 4 for *Life on Mars* and left shortly after they rejected it, only to pick it up again and co-executive-produce it with the brilliant *Dr Who* producer, Julie Gardner.

21 Home Again

1. To be fair, McGovern wasn't the only person involved, but the conflict came alive in his episodes in a way no other writer was able to match – and in those days *Brookside* had some of the very best writers on TV.

2. Jimmy McGovern, talk for BBC Writers Room, Leeds, 2009.

3. *Writing the Wrongs; The Making of 'Dockers'*, documentary, Channel 4, 1999.

4. T. W. Baldwin, *Shakspere's Five-Act Structure* (1947; later edition, 1963).

5. *Mad Men*, episode one, series one: 'Smoke gets in your eyes' by Matthew Weiner.

6. *The Journals of Arnold Bennett*, edited by Sir Newman Flower (1932), entry for 15 October 1896.

7. Allowing the antagonist 'equal rights' has the additional benefit of allowing a director myriad interpretations – another key to Shakespeare's longevity.

8. From Anton Chekhov, *Plays* (Penguin, 2002), Introduction by Richard Gilman.

9. It's instructive to compare Chekhov with Ibsen. *Hedda Gabler* is equally complex as *Uncle Vanya* or *Three Sisters*, but in *An Enemy of the People* the story is of just one man, of whom the author approves, denouncing everyone else as idiots. It's a very powerful work, but it's really – also – effectively propaganda. It would be interesting to pursue the idea of pushing Dr Stockmann's monomania to the fore (as noted above, it *is* possible to see his denunciations of local government

as a spiritual forebear of Glenn Beck and Fox News). It wouldn't be nearly so beloved by liberals, but I suspect it would be a more interesting work.

10. Andrew Stanton, Lecture, 'Understanding Story: or My Journey of Pain' (2006). Jimmy McGovern concurs with Andrew Stanton: 'For a story to be good it must be laden with themes, laden with argument.' But he adds a vital caveat: 'It ought not to intrude upon the story. You shouldn't be aware of the themes or the arguments until after you've watched it.' From *Mark Lawson Talks to . . .* , BBC 4, November 2010.

11. Lajos Egri, *The Art of Dramatic Writing* (1946).

12. Alan Yentob, to BBC Content Review, 2000.

13. Alistair Cooke: '60 Years . . . Behind the Microphone. Before the Camera . . . A Memoir', Royal Television Society lecture, New York, 1997.

14. 'What about Bohemian Rhapsody?!' Tony Jordan argued (discussion with author on reading first draft manuscript), October 2010.

15. Mark Cousins noted this in his always entertaining and provocative *The Story of Film* (More4, 2011). He also argued the case for *The Last Movie* (see below).

16. Reaction to the mainstream is an essential part of our make-up – it's how societies develop; from revolt into style one generation's fringe is the next generation's staple. It's thesis/antithesis again. However, when the film critic David Thomson described Dennis Hopper's *The Last Movie* (in *The New Biographical Dictionary of Film*) as 'a marker for pretentious nonsense', he skewered not only Hopper's folly, but also a universal tendency. Hopper, he said, had made the fatal mistake of believing that 'rebellion was some proof of artistic integrity'. It's a postscript that can be applied to much – though not all – work that seeks to differentiate itself from the norm. *The White Ribbon* is a great movie – is Damien Hirst great art? Certainly iconoclasm can pay dividends. While the tendency to break form can in the hands of a master end well, at its worst it's a classic illustration of how a jury, and (normally broadsheet) audience, will always be tempted to place *want* (how they wish to be seen – serious, arty, etc.) over *need*.

The composer John Adams said something very apposite in his introduction to his own work *Harmonielehre*:

Despite my respect for and even intimidation by the persona of Schoenberg, I felt it only honest to acknowledge that I profoundly disliked the sound of twelve-tone music. His aesthetic was to me an overripening of nineteenth-century Individualism, one in which the composer was a god of sorts, to which the listener would come as if to a sacramental altar. It was with Schoenberg that the 'agony of modern music' had been born, and it was no secret that the audience for classical music during the twentieth century was rapidly shrinking, in no small part because of the aural ugliness of so much of the new work being written.

Post-war German art's preoccupation with the smashing up of conventional form is particularly fascinating, and it's almost too tempting to ascribe it to the unique climate of a defeated nation. Whether politically (the Baader – Meinhof Gang), musically ('Krautrock') or theatrically (the 'post-dramatic theatre' movement in which narrative is viewed as betrayal), the urge to destroy the work of their fathers is an unusually dominant trait. Bertolt Brecht is another classic example, but his argument for *Verfremdungseffekt* – that an audience should experience his dramas intellectually and not emotionally – seems specious. It's humanly impossible *not* to empathize – unless the drama is awful or you are a psychopath. Fortunately his plays are far better than his theoretical adumbrations.

17. Richard Ford, *Canada* (2012).
18. From Mark Cousins' *The Story of Film*, More4, 2011.
19. Sometimes the work only *appears* to be radical. As Baz Luhrmann says, 'If you'd been used to the cinema being only about beautiful sets, wonderful costumes, sweeping shots and big emotions . . . and someone comes along and says . . . It's a girl in jeans and a white T-shirt that says *Herald Tribune* on it, you're gonna go like "yeah man, that's like life". Well, no, actually, it's just another cinematic device . . . Language is a living thing. It changes, it evolves. What you're saying never changes. People still say, "I love you" . . . "I will kill you". How they say "I love you", "I will kill you" – that is fashion.' Quoted by Mark Cousins in *The Story of Film*, More4, 2011.
20. David Frost, *Frost/Nixon: One Journalist, One President, One Confession* (2007).
21. Quotes from Michael Holroyd, *Bernard Shaw: A Biography* (1997).

22 Why?

1. From Joseph Campbell, *The Hero with a Thousand Faces* (1949).
2. Baroness Susan Greenfield, CBE, Professor of Synaptic Pharmacology, Lincoln College, Oxford. From her 'School of Life' lecture, Conway Hall, 11 December 2011.
3. This is very much Christopher Booker's argument in *The Seven Basic Plots*, as it is for Joseph Campbell and his disciples in the world of myth. Booker's argument, it seems to me, is undermined by a *Daily Mail*-like haranguing of the course storytelling has taken over the last two hundred years. He argues with some force that something was corrupted in human nature after the Industrial Revolution, and it was this that led to a break with the original archetypal journey towards emotional maturity. He cites the rise of the dark inversion as proof of this, and sees as foetid and immoral the work of Stendhal, John Braine, even *Frankenstein*, *Moby Dick* and *King Kong*. While it's true that there does seem to be an increase in these kinds of story, I think it's wrong to see them as works of approval; there is nothing in these works to suggest their authors condone Ahab, Joe Lampton or Victor Frankenstein. Indeed, each has a clear ancestral connection to classic mythology; *Frankenstein* is termed 'A Modern Prometheus' for a reason. These works are clearly responses to a changed society, artistic triumphs in their own way, and firmly rooted in the principles of Hubris and Nemesis he is so keen to praise in earlier, seemingly prelapsarian times. He harangues *Moby Dick*, *King Kong* and *Frankenstein* for having dark heroes and light monsters, but to all intents and purposes, isn't that a rather good definition of tragedy?
4. We depart once again from Lajos Egri here, who appears to suggest the triumph of thesis rather than synthesis – or that heroes learn nothing. A classical more than Hegelian dialectic.
5. A. A. Gill, TV column, *Sunday Times*, 2011.
6. 'The dialogue was ridiculous, the situations were unbelievable, the characters were parodical,' complained Tamara Rojo, herself a dancer and artistic director of the English National Ballet, in the *Observer*, 15 April 2012.

7. From Frank Thomas and Ollie Johnston, *The Disney Villain* (1993).

8. 'Mythology has been interpreted by the modern intellect as a primitive, fumbling effort to explain the world of nature (Frazer); as a production of poetical fantasy from prehistoric times, misunderstood by succeeding ages (Müller); as a repository of allegorical instruction, to shape the individual to his group (Durkheim); as a group dream, symptomatic of archetypal urges within the depths of the human psyche (Jung); as the traditional vehicle of man's profoundest metaphysical insights (Coomaraswamy); and as God's Revelation to His children (the Church). Mythology is all of these. The various judgements are determined by the viewpoints of the judges. For when scrutinized in terms not of what it is but of how it functions, of how it has served mankind in the past, of how it may serve today, mythology shows itself to be as amenable as life itself to the obsessions and requirements of the individual, the race, the age.' Joseph Campbell in *The Hero with a Thousand Faces*.

9. Friedrich Max Müller (1823–1900), who believed such abstract ideas were victims of the human desire to anthropomorphize.

10. Sir James George Frazer (1854–1941), *The Golden Bough* (first published in two volumes, 1890, then twelve volumes, 1906–15). It was to influence both *The Waste Land* and *Apocalypse Now*.

11. The order we choose to impose is a good illustration of character – and a disturbed or paranoid individual will impose a different interpretation of events than someone more balanced or with different mental make-up altogether. Charlie Kaufman's version of 'order' tells us much about him.

12. From Steven Pinker, *How the Mind Works* (1997).

13. Noel Gallagher, on viewing Jude Law's *Hamlet* in 2011, chose not to learn: 'It's four hours long and there wasn't one single minute that I knew what was going on. I was thinking, "I know they're speaking English but it's just all fucking gibberish." I can appreciate the acting and the way they learned all those lines but . . . what the fuck was going on?', *London Evening Standard*, September 2011.

14. Daniel Kahnemann, *Thinking, Fast and Slow* (2011).

15. The first version is probably epitomized by John Mills in the original film *Scott of the Antarctic* (1948); Roland Huntford's book for the second

see *Scott and Amundsen* (1979) (itself a TV series starring Martin Shaw); and for the most recent addition see Edward J. Larson's *An Empire of Ice: Scott, Shackleton, and the Heroic Age of Antarctic Science* (2011). There are, of course, other versions too.

16. One should add that the period they write it in can also be of massive influence. As the halo of victory at war wore off, the late 1970s was a period when many icons were smashed.

17. Polly Toynbee, 'If the *Sun on Sunday* soars Rupert Murdoch will also rise again', *Guardian*, 23 February 2012. She writes: '. . . before getting overly sanctimonious, journalism is not altogether a sacrament to truth. Even reputable journalism involves artifice in the very act of writing a "story", simplifying shades of grey into black and white, looking for an "angle" or a "peg". We précis a muddled reality into a narrative of right and wrong. We are all hungry for stories. I have never felt comfortable with over-lofty claims for the nobility or honour of our trade.'

18. See *Fairy and Folk Tales of the Irish Peasantry*, collected and published by W. B. Yeats. As might be discernible from the name Conn-eda (an amalgamation of those of his parents), the story is actually the foundation myth of the Irish province of Connacht.

19. Heinrich Zimmer, *The King and the Corpse: Tales of the Soul's Conquest of Evil*, edited by Joseph Campbell (originally published 1948; 2nd revised edition, 1971).

20. Syd Field touches on the idea of equal and opposite reaction in *Screenplay* (1979) but really uses it to illustrate the problems of a passive protagonist; he doesn't explore its deeper implications.

21. It is one of the great ironies that legal argument so often becomes not about the truth but rather which barrister can tell the best story. Jury trials seem, more often than not, merely competitions in storytelling. Peter Moffat dramatized this brilliantly in his BBC series *Criminal Justice*.

22. Hegel in *The Science of Logic* (1812–16): 'it is only because a thing contains a contradiction within itself that it moves and acquires impulse and activity. That is the process of all motion and all development.' Quoted by Lajos Egri in *The Art of Dramatic Writing* (1946), who expands: 'These three steps – thesis, antithesis, synthesis – are the law of all movement. Everything that moves constantly negates itself. All things change toward

their opposites through movement. The present becomes the past, the future becomes the present. There is nothing which does not move. Constant change is the very essence of all existence. Everything in time passes into its opposite. Everything within itself contains its own opposite.'

23. From Rafael Alvarez, *The Wire: Truth Be Told* (2010). Introduction by David Simon.

24. Theatre critic Michael Billington, recalling his memories of the 1973 production, *Guardian*, April 2000.

25. As the Friar noted in *Romeo and Juliet* (Act II, scene 3):

> For naught so vile that on the earth doth live
> But to the earth some special good doth give,
> Nor aught so good, but, strain'd from that fair use,
> Revolts from true birth, stumbling on abuse:
> Virtue itself turns vice, being misapplied,
> And vice sometime's by action dignified.
> Within the infant rind of this small flower
> Poison hath residence, and medicine power:
> For this, being smelt, with that part cheers each part;
> Being tasted, slays all senses with the heart.
> Two such opposed kings encamp them still
> In man as well as herbs – grace and rude will;
> And where the worser is predominant,
> Full soon the canker death eats up that plant.

He might well have been talking about Michael Corleone.

26. Frank Cottrell Boyce, 'How to write a movie', *Guardian*, 30 June 2008.

27. In *Story*, Robert McKee talks of 'the gap' where drama is born.

28. Campbell himself wrote (*The Hero with a Thousand Faces*):

> The standard path of the mythological adventure of the hero is a magnification of the formula represented in the rites of passage: *separation – initiation – return*: which might be named the nuclear unit of the monomyth.

Prometheus ascended to the heavens, stole fire from the gods and descended. Jason sailed through the Clashing Rocks into a sea of marvels, circumvented the dragon that guarded the Golden Fleece, and returned with the fleece and the power to wrest his rightful throne from a usurper. Aeneas went down into the underworld, crossed the dreadful river of the dead, threw a sop to the three-headed watchdog Cerberus, and conversed, at last, with the shade of his dead father.

29. Claude Lévi-Strauss posited that all myths were the result of binary oppositions. Influenced by Hegel, he argued in 'The Structural Study of Myth' (1955) (in *Structural Anthropology*, vol. 1): 'The purpose of myth is to provide a logical model capable of overcoming a contradiction (an impossible achievement if, as it happens, the contradiction is real).' It's a complex argument – sometimes absurdly so – and not altogether convincing, but it does appear to stumble onto an essential truth about stories.

30. Except, of course, if you slavishly copy it. Author Neil Gaiman stopped reading Campbell's *The Hero with a Thousand Faces* halfway through, reasoning, 'If this is true – I don't want to know . . . I'd rather do it accidentally than be told what the pattern is.'

31. Ian McEwan, 'Only love and then oblivion', first published in the *Guardian*, 15 September 2001.

32. For more, see Christian Keysers, *The Empathic Brain* (November 2011).

33. Aristotle, *The Poetics*, translated by Malcolm Heath (1996).

34. From George Eliot's review of W. H. Riehl's *The Natural History of German Life, Westminster Review*, July 1856.

35. From 'Aesthetic Culture' (1910) by Gyorgy Lukács. I am grateful to Alex Ross, *The Rest is Noise*, for the introduction to this work.

36. *The Poet Speaks: Interviews with Contemporary Poets*, conducted by Hilary Morrish, Peter Orr, John Press and Ian Scott-Kilvert (1966).

37. From Robert Hughes, *The Shock of the New* (1980).

Bibliography

Alvarez, Rafael, *The Wire: Truth Be Told* (US, 2004; UK, 2010)

Archer, William, *Play-Making: A Manual of Craftsmanship* (1912)

Aristotle, *The Poetics*, translated by Malcolm Heath (1996)

Aronson, Linda, *Screenwriting Updated* (2001)

Baldwin, T. W., *Shakspere's Five-Act Structure* (1947; later edition, 1963)

Bettelheim, Bruno, *The Uses of Enchantment: The Meaning and Importance of Fairy Tales* (1976)

Booker, Christopher, *The Seven Basic Plots: Why We Tell Stories* (2004)

Booth, Wayne C., *The Rhetoric of Fiction* (1961)

Bradley, A. C., *Shakespearean Tragedy: Lectures on* Hamlet, Othello, King Lear *and* Macbeth (1904; 2nd edn 1905)

Campbell, Joseph, *The Hero With a Thousand Faces* (1949)

Cousins, Mark, *The Story of Film* (TV series, More4, 2011)

Cunningham, Keith, *The Soul of Screenwriting: On Writing, Dramatic Truth, and Knowing Yourself* (2008)

Dancyger, Ken and Jeff Rush, *Alternative Scriptwriting* (2006)

Davies, Russell T. and Benjamin Cook, *Doctor Who: The Writer's Tale* (2008)

Davis, Rib, *Writing Dialogue for Scripts* (3rd edn, 2008)

Dethridge, Lisa, *Writing Your Screenplay* (2003)

Douglas, Pamela, *Writing the TV Drama Series: How To Succeed as a Professional Writer in TV* (2005)

Eco, Umberto, 'Narrative Structures in Fleming', in *The Role of the Reader: Explorations in the Semiotics of Texts* (1979)

Edgar, David, *How Plays Work* (2009)

Egri, Lajos, *The Art of Dramatic Writing* (1946)

Eisenstein, Sergei, *The Film Sense* (1942)

Field, Syd, *Screenplay: The Foundations of Screenwriting* (1979)

Field, Syd, *The Screenwriter's Workbook* (1988)

Field, Syd, *Four Screenplays: Studies in the American Screenplay* (1994)

Flinn, Denny Martin, *How Not to Write a Screenplay: 101 Common Mistakes Most Screenwriters Make* (1999)

Forster, E. M., *Aspects of the Novel* (1927)

Frazer, Sir James George, *The Golden Bough* (1890)

Frensham, Ray, *Teach Yourself Screenwriting* (1996)

Freud, Anna, *The Ego and the Mechanisms of Defence* (1937; revised edition, 1966)

Freytag, Gustav, *Technique of the Drama: An Exposition of Dramatic Composition and Art. An Authorized Translation from the Sixth German Edition*, by Elias J. MacEwan (3rd edn, 1900)

Frost, David, *Frost/Nixon: One Journalist, One President, One Confession* (2007)

Frye, Northrop, *Anatomy of Criticism* (1957)

Frye, Northrop, *The Great Code* (1981)

Garfinkel, Asher, *Screenplay Story Analysis: The Art and Business* (2007)

Goldman, William, *Adventures in the Screen Trade: A Personal View of Hollywood and Screenwriting* (1983)

Gulino, Paul, *Screenwriting: The Sequence Approach* (2004)

Harmon, Dan, Channel 101 (www.Channel101.com), in particular 'Story Structure 101 – Super Basic Shit', and the articles that follow it

Hauge, Michael, *Writing Screenplays That Sell: The Complete Guide to Turning Story Concepts into Movie and Television Deals* (1988)

Hegel, Georg, *The Science of Logic* (1812–16)

Highsmith, Patricia, *Plotting and Writing Suspense Fiction* (1989)

Hiltunen, Ari, *Aristotle in Hollywood: The Anatomy of Successful Storytelling* (2002)

Hughes, Robert, *The Shock of the New* (1980)

Hulke, Malcolm, *Writing for Television* (1980)

Indick, William, *Psychology for Screenwriters: Building Conflict in Your Script* (2004)

Isaacson, Walter, *Steve Jobs: The Exclusive Biography* (2011)

Jewkes, Wilfred T., *Act-Division in Elizabethan and Jacobean Plays 1583–1616* (1958)

Kahneman, Daniel, *Thinking, Fast and Slow* (2011)

Kelly, Richard T. (ed.), *Ten Bad Dates with De Niro: A Book of Alternative Movie Lists* (2007)

Keysers, Christian, *The Empathic Brain* (2011)

King, Stephen, *On Writing* (2000)

Kott, Jan, *Shakespeare Our Contemporary* (1962)

Kuleshov, Lev, *Kuleshov on Film: Writing of Lev Kuleshov* (1974)

Larsen, Stephen and Robin, *Joseph Campbell: A Fire in the Mind* (2002)

Lawson, John Howard, *Theory and Technique of Playwriting* (1936)

Lévi-Strauss, Claude, 'The Structural Study of Myth', in *Structural Anthropology*, vol. 1 (1955)

Lodge, David, *The Art of Fiction* (1992)

Logan, John and Laura Schellhardt, *Screenwriting for Dummies* (2008)

Lumet, Sidney, *Making Movies* (1995)

McKee, Robert, *Story: Structure, Style and the Principles of Screenwriting* (1999)

Mamet, David, *Three Uses of the Knife* (1998)

Mamet, David, *Bambi vs. Godzilla: On the Nature, Purpose, and Practice of the Movie Business* (2007)

Morris, Elisabeth Woodbridge, *The Drama; its Law and its Technique* (1898)

Norman, Marc, *What Happens Next: A History of American Screenwriting* (2007)

Ondaatje, Michael, *The Conversations: Walter Murch and the Art of Editing Film* (2004)

Perry, Bliss, *A Study of Prose Fiction* (1902)

Pinker, Steven, *How the Mind Works* (1997)

Price, William Thompson, *The Technique of the Drama* (1892)

Propp, Vladimir, *Morphology of the Folk Tale* (1928)

Ross, Alex, *The Rest is Noise: Listening to the Twentieth Century* (2007)

Sargent, Epes Winthrop, *The Technique of the Photoplay* (1912; 3rd edn, 1916)

Schlegel, A. W., *Lectures on Dramatic Art and Literature* (1808)

Schmidt, Victoria Lynn, *45 Master Characters* (2007)

Scott, Kevin Conroy (ed.), *Screenwriters' Masterclass* (2005)

Seger, Linda, *Making a Good Script Great* (1987; 3rd edn, 2010)

Seger, Linda, *And the Best Screenplay Goes To . . . Learning from the Winners: Sideways, Shakespeare in Love, Crash* (2008)

Simmel, Georg, *The Sociology of Georg Simmel*, translated by Kurt H. Wolff, Part IV, 'The Secret and the Secret Society (1950)

Bibliography

Snyder, Blake, *Save the Cat! The Last Book on Screenwriting That You'll Ever Need* (2005)

Snyder, Blake, *Save the Cat! Goes to the Movies. The Screenwriter's Guide to Every Story Ever Told* (2007)

Stanton, Andrew, 'Understanding Story: or My Journey of Pain', lecture (2006)

Stefanik, Richard Michaels, *The Megahit Movies* (2001)

Surrell, Jason, *Screenplay by Disney* (2004)

Sutton, Shaun, *The Largest Theatre in the World* (1982)

Taleb, Nassim Nicholas, *The Black Swan: The Impact of the Highly Improbable* (2007)

Taylor, John Russell, *The Rise and Fall of the Well-Made Play* (1967)

Thomas, Frank and Ollie Johnston, *The Disney Villain* (1993)

Thomson, David, *The New Biographical Dictionary of Film* (2002)

Tierno, Michael, *Aristotle's Poetics for Screenwriters* (2002)

Tilley, Allen, *Plot Snakes and the Dynamics of Narrative Experience* (1992)

Truby, John, *The Anatomy of Story: 22 Steps to Becoming a Master Storyteller* (2007)

Vaillant, George E., *Adaptation to Life* (1977)

Vogler, Christopher, 'A Practical Guide to *The Hero with a Thousand Faces*', (1985)

Vogler, Christopher, *The Writer's Journey* (1996)

Voytilla, Stuart, *Myth and the Movies: Discovering the Mythic Structure of 50 Unforgettable Films* (1999)

Waters, Steve, *The Secret Life of Plays* (2010)

Yeats, W. B., *Fairy and Folk Tales of the Irish Peasantry* (1888)

Zimmer, Heinrich, *The King and the Corpse: Tales of the Soul's Conquest of Evil*, edited by Joseph Campbell (1948; 2nd edition, 1956/1971)

Acknowledgements

This book could not have been written without following the path laid down by those who have wrestled with story structure before. It would be unfair not to mention Joseph Campbell, Syd Field, Northrop Frye, William Archer, Robert McKee, Christopher Booker, Epes Winthrop Sargent, Vladimir Propp, and Christopher Vogler – alongside valuable additional insights from Laurie Hutzler and William Indick. All are worth reading, but I would particularly recommend Lajos Egri, whose *How to Write a Play* (1942) contains the first real insights into dialectical structure, and David Mamet, who picked up the baton. Everything contained in this book is built on their foundations. If he weren't so busy writing plays that so peerlessly embody it, Mamet would have produced the definitive book on storytelling. As it is, his *Three Uses of the Knife* (1998) comes closer than anyone.

I have attempted to acknowledge my debt to them all wherever possible, and where I have disagreed with them it has been in the spirit of creative opposition the book espouses. As Egri himself said in his own Preface, it's all dialectical; someone will – and should – disagree with me now.

I must acknowledge David Lodge, whose book *The Art of Fiction* (1992) introduced me to both Leonard Michaels and symmetry, Wayne C. Booth for his definitive work on showing and telling, *The Rhetoric of Fiction* (1961), and Vladimir Propp's *Morphology of the Folk Tale* (1928) for blazing the trail. Dan Harmon's entertaining website (Channel101.com) contains some very smart observations on story structure and was valuable in underlining my own thoughts – for a lightning 'how to' guide it's well worth a look. For parallels with the worlds of art and music, Robert Hughes's *The Shock of the New* (1980) and Alex Ross's *The Rest is Noise* (2007) were indispensable. None of these, however, would have made any sense without one criminally under-acknowledged lecture by Andrew Stanton: 'Understanding Story: or My Journey of Pain' (2006). It unlocked everything.

Professor John Mullan at University College London was incredibly generous with his time and patience and pointed me towards the Russian formalists; Dominic Dromgoole at the Globe Theatre added a healthy dose of scepticism on Shakespearean act design. Professor Linda Anderson at the University of Newcastle-on-Tyne taught me, gave me confidence in my own opinions and remains a boundless inspiration. I left Newcastle with a love of literature, but no real sense of what to do with it. There were key meetings once the journey had begun: Jimmy McGovern, who inspired me, Tony Jordan, who taught me, Paul Greengrass, who introduced me to five acts, and Paul Abbott, who did it all in front of me, dazzlingly, without the aid of a safety net; between them they inspired the curiosity that led to this book.

The writers it's been my privilege to work with over many years have been my real – unacknowledged – tutors. Jed Mercurio (who was incredibly patient and generous in the early days), Stephen Moffat, Dominic Minghella, Guy Hibbert, Ashley Pharoah, Matthew Graham, Debbie Horsefield, Sarah Daniels, Juliet Ace, Neil Cross, Mike Bullen, Abi Morgan, Peter Morgan, Simon Burke, Peter Bowker, Terry Johnson, Tony Grounds, Kate Brooke, Mark Catley and Justin Young were incredibly significant, as were those who were just happy to chat away – in particular Russell T. Davis, Alan Plater and Richard Curtis, all of whom were more than generous with their time, criticism and support.

From the Writers Academy I have to thank Rumu Sen Gupta, Helena Pope, Belinda Campbell, Kathlyn McGlyn, David Roden, Neil Irvine, Caroline Ormerod and the students. Tony Jordan once described them as 'Beagles you are forcing to smoke'. What I learned from their incredible appetite for knowledge (and argument) was immeasurable. At the heart of it all was Ceri Meyrick, who, despite having two small children, was always there to patiently tell me when I was wrong, particularly when I was behaving like a third.

Acknowledgements

Mike and Bernadette Octigan provided spiritual nourishment and Irish hospitality beyond the call of duty. Then there were Jenny Robins, Ian Critchley, Claire Powell, James Dundas, Lucy Richer and in particular Ben Stephenson – none of whom had to, but all of whom went out of their way to find me a place to think.

As and when drafts arrived, Jimmy McGovern, Tony Jordan, Simon Ashdown, Rachel Wardlow, Rosie Marcel, Paul Unwin, Victoria Fea and Lucy Dyke read and gave invaluable advice. There are few worse sentences in the English language than 'Will you read my book?'. The fact that all of them did remains to me incredibly touching. All were incisive and critical, all – as experts in their field should be – were robust equally in their praise and blame.

Into the Woods wouldn't exist if it hadn't been for Rob Williams, who badgered me to write it, then held a gun to my head until it was finished. Both he and Emma Frost provided brilliant notes and boundless enthusiasm over too many drafts and too many years; both were there from the very start and never went away. Sara Turner, too, should be mentioned, for she was the first to make me believe any of this was worthwhile – there aren't enough thanks for them.

And finally, of course, Patrick Loughran, Jane Robertson and Helen Conford at Penguin, who showed me what editors *should* do; Gordon Wise who did the same for agents; and my father and mother who surrounded me with books. And Jennifer, without whom . . .

Credits

p. 32 – 'Yummy Mummy Lit' satire, reproduced by kind permission of Rafael Behr and Guardian News and Media Limited

p. 77 – Jackson Pollock, *Number 1, 1950 (Lavender Mist)*, reproduced by kind permission of National Gallery of Art Images

p. 84 and 158 – extracts from *Apocalypse Now*, screenplay by John Milius and Francis Ford Coppola, reproduced by kind permission of Faber and Faber Ltd

p. 92 – extract from *EastEnders*, by Tony Jordan, reproduced by kind permission of the author and the British Broadcasting Corporation

p. 111 – 'VW Lemon', reproduced by kind permission of Volkswagen plc

p. 115 – Willem de Kooning, *Excavation*, 1950, copyright © The Willem de Kooning Foundation, New York/ARS, NY and DACS, London, 2012

p. 123 – extract from *Tinker Tailor Soldier Spy* (1979), screenplay by Arthur Hopcraft, reproduced by kind permission of the estate of Arthur Hopcraft and the British Broadcasting Corporation

p. 125 – extract from *Butch Cassidy and the Sundance Kid*, screenplay by William Goldman, reproduced by kind permission of the author, ICM Partners and Applause Books

p. 135 – extract from Chris Rock, *Bigger & Blacker* reproduced by kind permission of Chris Rock

p. 153 – extract from *Holby City* reproduced by kind permission of the British Broadcasting Corporation

p. 157 – extract from *Cardiac Arrest*, screenplay by Jed Mercurio, reproduced by kind permission of the author and the British Broadcasting Corporation

Credits

p. 165 – extract from *The Curse of Steptoe*, screenplay by Brian Fillis, reproduced by kind permission of the author and the British Broadcasting Corporation

p. 200 – extract from *Canada*, by Richard Ford, reproduced by kind permission of Bloomsbury plc, copyright © Richard Ford and Bloomsbury Publishing plc

Index

Index